8/87

The Dawn
of
Modern Warfare

The Dawn of Modern Warfare

Albert Sidney Britt, III
Jerome A. O'Connell
Dave Richard Palmer
Gerald P. Stadler

Thomas E. Griess
Series Editor

DEPARTMENT OF HISTORY
UNITED STATES MILITARY ACADEMY
WEST POINT, NEW YORK

AVERY PUBLISHING GROUP INC.
Wayne, New Jersey

Series Editor, Thomas E. Griess.
In-House Editor, Joanne Abrams.
Cover design by Martin Hochberg.

All original artwork by
Edward J. Krasnoborski and F. Mitchell.

Contents

To the professional practitioners of the military art—
past, present, and especially future.

Illustrations

Chapter 7

Chapter 8

Maps

Acknowledgements

All authors are indebted in varying degrees to those persons from whom they have received assistance and advice. Perhaps more than most, we are obliged to acknowledge the guidance, inspiration, and helpful criticism of a large number of people who have contributed to *The Dawn of Modern Warfare*.

In particular, we would like to extend our gratitude and appreciation to our colleagues in the Department of History who made an immeasurable contribution to the quality of this book. If it measures up to their tradition of excellence, a hope will have been realized.

We are also indebted to those resourceful staff members of the department whose patience, hard work, and cheerful flexibility have made the preparation of this book both enjoyable and professional. We would be remiss not to mention the artistic treatment of the maps and sketches which is due to the talent and industry of Mr. Edward J. Krasnoborski. His contribution has improved the book in a most direct and invaluable way. Manuscript preparation and other administrative chores were carefully and competently handled under the overall direction of Mrs. Dorothy H. Waterfield.

Hopefully, several scholars will see in the text some of the results of their teaching efforts. The impact of Professor Theodore Ropp is evident throughout the book. Professors Jay Luvaas and Peter Paret influenced strongly that portion pertaining to Frederick the Great.

In one area only we claim complete originality and absolute responsibility—the mistakes are ours.

Albert S. Britt, III
Jerome A. O'Connell
Dave R. Palmer
Gerald P. Stadler

West Point, New York
January 1973

Foreword

Cadets at the United States Military Academy have studied military campaigns and institutions for approximately a century in a course entitled History of the Military Art. Beginning in 1938, that study of history was supported by texts and maps that were prepared by members of the departmental faculty under the direction of T. Dodson Stamps, who was then head of the Department of Military Art and Engineering. The coverage of military developments from the fourteenth to the eighteenth centuries, however, was fragmentary and incomplete. This was because the course of instruction emphasized military campaigns and principles, and devoted little time to the broader aspects of military history. The present text, *The Dawn of Modern Warfare*, was designed to correct that deficiency by expanding the scope of coverage.

The readings collected in this text offer a historical survey of the evolution of western warfare over nearly five centuries. In writing about events that occurred over such a broad period of time, the authors have exercised selectivity and concentrated on significant developments, thereby establishing a foundation of knowledge upon which the reader can build in later studies. They have not attempted to tell a carefully connected and detailed chronological story except in their attention to warfare as a whole and to meaningful elements of continuity that connect one era to another. Since the title of this text may seem to make a flat assumption, some readers will question that modern warfare commenced during the period covered herein. Hopefully, these same readers will grant, however, that prior to Napoleon's time there were important social, political, and military developments that nudged warfare into the modern epoch.

Four faculty members of the Department of History at the United States Military Academy shared in the writing of this text. Relying primarily upon sound secondary sources, they performed the detailed research, designed supporting maps, and wrote the narrative. The Department of History and many West Point graduates are indebted to them for their efforts, which were made under the pressure of time and with minimal resources. In the first chapter, which includes coverage of the Middle Ages, Gerald P. Stadler traces the re-emergence of infantry as a decisive arm on the battlefield. In Chapter 2, Jerome A. O'Connell surveys developments in early naval warfare. In the next four chapters, Dave R. Palmer deals with the revolution in warfare wrought by Gustavus Adolphus of Sweden, and the emergence and decline of France under the rule of Louis XIV. The text concludes with the two chapters written by Albert S. Britt, III, that cover the art of war as practiced by Frederick the Great of Prussia.

The present edition of *The Dawn of Modern Warfare* is essentially the text that was printed for use at the Military Academy in 1973. As editor, I have attempted to clarify certain passages for the general reader, amplify purely military terminology, and improve the evenness of the narrative. The editor is grateful for the advice and suggestions that were tendered by Rudy Shur and Joanne Abrams of Avery Publishing Group, Inc. Their assistance was timely and helpful. Ms. Abrams immeasurably improved the narrative through her painstaking editing, corrections of lapses in syntax, and penetrating questions related to clarity of expression.

Thomas E. Griess
Series Editor

Introduction

At the end of the thirteenth century, warfare suffered from a lack of imagination on the part of the men who waged it. Unlike the Roman and Byzantine practitioners of the art of war, the men who wielded force in this later period of history were helpless for the most part to counter the effects of their crumbling civilization, and thus allowed stagnation to set in. The student of the art of war, however, can begin to perceive the glimmer of change that appeared in the fourteenth century. At that time, the threads that comprise the entire fabric of war began to take on different shapes as western mankind emerged from the Middle Ages and renewed the relentless drive to progress in all aspects of life. This text commences with that renaissance, and concludes with events that occurred on the eve of the profound social and political revolution that shook western Europe five centuries later.

While Napoleonic warfare shattered many military concepts that were deeply rooted in the period treated in the latter portion of this text, there are, nevertheless, valid reasons for studying the earlier era. It was during this era that England gained the ascendancy on the high seas that would immediately begin to influence European developments. This was also the period during which great captains flashed across the pages of history, and generalship was deeply influential and personal. Then, too, the concept of limited war was practiced as an art, a subtle balancing act from which modern leaders can learn more than a little. This was the epoch ushering in another, more lengthy and world-wide clash between England and France which, alternately smouldering and flashing, engulfed the Hapsburgs, Russia, American colonists, and that staunch Soldier-King, Frederick the Great. The science of fortification flourished and ultimately exerted undue influence on the waging of war. At the same time, armies grew more professional, and governments learned how to better manage them. Stagnation in tactics disappeared under the influence of Gustavus Adolphus of Sweden, only to appear again as imitators sought to duplicate the precise linear tactics practiced so effectively by Frederick.

Another theme that makes the study of warfare as waged during that period profitable is the restoration of the combined arms concept to the battlefield. It occurred only gradually, because there had to be first a resurgence of the infantry—a revitalization that was sufficiently powerful to counter the accepted supremacy of the cavalry. Initially utilizing existing weapons and later adopting the first crude gunpowder-activated handguns, the foot soldier restored balance to the practice of war. At the same time, improving technology made available primitive field artillery pieces that could accompany armies and fire gunpowder-propelled missiles. As the infantryman became more effective and the cavalryman's dominance declined, tactics used to fight battles became more flexible. Our story begins with one of the early challenges to the supremacy of the mounted knight.

Changing Tides
in Warfare

The Beginning of Modern Warfare 1

Even as the results of battles in the thirteenth century served to emphasize the superiority of medieval cavalry in the hands of a skillful commander, some evidence began to suggest the resurgence of infantry as a competitive arm on the battlefield. No single battle or campaign heralded the ascendancy of infantry. Rather, the process was slow, irregular, and disordered by the vagaries of national attitudes, the wide variations in qualities of generalship, and the influences of different and incomparable circumstances. Unsophisticated medieval communications produced a barrier to the exchange of ideas and the discovery of trends concerning the evolution of warfare. Yet the unmistakable movement toward greater participation of infantry on the battlefield emerged in different corners of Europe, and would not be suppressed.

An example of this trend can be seen upon examination of the Battle of Courtrai, which jolted the traditional outlook of the cavalry-minded soldiers of France and cast doubts on the invincibility of the mounted warrior. Hurrying to its southern frontier in July of 1302, the Flemish Army drew up in an excellent defensive position near Courtrai to challenge the French threat to that city. Robert of Artois, the French commander, brushed aside suggestions from his advisors, who urged him to bypass the insignificant castle at Courtrai and push on to Ghent. Instead, Robert resolved to attack what he considered contemptible and inferior infantry.

The Flemish took advantage of existing terrain in selecting their defensive position. In front of the position ran a small watercourse. Between this and their front lines, the Flemish dug *pottes*, or holes, each approximately three feet deep and covered with grass and branches—to serve as traps for the French knights. Over 10,000 Flemish infantrymen deployed in a solid mass along a 1,000-yard front. Swampy meadows and a deep ditch protected the right flank, while the Lys River and a Franciscan nunnery shielded the left. A small number of *arbalesters*, or crossbowmen, deployed to the edge of the stream to fire their shafts at the French as they advanced, but

the vast majority of the Flemish army was infantry. A small reserve waited behind the center of the massed formation. Wearing metal hats, the only other protective armor the Flemish could boast of was a heavy cloth or leather coat, called a *gambeson*. Their weapon was a peculiar sort of pike, the *goedendag*, a heavy, long-shafted club with a spike protruding from the end.

Opposing the Flemish was a typical French field army of the late thirteenth or early fourteenth century. It consisted of a combination of light infantrymen, mainly Genoese armed with the crossbow, and a sizable number of heavy cavalrymen, grouped in ten squadrons and arrayed in three lines. Though substantially less numerous than their Flemish opponents, the French knights entertained no doubt that the battle would be won by their mounted warriors.

Robert of Artois opened with a fusillade of arrows from his Genoese crossbowmen, who drove back their Flemish counterparts after a long exchange of missiles. From their side of the stream, the Genoese crossbowmen were near enough to pour their shafts into the mass of Flemish infantry. Two of the subordinate Flemish commanders ordered their troops to draw back to get out of the range of the Genoese archers, and the fact that the Flemish accomplished the movement without confusion or panic testifies to their steady discipline.

The reason for the next occurrence is not entirely clear. Either tempted by the retirement of part of the Flemish infantry or determined that his heavy cavalry and not his crossbowmen would deal the decisive blow to the enemy, Robert ordered his infantry aside and launched the vanguard of his cavalry at the Flemish. The results were chaotic. Unable to dodge or clear the way, retiring crossbowmen either were ridden down or created confusion in the ranks of the advancing knights. The small waterway in front of the Flemish position proved to be deeper and muddier than anticipated. The marshy meadow on the Flemish right also proved troublesome. Many of the frustrated knights who finally negotiated these two obstacles became unseated when their mounts stumbled in the concealed *pottes* dug by the Flemish. Looking up the slope, they saw, coming toward them, the whole Flemish phalanx with pikes leveled. Flemish commanders had decided to take advantage of the obvious disorder and loss of momentum in the French mounted charge. Pushed back to the stream, Robert angrily ordered the main body of his cavalry to attack. Stream, marsh, retiring crossbowmen, and retreating knights helped to frustrate the impulse of the main body of cavalry. At one point the center of the Flemish formation was driven in by the knights who reached it, but the timely reinforcement by the reserve re-established the wall of bristling pikes. Too late the French cavalry tried to withdraw, but neither the exhausted mounts nor the heavily armored knights could avoid the irresistible pressure of the advancing Flemish, who slashed and stabbed the horses and killed dismounted knights, including Robert of Artois. Following their infantry, the third line of French cavalry galloped off the field.[1]

The Decline of Cavalry

Notwithstanding the impetuosity of the charge of the French cavalry over obviously ill-suited terrain, the defeat of cavalry by infantry at Courtrai sounded a new note in the evolution of warfare in western Europe. Not since the defeat of the Roman infantry by cavalry at Adrianople in A.D. 378 had such an important development in warfare emerged. Nor was it an isolated matter. A few years later, in 1314, Robert the Bruce of Scotland actually dismounted the bulk of his knights to take advantage of the marshes and trees through which the opposing English must pass. Like the French cavalry at Courtrai, the English mounted men-at-arms at Bannockburn disdained the use of their supporting infantry and left it far behind. Bogs, steep slopes, and scattered woods disorganized the English knights and they floundered, becoming easy prey for the pikes and axes of the Scots who fought under Robert.[2] Neither Courtrai nor Bannockburn turned the course of military history in a new direction or signaled the rise of the Flemish or the Scots as a formidable military power in the latter part of the Middle Ages. Yet each incident marked a step on the path toward the realization that disciplined infantry could be an effective counterforce to the traditional superiority of the feudal knight.

More profound and fundamental forces than the disciplined and well-armed infantry force, however, were at work to dislodge the feudal knight from preeminence in western European warfare. Encouraged by the popular response to the call to crusade and backed by the powerful moral and economic strength at its disposal, the papacy became increasingly involved in the secular as well as the religious course of Europe. Its increased participation in dynastic quarrels led to a discrediting of spiritual power used politically to gain aims only remotely connected with the perceived role of the Church. As a result of this and other factors, a new nationalist-monarchical system was beginning to emerge in western Europe, and inevitably it collided with the old theocratic-feudal order of the Middle Ages.

In addition, other forces influenced both the style and intensity of warfare. No longer was war the private province of the aristocracy. With the initiation of the crusades, warfare became an increasingly commercial undertaking. The growth of commercial cities and trading centers not only added a new source of revenue for use in waging war but also introduced another voice to be heard in the councils of war. The wealth of cities and individuals offered the monarch a potential escape route from his former dependence on the nobility or aristocracy. Guilds, crafts, citizen militias, and the unrest that triggered the dramatic signing of England's Magna Carta in 1215 signaled a growing participation of a larger segment of the population in the government in general, and in the prosecution of war in particular.

From their travels on the crusades, returning warriors brought back advanced methods of fortification learned in the eastern half of Christendom. Castle building increased in western Europe until the feudal fortress dominated the countryside of France and England. More wealth in the hands of towns and cities permitted them to provide their own local militia—bodies of troops like the Flemish militia that fought at Courtrai. Special mercenary soldiers proved useful for the defense of fortress walls, where skilled crossbowmen were in high demand. Since the feudal knight could perform essentially one function, and that function was not directly useful in either the attack or the defense of a fortress, more emphasis was placed on procuring troops who could mine, dig, batter, or operate the large siege machines needed to attack a castle.

In his own way, the feudal knight contributed to the increasing importance of mercenaries. Improving his means of protection from the twelfth through the fourteenth centuries through the use of plate armor instead of mail,* the knight became an increasingly expensive soldier, and his international commercial value could persuade him to subordinate his own personal or national loyalty. In addition, the standard contract between lord and vassal usually prescribed the annual length of service—ordinarily 40 days—that the armored warrior owed to his lord. In the latter part of the thirteenth century, the Kings of both France and England found the reliability

---

*Mail armor consisted of a flexible covering made of interlocked metal rings.

of a paid force, whether feudal or mercenary, worth the additional cost. As trade and commerce revived and the supply of money grew in western Europe, the bond between monarch and commercial interests strengthened. A king's ability to pay for the services of his warriors was a key factor in the decline of the feudal system. Economic, social, and governmental forces speeded the disintegration of feudalism and accelerated the trend toward achieving unity and central power in the dynastic states of France and England.[3] The process became strikingly evident during the long struggle between England and France, the Hundred Years' War (1337–1453), but before that lengthy struggle embroiled Europe in war, there was another significant step in the decline of cavalry.

The Resurgence of Infantry

Like an echo from the past, the Swiss of the fourteenth century developed a formation much like the Macedonian phalanx, and stunned the cavalry-minded soldiery of western Europe. The formation by itself, however, was not the sole reason for Swiss success. In the early organizational stages, Swiss forces were almost entirely equipped with the *halberd*, an 8-foot weapon with a sharp point at the end of a heavy head, a blade on the front, and a spike or hook on the back. The point on the end enabled the infantryman to use the *halberd* like a pike; with the blade he could slash, and the hook was ideal to unseat a mounted warrior, or at least to pull the reins out of his hands. Strong arms could give the cutting blade of the *halberd* more power than any sword, slicing through helmet or plate armor or decapitating a horseman with a single blow. Finally, the superb discipline of the Swiss produced compact, deep columns that could adjust to the peculiarities of terrain and yet retain solidity for rapid movement and unyielding impact. For about two centuries (ca. 1315–1515), the Swiss phalanx proved its worth on western European battlefields.

An Ambush at Mortgarten

Led by elected or nominated "captains," the Swiss infantry surprised and butchered a punitive expedition of Austrians at Mortgarten in 1315. *(See Map 1.)* Duke Leopold of Austria had mobilized an army of 4,000–5,000 men at the entrance to the Swiss passes in order to chastise the Swiss for plundering the abbey at Einsiedeln and carrying off a number of monks as hostages. Of the two passes available to the Austrian Duke, one was blocked by Swiss fortifications, so Duke Leopold chose the other, which led through the defile of Mortgarten. With a force numbering between 1,500 and 2,000, the Swiss threw up a hasty obstacle—a wall of loose stone—across the road and guarded it with a small party. But the bulk of their

The Swiss Halberdier

force hid in the woods and ravine above the road. Below the road, a lake served as another obstacle to complete the textbook ambush site. Advancing without the benefit of reconnaissance scouts, Leopold was unaware of what lay ahead until his vanguard of horsemen reached the stone obstacle. Ordering his soldiers to storm the wall, he apparently intended for them to accomplish the feat dismounted, for his infantry was at the rear of the column in the typical medieval fashion.

At about this time, boulders and trunks of trees rolled out of the woods above the road, followed by the main body of Swiss in tight formation, driving into the flank of the cavalry with their *halberds*. Unaware of what was happening in front, the rest of the Austrian army continued to push forward, so packing the cavalry together that it was incapable of maneuvering. Turning around to flee, part of the cavalry at the rear only added to the confusion, as it became intermixed with the infantry; meanwhile, the knights in front were hacked by *halberds* or driven into the lake. Some, one chronicler relates, "threw themselves in panic into the lake, preferring to drown rather than to be hewn about by the dreadful weapons of their enemies."[4] Like Hannibal's Carthaginians at Lake Trasimene (217 B.C.), the Swiss combined imaginative tactics with careful use of terrain to defeat a superior and more mobile force.[5]

Reluctant to admit that well disciplined and properly armed infantry could best a cavalry force, the Austrians, like the French after Courtrai, chose to believe that poor generalship and the peculiarities of the terrain deprived them of a fair test against the Swiss. At the same time, there were no dark mysteries about the methods or ability of the Alpine infantrymen. Organized along the political lines of the existing cantons (states) of the Swiss Confederation, the Alpine soldiers had no permanent generals or standing army. *(See Map 1.)* In times of danger, the troops of one canton would come to the aid of another, and from among the collective leadership, one commander would be chosen to lead in battle. The Confederation included both peasant and city republics, founded along the lines of the original three forest cantons that were allied before the Battle of Mortgarten. Soon the success of the forest cantons encouraged the city of Lucerne and the urban community of Bern to join in alliance. Others followed. Anything but peaceful, the cantons quarrelled and warred among themselves frequently, interrupting their own internal disputes to unite whenever an outside intruder threatened the integrity of one of the cantons.[6]

The Battle of Laupen

Although at Mortgarten the Swiss demonstrated their ability to fight an effective defensive battle against a mounted enemy, the strength of their phalanx was not limited to this form of battle. In 1339, at Laupen, a Swiss army met the forces of a combination of feudal chiefs from the valleys of the Rhone and Aar Rivers, under the command of Count Gerard of Vallangin. *(See Map 1.)* The battlefield was an open plain at the foot of the Alps. By this time, the Swiss had learned that infantry armed with the *halberd* alone were at a disadvantage in disputing charging cavalry. The 8-foot *halberd* allowed mounted warriors to come too close to the formation, where the horsemen could use their lances. Consequently, they had taken to arming a sizable portion of the Alpine infantrymen with an 18-foot, metal-tipped pike, and placing them in the outer ranks of the formation. Those armed with the *halberd* took their place in the interior ranks of the dense phalanx. By now, also, the Swiss had developed their normal order of battle—echeloned deployment in three heavy columns. Usually four rows of pikemen formed the outer ranks of the phalanx. *(See Diagram with Map 1.)* Within the formation, the halberdiers awaited the outcome of the first and subsequent impacts with the pikes. After the pikemen sufficiently disorganized the opposing cavalry or infantry, the halberdiers moved forward with a will and closed in to finish the work of the pikemen. Each column, which was in effect a phalanx with a narrow front, included the troops of one canton.

At Laupen, the Swiss commander, Rudolf von Erlach, advanced with his center column forward and the two columns on the wings drawn back, but he did not begin his advance until the feudal chiefs were already committed and had started their charge. Count Gerard's infantry, on his left and in the center, was no match for the relentless advance of the Swiss, and was soon driven from the field with severe losses. But on the Swiss left the men of the forest cantons were rapidly surrounded by the attacking cavalry, although they managed to hold their own. When they had driven the feudal infantry from the field, however, the other two columns turned to come to the aid of the column that faced Gerard's cavalry, hitting the horsemen from their left and rear. Exhausted by their charge and discouraged by the assault of the other two Swiss columns, Gerard's cavalry wing quit the field.[7] Laupen marked the beginning of an era in which the Swiss phalanx emerged as an effective offensive as well as defensive system with which cavalry could be defeated.

The Swiss System

Recognizing that the Swiss had recovered the tactical strength of infantry, the opponents of the Alpine soldiers searched for ways to challenge the superiority of the well-disciplined Swiss foot soldiers. Some resorted to imitation, generally with poor results, for superficial imitation (e.g., simply dismounting knights to fight as infantry) could not equal the substance of the Swiss system, which drew sustenance from the entire resources of the state. The Alpine infantrymen marched to battle in the same formation in which they expected to fight—the dense, compact phalanx. In addition, mobilization time was reduced to the bare minimum since the Swiss Army had no need to assemble before marching to battle, but could march from the cantons by various routes after being alerted, and join other contingents near or on the battlefield. Although this could, and sometimes did, result in concentration on the battlefield, a practice alternately condemned and emulated in the history of the art of war, the capability of the opponent to take advantage of the Swiss piecemeal commitment was an important consideration. Neither the Austrians at Sempach nor the Milanese at Arbedo were able to exploit the fleeting weakness of this method of Swiss concentration.[8] One reason for such failures on the part of Swiss opponents was the unremitting willingness of the Alpine soldier to fight, coupled with his dispiriting tendency neither to give nor to expect quarter. For example, when a French army of mercenaries invaded the Swiss Confederation in 1444, a body of Alpine infantrymen less than 1,000 strong boldly attacked the French,

who were 15 times their number. Quickly surrounded, the Swiss used a hollow square to repel cavalry and archer alike. When the entire Swiss force was finally annihilated, the French commander withdrew, leaving 2,000 of his own dead on the battlefield and soberly judging that his army could not stand many victories as costly as that one.[9]

Audacious and perhaps even brilliant in their adoption of discarded tactics, the Swiss nevertheless were destined to be eclipsed on the battlefields of Europe. For the first 150 years that they occupied the spotlight and won the respect of the soldiers of western Europe, the Swiss could credit part of their remarkable success to the fact that they did not meet either a resourceful general or a tactical system to rival their own. The outstanding features of their military superiority were its efficiency and its simplicity, neither of which, unfortunately, could stand unchallenged against the march of technology. Nor did they seriously study the art of war. Finally, no great leader apparently ever aspired to permanent generalship. This is not to say that in local situations there

Swiss Infantry in Close Combat

was not occasionally a display of a respectable caliber of generalship and a competent grasp of strategy. In clashes with Charles the Bold, Duke of Burgundy—one ruler who was not intimidated by the Swiss reputation—the Swiss showed an ability to maneuver skillfully and to utilize the terrain cleverly. The battles at Morat and Nancy are examples in point.[10]

The disregard by the Swiss for the study of warfare or the important contributions of technology in the fifteenth and sixteenth centuries were destined to undermine the superiority of their renowned columns. More efficient opponents, more capable generals, and the beginning of the use of gunpowder forecast disaster for a military system that clung tenaciously to the tactics of its ancestors. While the Swiss mercenary remained an important military commodity on the battlefields of Europe, the period of decline of the Swiss method of warfare had already begun in the latter part of the fifteenth century.

The Hundred Years' War (1337–1453)

The Swiss were not alone in their discovery of a method to challenge the superiority of mounted, armored knighthood. Elsewhere in Europe, a different method emerged to dispute the supremacy of the soldier on horseback. That development is best highlighted by an examination of the contest between the two most formidable powers in Europe.

In the early part of the fourteenth century, the growing power of the kingdoms of France and England, the concurrent decline of the influence of the papacy, and the peculiar relationship between the rulers of the two nations led to a long period of conflict between those two kingdoms, which only terminated with their cooperation in World War I.

A sovereign in his own right, the King of England also occupied the unenviable position of being a vassal of the King of France by virtue of land holdings of England on the Continent that were, through the long development of feudalization, fiefs under the control of the French king. Edward III, while still a prince, received the Duchy of Aquitaine from the King of France, Charles IV, in 1325. *(See Map 2a.)* The reason for this unusual transfer was the fact that the prince's mother was not only the wife of the English king, but also the sister of Charles, King of France. Two years later, Edward III became King of England when his father, Edward II, was forced to abdicate. Charles IV died about a year later and left no male heir for the throne of France. Consequently, the French barons and peers chose Philip of Valois, a nephew of Charles IV, as the new king, Philip VI. The English court, however, felt that Edward III had a legitimate claim to the French crown through his mother, the sister of the former

King of France. But England's Army and Navy were too weak to enforce Edward's claim.

Edward III's acceptance of the situation did not mean that he was satisfied with it. Aquitaine was an English bridgehead in France, and Edward had no intention of relinquishing it. Nor was he eager to submit as a vassal to the new French king, which he ought to have done as lord of Aquitaine. On the other hand, the existence of an English duchy in France was unsettling to Philip, and he used every device at his disposal to coerce Edward into submitting to him as vassal to liege lord. An alliance between Scotland and France aggravated matters, since the battling between the Scots and English, encouraged by France, served to weaken and harass England. Edward countered with an alliance with the Flemish, who were dependent on the English for wool for their weavers. Flanders was also in a threatening, strategic position on the frontier of France. Incident followed incident, bringing the two proud kingdoms closer to the brink of war. Finally, the declaration by Philip in 1337 that Aquitaine was forfeited ended the nervous diplomatic sparring and plunged England and France into open conflict.

Yet, to view the dynastic struggle between the two kings as the sole cause of the Hundred Years' War would be misleading and inaccurate. More profound influences that helped to drag the two kingdoms into an armed clash are mentioned by the British historian, J. F. C. Fuller:

> Seen in focus, the causes of the Hundred Years War were by no means rooted solely either in the dynastic or in the feudal questions, but rather in the multiple conditions of the age which gave it birth. The authority of the papacy was on the wane; the influence of the [Holy Roman] empire was all but spent; kingdoms were rising into power; trade was becoming increasingly a cause of contention between kingdoms; the command of the sea was looming over the horizon; the spirit of chivalry, begotten during the crusades, had become blatantly bellicose; and, above all, there was not sufficient room for two would-be dominant powers in western Europe. All these things, under the cloak of Edward's feudal claim to the crown of France, precipitated the Hundred Years War, the greatest tourney of the middle ages, which, in spite of its follies and disasters, sowed the seeds which were to sprout into a greater England and a greater France.[11]

Viewed in perspective, then, the seizure of Aquitaine was simply the spark that ignited the conflagration which would occupy the attention of much of Europe for over a century.[12]

The Battle of Crécy

The beginning of the Hundred Years' War is normally dated

from the time that Philip seized the Duchy of Aquitaine for the French in 1337 in response to growing signs of preparation for war by Edward III in England. Yet the first significant clash between the two kingdoms did not occur until Edward quieted the turbulence with the Scots on his own borders and gathered sufficient strength and support at home to launch an invasion of France in 1346.[13]

Just as the *halberd*, and to some degree the pike, had given the Swiss phalanx weapons around which a strong and decisive formation was able to emerge, the English had developed a weapon of their own that bridged the gap between the supremacy of feudal cavalry and the beginning of modern warfare. For over 50 years before the first major contest of the Hundred Years' War, English yeomen had been perfecting the longbow, a weapon that gave them a decided advantage over a variety of opponents until well into the sixteenth century.

Made of yew and approximately 6 feet in length, the longbow was remarkably accurate at the normal tournament range of 220 yards, and could launch its arrow easily twice that range. It had proved its value in the border conflicts between the English and the Scots. Larger and more powerful than the contemporary crossbow, the longbow fired its shaft more accurately and over a far greater distance. Equally important was the fact that a trained yeoman could fire three arrows with his longbow for every one that the crossbowman could launch, even after the latter improved his loading time with the help of a winch, which was an integral part of the crossbow. The only major drawback of the longbow, and the one that may account for the failure of other European nations to adopt it, was the length of time required to develop the skill and strength to operate it properly—six years according to some contemporary accounts.[14]

When Edward III contemplated the campaign that he was about to initiate against France, he must have been aware that France was both more populous and more wealthy than England. To be successful, he had to overcome the inherent strengths of France with the quality of his army. Accordingly, to obtain the numbers that he would need to invade France, Edward borrowed from both the mercenary system and what lingered of the feudal system in England. He recruited using the method of indenture, by which he contracted with individuals to raise a specified number of troops for a given period of time; the individual who raised the troops received a sum of money from the royal treasury. In this way he took advantage of the loyalty of his subjects to rally to his cause. The contractors who raised the troops were generally of the class of the more powerful and adventuresome vassals, the remnants of the feudal class.[15] The major fighting elements of his army were 6,000 to 7,000 men-at-arms, about 10,000 archers, and

A Crossbowman

A Longbowman

3,000 to 4,000 Welsh infantry. Armed attendants and squires brought the total of the force with which he crossed the Channel to around 35,000.

Edward III displayed respectable tactics during the campaign, but the mediocrity of his strategy nearly cost him the expedition. *(See Map 3a.)* Landing unopposed near the tip of the Cotentin Peninsula, he moved across the wealthy Duchy of Normandy in what can only be described as a huge raid, gathering enough plunder and ransom money along the way to substantially defray the cost of the expedition. From the direction of his movements, it does not appear that Edward was overly anxious to meet and fight the French Army, which he knew, when assembled, would outnumber his invading force.[16]

Slow concentration of the French and indifferent reconnaissance permitted Edward to move all the way to the Seine River, where someone had possessed enough foresight to destroy the bridge at Elboeuf. Therefore, on August 7, 1346, Edward was faced with a difficult choice. Because he knew he might face a stronger French army, it was imperative that he keep open a line of retreat. However, he had already sent his fleet home and calculated that the only likely ports from which he could evacuate his army, if the need arose, were north of the Seine along the Channel coast. No usable crossing sites were available downstream along the Seine, and the French army was concentrating near Paris. Carefully he started working toward Paris until he found a partially destroyed bridge at Poissy, 50 miles upstream from Elboeuf and only 13 straight-line miles from Paris.[17]

Thanks to inadequate French scouting and security, Edward's engineers were able to repair the bridge, and his troops began their crossing on August 15. Once Philip learned of Edward's crossing, he displayed his chivalric bent by sending a formal challenge to Edward, inviting the English to battle near Paris. Edward's reply suggested that he would consent to fight far to the south, but instead he marched his army northward, gaining a day and a half while the French waited in good faith. A hurried march took his army north to an area near the mouth of the Somme River, where, again, lax French security permitted him to make another river crossing on the twenty-fourth and finally gain a clear line of retreat to the Straits of Dover, should he need it. No longer could Edward avoid battle, for the French army was breathing down his neck even as he slipped unopposed across the Somme. On August 26, he chose an excellent defensive position on a rise of ground and braced himself for the inevitable French attack.[18]

Edward deployed his troops in the usual groups of the period, with two on line to receive the attack of the French and one held in reserve under his direct control. *(See Map 3b.)* Dismounted men-at-arms made up the strong nucleus of

each of the frontline groups and were formed in a solid line, probably six or eight deep. On each wing and between the two groups of the men-at-arms stood the archers, placed there so that they would not get in the way of the men-at-arms. Infantry armed with the spear were placed behind the archers. The reserve that Edward retained contained 700 mounted men-at-arms, 200 archers, and about 1,000 Welsh infantry spearmen. The right of Edward's line was securely protected by the village of Crecy and the small marshy valley of the river Maye. On his left, Edward extended his frontline until it joined the small village of Wadicourt, thereby denying the French the opportunity to turn either flank without difficulty.[19]

Expecting to see Edward's army still retreating northward, King Philip's advance elements were surprised when they sighted the entire English force drawn up in battle array. Realizing that his army was still strewn over several miles of road, Philip ordered the vanguard to halt; since it was late in the day, he did not plan to begin the battle until the following day. But the confusion of the poorly disciplined conglomeration of French units overrode Philip's judicious caution. As the vanguard of the French men-at-arms halted and pulled back slightly in the face of the English army, those following them assumed that the battle had already begun and that their leading elements had been pushed back. Secure in the knowledge that they outnumbered the English by at least 2 and perhaps 3 to 1, the subordinate French commanders pushed their troops forward and scrambled into whatever gaps could be found in the frontline, creating confusion and bringing the leading elements to within bowshot of the English lines. Philip finally struggled to the front himself, and found the entire open area facing the English filled with his own army, which was in great disorder and too close to the English to withdraw safely. He decided to attack with what he had.

Philip opened the attack with the 6,000 Genoese crossbowmen at his disposal. They halted twice to check their alignment, shouted their defiance, and started moving a third time as they let their arrows fly. English accounts generally agree that this opening fusillade fell short of the mark and did little damage. But the response of the English longbowmen took a heavy toll of both the crossbowmen and the horses of the men-at-arms. Disgusted by the unequal contest between the competing archers, the commander of the French men-at-arms ordered the charge. As the French had done at Courtrai, they rode down those crossbowmen who were unable to dodge or clear the way, and struggled up the slope, which had been made slippery by a recent rain. No doubt the French horses found the going difficult at best, as each carried a knight with his heavy armor, was burdened by the additional 140 pounds of armor on the horse, and stumbled in potholes that had been dug by the English. Even though additional mounted French troops arrived on the field after the action started and pressed to the front, they could not appreciably change the tide of the battle. Confusion from the retreating horsemen, wounded horses, and fleeing crossbowmen broke up their ranks. As the French troops approached the English position, the accuracy and volume of fire of the English longbowmen crippled their horses, giving the English dismounted men-at-arms the opportunity to surge forward and complete the repulse begun by the longbowmen. The battle that had started just before dark continued with the arrival of fresh French men-at-arms, but the French were exhausted by midnight. Finally the futile attacks stopped, and Edward chose not to pursue Philip's battered, retreating army.[20]

Edward continued his retreat to Calais unchallenged, besieged that city for a year, and finally captured it—the one positive result of his campaign.

As so often happens in history, the impact that the Battle of Crécy had on subsequent battles was less a result of the actual cause of the French defeat and more a result of what the French perceived to be the cause of their defeat. Ignoring the obvious advantage of the longbow over the crossbow and focusing their attention on the incomprehensible inability of their mounted cavalry to carry the day, the French decided that the cause of England's success lay in clever use of their men-at-arms on foot. It made some sense. One of the reasons that the French cavalry had fared so badly was that their horses were vulnerable to the English arrows, and could not reasonably carry more armor for protection. But the tactics that the French adopted at their next meeting with the English, at Poitiers in 1356, were, if anything, even worse than those used at Crécy.[21]

The Battle of Poitiers

The commander of this English expedition, which took place 10 years after Crécy, was Edward, the Black Prince, son of Edward III. Landing in France near the Pyrennes, he pushed northward into central France, leisurely plundering as he went. King John of France mobilized a force to intercept him.

The curious wanderings of the two armies, neither one of which was very large, are difficult to understand, and bring little credit to either commander. At times the two armies were only 15 miles apart; but they either encamped, awaiting the next move of the other, or veered off in different directions. *(See Map 3c.)* Finally, through poor reconnaissance on both sides, the English advance party unexpectedly encountered the French rearguard about two miles east of Poitiers.[22] At dawn on the next day, September 18, 1356, the Black Prince assured himself that he had indeed struck a part of the main French army, selected a defensive position to receive battle, and began busily looking for a route of withdrawal. After the

initial contact of the first day, the French army had withdrawn toward Poitiers. King John had the English in such a position that he could have maneuvered across their line of communication and forced the Black Prince to fight on a battlefield of French choosing, but the chivalric instinct that guided John's thinking compelled him to engage once contact was made. All of the eighteenth was spent in fruitless negotiations, because the terms offered by the French were unacceptable to the Black Prince. Edward used the time well to search for a crossing site over the Moisson River, to his rear, so that he could avoid battle by timely escape. Disposing his force not to fight a battle but to cover his retreat across the river, he hoped to make the crossing before the French struck. In his preparation for withdrawal, he was admirably assisted by the peculiar type of terrain that bordered the river. A considerable portion of the position was covered by a vineyard. In that part of France, the vines grew on wooden stakes about four feet high and so close together that a horse could not pass between them. In this vineyard, Edward dispersed his longbowmen, reinforced by dismounted cavalry and infantry armed with spears.

The battle turned on a decision made by John in an effort to overcome the vulnerability of his cavalry mounts. The French king divided his army into four battles, or divisions, the first of which he dismounted a distance from the rise that the English longbowmen occupied. He intended to reduce his men's vulnerability by removing their mounts, but the weight of the armor that the knights wore apparently did not enter into his calculations. As the dismounted men-at-arms struggled up the slope toward the top of the hill, a rain of arrows from the longbowmen greeted them. In addition, the vanguard of John's army, still mounted, noticed that the Black Prince, his banner, and his entourage disappeared over the back of the hill at about the same time. Just as the French surmised, the Black Prince was going to the river to check the crossing site for the retreat. In haste, the French troops urged John to let them charge what they prematurely judged to be a retreating army. As they charged up the slope, channelized by the narrow, sunken trails, hedges, and brush that covered the hillside, the longbowmen shifted their aim to the mounted charge and so disorganized it that only a handful were still mounted when they reached the vineyard, where they were promptly unhorsed by spearmen and English cavalry on foot. As the first element of John's dismounted troops continued to struggle up the slope, the Black Prince grasped the seriousness of the situation and hurried troops back from the crossing site to bolster his line. The continued fire of the English archers and these reinforcements routed the exhausted and unfortunate dismounted knights by striking them in front and flank. Two more divisions of dismounted men-at-arms still remained at John's disposal, but the first of these, seeing the results of the initial two attacks and judging that the continuation of the battle was hopeless, broke and fled.

The last of the divisions remained to be spent, and spend it John did. Dismounting about a mile from the English position, the armor-clad cavalry began the same long, torturous climb up the slope, led by the King himself. Sensing that the moment for a counterstroke had arrived, the Black Prince prepared to counterattack and sent a small detachment of cavalry out on the flank, well out of sight. His archers had nearly exhausted their arrows, and, when these were expended, he threw them forward in hand-to-hand fighting against John's last wave of weary hill climbers. The French withstood the shock of the attacking archers well, and the battle surged back and forth on the hillside until the Black Prince's 200 cavalrymen burst upon the French flank and turned the tide, probably as much through the psychological effect that they had on John's troops as their physical contribution to the battle. Throughout the battle, the French crossbowmen never seriously challenged the longbows of the English in range or volume of fire, and played a predictably minor role in the outcome. The remainder of the French army was destroyed, and King John was captured.[23]

Despite the distinct military success of the English at Crécy and Poitiers, it would be inaccurate to link subsequent political advantages of the English with their victories on the battlefield. Four years after Poitiers, for instance, the Treaty of Bretigny (1360) between the French and English tripled the holdings of the English on the Continent at the expense of the French. (See Map 2b.) Yet the reason for the advantageous treaty for the English is more correctly identified as being King John's willingness to exchange territory for his release from English captivity than the military success of the English.[24] In addition, the errors in tactical employment of the French in both battles strongly suggest that the English Army may simply have been the fortunate benefactor of unworthy opponents. This view, however, ignores the impact of the longbow on the direction of warfare in the fourteenth and fifteenth centuries. Used by itself in the hands of a force exclusively composed of infantry, the longbow might well have disappeared into obscurity as another gimmick, full of promise but lacking practicality. Visualize the vulnerability of a host of English longbowmen facing a determined mounted charge after the archers had expended their arrows. The importance of the longbow in the march of technology is the contribution of unrivaled firepower—in range, accuracy, and volume—that the weapon offered to a *combined* force of cavalry and infantry. As long as the French, or, for that matter, any other army, attempted to challenge an English army built around the longbow without using a weapon that could equal the firepower of that weapon, the English continued to enjoy consistent success on the battlefield.

As different as the systems of the Swiss and the English were, each method was a distinct step in the direction of elevating the value of infantrymen at the expense of the mounted soldier. Neither the *halberd*—or the combination of *halberd* and pike which the Swiss adopted later—nor the longbow survived as the ultimate weapon. Both capitalized on the freedom of movement and action of the individual soldier as he dropped one piece of body armament after another. Yet each weapon enjoyed only passing superiority until other weapons offering greater range, accuracy, or destructive capability appeared on the battlefield.

Combined Arms Application

The tactical superiority of the Swiss earned respect for the Alpine infantry, but never elevated Switzerland to the position of a major power in Europe. Swiss mercenaries fought all over Europe, but not as a part of a Swiss army. Near the end of the fifteenth century, it was not unusual for the Swiss to find themselves fighting against their own countrymen, as Italy became the battleground of two leading military powers of Europe—Spain and France. Not only internal strife but also mutual jealousies prevented the Italian states from mounting an effective resistance against a determined invader. No doubt the wealth of the Italian states was also an irresistible lure to both Spain and France. When Charles VIII came to the throne in France (1483), he resolved to press his claim to the Kingdom of Naples, which was ostensibly in the hands of its king, but was actually controlled by the Spanish through family ties. (See Map 4a.)

The Army of Charles VIII

While the earliest European mention of a substance that appears to be gunpowder is attributed to the Englishman Roger Bacon (ca. 1260), the explosive mixture did not make a substantial impact on European warfare until some time in the fifteenth century. Earlier evidence of the use of gunpowder in Asia and Europe exists, but the siege of Constantinople in 1453, during which the Turkish Sultan used enormous 25-inch cannon to hurl 1,200 to 1,500-pound projectiles at the fortress walls, ushered in a new era of warfare.[25]

Although some reports suggest that the English employed a few cannon as early as Crécy in the Hundred Years' War, they appear to have had little effect on the outcome. By far the more important effect of the Hundred Years' War was that it helped to accelerate the growth and power of both England and France. In addition, the consistent success of the English led the French to search for ways to overcome

Charles VIII of France

the growing strength of infantry supported by cavalry, whether the infantry were armed with the longbow, as in the case of the English, or with *halberd* and pike, as in the case of the declining Swiss phalanx.

When Charles VIII of France led his army to Italy in 1494, the organization and efficiency of his force impressed the leading powers of Europe. Swiss mercenaries drilled the infantry of his army, while Swiss pikemen and Scottish archers marched side by side with French heavy cavalry. But the remarkable feature of Charles' army was the artillery train, which was more reliable, more mobile, and larger than anything witnessed before. Clearly, France led Europe in the development of artillery in the late fifteenth century; the artillery train of Charles' army reveals the degree of progress the French had made in artillery materiel development.

The largest weapons that accompanied Charles' army weighed approximately 6,000 pounds, were mounted on four-wheeled carts, and were drawn by a team of 12 horses. At the other end of the spectrum were small guns on two-wheeled carriages, firing balls that could not have been much larger than those fired by the cumbersome shoulder weapons of the time. The most useful artillery pieces, however, were the variety of weapons between the two ends of the spectrum, exhibiting the development of functional gun carriages by the French. In the first place, the French succeeded in reducing the weight of gun carriages sufficiently to allow the field guns to keep up with advancing troops. Mounted on two wheels and a trail, the gun carriage also provided a rudimentary means of elevating the tube at least a few degrees with the help of very basic trunnions and a two-section trail hinged at the front. While the gun was mounted solidly in the upper section of the trail, the rear of the upper section could be raised and lowered with some difficulty to vary the angle of fire—a singular advance in artillery carriage construction that enabled closer cooperation between the artillery and either cavalry or infantry. Stone projectiles were obsolete, and had been replaced by cast iron shot. The gun tubes of early bombards, usually made of wrought iron and secured against bursting by metal hoops, were superseded by muzzle-loading cannon of cast iron and even bronze, providing the advantageous combination of greater strength and reduced weight. Taken together, the improvements inherent in Charles' artillery were keyed to the growing use of gunpowder and offered a technological departure from earlier siegecraft and the almost total lack of field pieces. Still heavy and not without the associated problems of transport, the artillery that Charles took to Italy gave his army a dimension that had previously been lacking.[26]

Charles crossed the Alps and entered the Italian states with an army of approximately 65,000 troops, 40,000 of whom were infantry. *(See Map 4b.)* Ten thousand of the foot soldiers—German and Swiss mercenaries armed mainly with the pike—formed the backbone of the infantry. But a part of the infantry carried another weapon, a variation of the arquebus, which in turn was an improved version of the hand cannon. Designed with a stock to absorb the shock and equipped with a mechanical device for applying the match to powder, this early hand weapon was the forerunner of the musket. Heavy and awkward, the arquebus was slow to load and fire. When introduced on the battlefield, its impact must have been more psychological than real, for it was less accurate than the arrow shot from a bow. Nevertheless the arquebus could fire a ball weighing less than an ounce over 200 yards. Further improvements in design over the next two or more centuries would be needed before the hand weapon using gunpowder would finally displace the pike, bow, and sword.[27]

The French Success

Against little resistance, Charles took Florence and marched on Rome. The following year he took Naples. Charles' artillery made short work of Italian fortresses at each step of his campaign, a rude awakening for the disorganized Italians. But what shocked the Italians more profoundly was the rapidity and violence of the French campaign. Having grown accustomed to the long, protracted, limited wars among the five leading Italian states—Naples, Venice, Milan, Florence, and the Papal States—the Italians were hardly prepared for the devastation of their states or the fearful casualties inflicted by Charles' army. Although he withdrew in 1495 after shattering an Italian army that tried to block his route of march at Fornovo, Charles completely disrupted the political system of the states of Italy and left their rulers bewildered by the result of what Charles' invasion had done to their nicely balanced and secure political and social systems.[28]

Charles VIII's invasion of Italy in 1494 left a trail of broken castles and dejected castle-owners in its wake. His campaign undoubtedly accelerated the trend toward the improvement of permanent fortifications. He also shattered the carefully balanced political framework of Italy, and exposed the weakness of her collective and individual military organizations. This political and social upheaval was not temporary, but lasted over two centuries.

The Military Critic

What happened and what it inspired occupied the thoughts of one Italian writer for the latter two decades of his life. A bureaucrat, a brain truster, an idea man, a dejected and discarded liberal—he was these and more. Niccolo Machiavelli (1469–1527) was a political scientist, a philosopher, a commentator on strategy, and perhaps the first prophet of power politics.

In 1498, the Medici family was ousted from power in Florence and the Soderini family moved in. Having developed a reputation as a capable administrator, Machiavelli found himself with a job, a bureaucratic post of modest importance in the government of Florence. While in this post, Machiavelli was an attentive observer of Florentine politics, and saw at first hand how the Italian political and military machinery operated. He did not like what he saw. When the Soderini family fell from power in 1512, Machiavelli lost his job, as the Medici family regained control. Although he returned to public life briefly in 1515, the major part of his later life was devoted to writing.

Machiavelli's four principal works were composed between the years 1513 and 1515. They are: *The Discourses on the First Decade of Titus Livy, The Art of War, The History of Florence,* and *The Prince.* The latter two were not published until 1532, after his death, although a plagiarized and edited version of *The Prince* appeared in 1523 under a different title. Each of his primary works differs in its approach, but, with the exception of *The History of Forence,* they all offer guidelines for a ruler in the areas of politics, administration, and military policy. "There cannot be good laws where there are not good arms," he wrote in *The Prince,* "and where there are good arms there must be good laws. . . ."[29] Machiavelli proceeded to state one of his basic contentions: that the foundation of states is a good military organization. Machiavelli leaned heavily on the earlier model of the Roman Empire as the basis for his philosophy of government and military policy. To him, that period represented one of the most efficient eras

in the history of civilization. He strongly believed that important lessons could be learned from history. Machiavelli also proposed that history, in fact, repeats itself, causing numerous critics to pounce on the conclusions that he drew.[30]

Machiavelli severely criticized the *condotierri,* companies of footloose mercenary soldiers who virtually hired themselves out to the highest bidder among the Italian states. He believed that their mercenary interest was the controlling factor in their performance, and that service to the state was the least of their motivations. He had seen how ineffective they had been against the French during the invasion of Charles VIII.

He also discussed the relationship between Italy's fragmented political system—five roughly equal entities—and the inadequacy of her military capabilities. Machiavelli saw that Italy was strategically placed in respect to the world trade routes. These avenues of commerce had rapidly grown in importance as a result of the opening of the East through the crusades, the breakup of the manorial economy throughout western Europe, and the general growth of handicraft manufacture and trade. What troubled Machiavelli was that he could see that the political and military organizations in France, England, and Spain were keeping abreast of economic expansion, but that no similar united political structure was emerging in Italy. He identified the correlation between financial and military power, but he rated the ability of generals and the courage of soldiers as more important than the financial power of the state, a point of view challenged by a number of his critics.[31]

Niccolo Machiavelli

In the same way, critics cite Machiavelli's lukewarm approach to the importance of field artillery as another indication of his lack of modernity, pointing out that artillery was about to revolutionize warfare, as Charles VIII had amply demonstrated. A close reading of Machiavelli in his *Discourses*, however, shows that he cautioned against sole reliance on artillery no matter how good it was, and argued that efficient infantry was the backbone of any army that adhered to a combined arms concept. In addition, he argued that early use of artillery was more important for the psychological effect it had on men and horses than its physical effect, another observation that few could seriously challenge. Finally, Machiavelli reminded his readers that no matter what the weapons are in the hands of the troops, it is the courage of the troops and the skill of the commander that are decisive, not the weapons themselves.[32]

Machiavelli displayed little awareness of the latent power of nationalism, although he favored and advocated universal conscription of male youth. Perhaps he failed to appreciate the full force of nationalism turned loose in war. For whatever reasons, Machiavelli favored the state that is administered by a powerful monarch, and not by a representative government of the people.

At a time when Italy had developed its military system to fight very controlled and limited wars, Machiavelli proposed reform. "To him," writes Felix Gilbert, "political life was a struggle for survival between growing and expanding organisms. War was natural and necessary; it would establish which country would survive and determine between annihilation and expansion. War, therefore, must end in a decision, and a battle was the best method of reaching a quick decision, since it would place the defeated country at the mercy of the victor."[33] Machiavelli's attempt to blend and direct all military efforts toward the attainment of one supreme goal was probably the beginning of strategical thought as we understand it today. He proposed the application of power politics, thereby directly or indirectly influencing generations for years to come. Among many people, there is the tendency to view with uneasiness the philosophy of a man who wrote so frankly about bending all national power to the will of the state. Perhaps the reason for the uneasiness is Machiavelli's realism. He unmasked the implements with which "The Prince" would direct the affairs of state.

When representative governments began to displace monarchies, Machiavelli's description of the relationship between political and military power was a remarkably accurate guideline for statesmen and soldiers. Undoubtedly, the Florentine missed the mark in some areas, but he challenged his successors to explore further both the evolution of military institutions and the link between military and political power.

Fortifications

The increased power and adaptability of cannon and siege artillery prompted a critical review of the methods of attack, defense, and construction of fortifications. Even though the old patterns of medieval defense and construction persisted for some time, two general developments emerged in response to the wider use of gunpowder weapons. In the modification of old forts and the construction of new forts, a variety of measures were used to strengthen the defense of the fort against artillery. At the same time, construction in the fifteenth and sixteenth centuries revealed new efforts to incorporate artillery into defense of the castle.

For centuries, the tall, stately walls of the castle and the imposing height of corner towers typified the architecture of medieval strongpoints. During the fifteenth and sixteenth centuries, however, the battering power of artillery forced the construction of lower walls, thereby adding strength to the vulnerable area of the fort. New construction tended to place half of the wall below the ground. If terrain prevented such construction, earth from the surrounding area was banked against the lower part of the wall. Thicker walls—some as thick as 40 feet—became common. Gradually an outer enclosure emerged in castle construction. This enclosure was separated by a ditch from the main works of the fort, and it was not unusual for the ditch to be turned into a water-filled moat. Finally, the impressive vertical walls of the fort gave way to sloping walls, which were better suited to withstand the impact of larger projectiles.[34]

When renovating old forts or building new forts, ramparts were placed immediately adjacent to the top of the wall, thereby facilitating the emplacement of artillery, which was used to sweep the area around the fort with fire. Cannon on the ramparts, however, could not discourage attackers who managed to advance to the area immediately next to the wall. An expedient was adopted, therefore, by making gun loops, or openings, at the base of the tower, where arrow loops had been located earlier. From these openings, cannoneers had fields of fire along the base of the wall. While gun loops in the walls would have been more effective, the thickness of the walls usually made this alternative impossible. Gradually towers became stronger and larger, providing better defense against cannon shot and offering an inside platform for defending artillery.[35]

Perhaps the most artistic yet functional construction of fortifications during the period occurred in England. After Henry VIII (1509–1547) managed to antagonize both the papacy and the Holy Roman Emperor, he began to prepare for what he considered imminent invasion. A flurry of activity followed, in which old forts along the coast were renovated

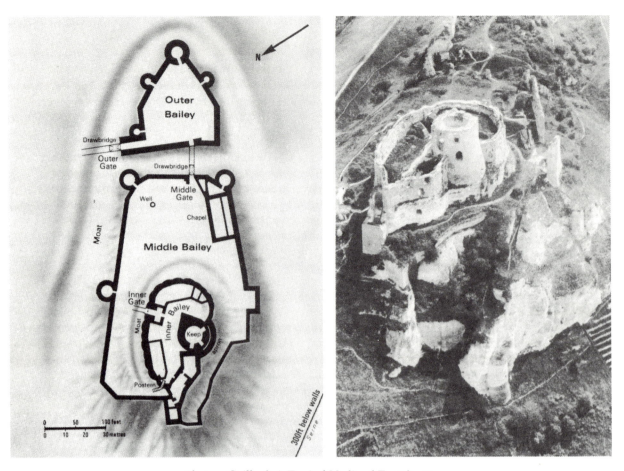

Chateau Gaillard, A Typical Medieval Fortification

and new ones added. The basic design of the new fortification was a concentrated compact block that could be defended from any direction by internal artillery. Examples of Henry's forts, built around 1540, still exist today in Kent, Sussex, and Cornwall. The King equipped his castles with the modern artillery available, and mounted them in tiered platforms, each of which rose higher than the platform in front of it. The Deal castle at Kent is one of the largest remaining examples of this type of construction, boasting sufficient gun emplacements to rake its outer moat with over 50 cannon. Like many of the castles and forts built durng the era, Deal Castle exposed only one access route to the inside over a drawbridge. Attackers soon found that this entryway was usually the best defended part of the fort, and were forced to search for a weak part of the wall and concentrate their fire on that vulnerable area. More often, attackers turned gunpowder to their own advantage and dug tunnels where a mine could be placed to blast a breach in the wall.[36]

Yet the attack, defense, and construction of fortifications had not yet reached full efficiency. The development of fortifications and countermeasures would continue until it reached its peak in the skill of the brilliant French engineer, Vauban, in the latter part of the seventeenth century.

The Spanish Ascendancy

While Charles VIII paved the way for the improved use of artillery in the army he took to Italy, the potential of the hand weapon, the arquebus, was barely tapped. The man who understood the value of the arquebus and who found a way to integrate it into a tactical formation was a Spaniard, Gonzalo de Cordoba, called "El Gran Capitan" by his countrymen. He, too, fought on the Italian peninsula, having been sent there in 1495 to defend Spanish interests in southern Italy against the onslaught of Charles VIII.

Defeated at Seminara *(see Map 4b)* by a French army of heavy cavalry and pikemen, Gonzalo considered alternatives that would strengthen the Spanish Army. The one that he adopted combined what he felt were the best aspects of tactics, organization, and equipment available at the time. Part of his army he modeled on the Swiss pikemen to take advantage of the shock of the pike and the impact of a disciplined infantry formation. Another part of his army was composed of well equipped arquebusiers, thereby capitalizing on the firepower of the best and latest handguns he could procure. He adopted the Italian method of using at least rudimentary field fortifi-

Deal Castle

cations, primarily to exhaust the attack of his enemy before launching his own. In his increased emphasis on the arquebus, Gonzalo benefited from the concurrent technological improvements of the weapon. Early handguns varied in size, shape, length of barrel, and caliber, almost according to the whim of the manufacturer. In the fourteenth century, some handguns weighed as much as an amazing 50 pounds, and it was not uncommon to find hand weapons at the time of Charles' invasion of Italy that weighed as much as 30 pounds. Understandably, such a weapon was usually rested on a fork or some sort of support when fired. But weight alone was not the most serious drawback of the early arquebus; the weight of weapons was steadily reduced as more durable metals permitted the use of less cumbersome trigger housings and barrels with thinner walls. The more basic disadvantages of the weapon were its extremely slow rate of fire—a round every several minutes—poor accuracy, and awkward operation. Once the weapon was loaded and the match (a twisted, smouldering cord several yards long) was lit, the operator needed, as one writer has said, "three hands and three eyes."[37] The requirement for one of the hands and one of the eyes disappeared with the introduction of the matchlock. Grasped in a mechanical arm called a serpentine, which was fixed to a pivot on the side of the stock, the glowing match, or cord, was automatically lowered into the powder in the pan with the pull of the trigger. A seemingly simple and obvious improvement, perhaps, to a soldier accustomed to the complex igniting mechanisms of the twentieth century, the matchlock nevertheless was slow in being developed and adopted. Once perfected, however, it permitted more consistent aiming and easier operation.[38]

Although recognizing the merits of the improved arquebus by increasing the number in his army and integrating its use into his tactical scheme, Gonzalo also acknowledged the limitations of the arquebus, some of which he could not overcome. For one important limitation, however, he found a remedy. Because the many steps involved in loading and firing the weapon consumed an inordinate amount of time, the arquebusier was helplessly exposed to the enemy between firings. To afford protection to the arquebusiers while they were reloading, Gonzalo wisely retained a sizable number of pikemen, and thus achieved a revolutionary blend of pike and shot that would persist in one form or another for at least two more centuries.

It took some time for Gonzalo to organize and perfect the tactics employed by his army, but he was ready to test his system against the French in early 1503, near the small Italian town of Cerignola. Gonzalo chose a defensive position on a slope covered with vineyards. At the base of the slope ran a ditch, which his infantry occupied after extending and deepen-

Spanish Arquebusier

ing it by throwing up a parapet along the bank. Behind the ditch he placed a few ranks of arquebusiers and pikemen, reinforced with 13 pieces of artillery. (As it turned out, he gained little from the artillery, for soon after the battle opened a chance spark ignited all of the loose powder they were using.) To induce the French to attack him, he sent forward his light cavalry—used by the Spanish commander for harassing, skirmishing, and scouting—and kept what heavy cavalry he had (less than a 1,000) as a reserve.

Encouraged by the thin lines that appeared before him, the French commander attacked with ranks of mixed men-at-arms and infantry. The combination of the ditch and the steady fire of arquebusiers broke up the French assaults. Since the attack began late in the day, the growing darkness added to the confusion, and, at the moment when he judged the French demoralized, Gonzalo launched the counterattack with heavy cavalry and the men from the entrenchments. The victory, as well as the artillery train of the French, belonged to the Spaniards.[39]

Although Cerignola was a small battle and had no important political results, it is nevertheless another landmark on the path of the growing importance of infantry in land warfare. The infantry soldier armed with the hand weapon had earned a place of respect on the battlefield.

The French had no intention of letting Gonzalo rest on his laurels. The Spanish had been outnumbered when they had met the French at Cerignola, and later in that same year, recognizing that he still outnumbered the Spanish, the French commander in chief, the Marquis of Mantua, struck a course along the western coast of Italy for Naples. *(See Map 4b.)* Hurrying across the mountains through torrential autumn rains, Gonzalo blocked the French route when he pulled up just ahead of them on the swollen banks of the Garigliano River. A hasty French river crossing attempt using a pontoon bridge failed in the face of Spanish arquebus and artillery fire. Both armies settled down to glare at each other across the Garigliano for nearly two months, as November and December weather became increasingly cold and wet.

In the difficult and nervous game of chess in which he was now engaged, Gonzalo de Cordoba was probably at his best, demonstrating that he was not only a tactical and organizational innovator, but also a solid troop leader. While his French counterparts escaped from the mud and cold along the banks of the Garigliano by moving to comfortable quarters in nearby towns, Gonzalo shared the privations of his soaked troops and visited the lines daily to bolster the morale of his army. His constant presence at the front gave Gonzalo another advantage—an opportunity to make daily assessments of French morale, which was steadily deteriorating among troops who were, in many cases, far from home, and whose misery was apparently of little interest to their officers. Gonzalo carefully planned a surprise attack.

In preparation for the river crossing, Gonzalo had directed his engineers to develop a pontoon bridge composed of sufficiently small parts to enable it to be carried on the backs of mules and then assembled quickly on the spot. Fraternization between French and Spanish troops during a two-day Christmas truce confirmed Gonzalo's suspicion that morale was low and security lax in the French army. The site selected for the crossing was at the extreme left of the French line, offering not only drier ground and a narrower portion of the river, but also a position at which the initial stages of the preparation for the crossing could be concealed. *(See Map 4c.)* Gonzalo planned to command personally the main element

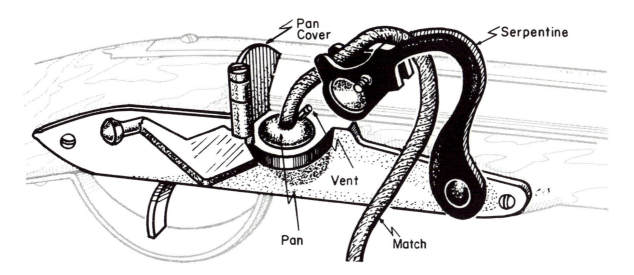

The Early Matchlock

that crossed the pontoon bridge after the vanguard secured the opposite bank. Directly opposite from the French main lines another contingent waited to cross by a permanent bridge as soon as they received word that the surprise crossing had been successful.

The entire plan worked to perfection. Neither the Swiss infantry nor the French men-at-arms expected the attack, and both were unable to make a stand before being swept before Gonzalo's light cavalry and the eager infantry that followed. The French offered limited resistance several miles back from the river at the defile at Formia, but even this disintegrated after an hour's hard fighting. The Spanish light cavalry continued the pursuit to the port of Gaeta.[40]

Gonzalo de Cordoba, El Gran Capitan, fought his last campaign at Garigliano, but the system that he had perfected served Spanish armies well long after his death in 1515.

The Growth of Spanish Superiority

In 1504, shortly after the French defeat on the banks of the Garigliano, France and Spain agreed to end hostilities, and Italy enjoyed a short rest from the battling of the two powers on her soil. When the Holy Roman Emperor died in 1519, however, the contest over his successor erupted into war between Spain and France; as usual, it was fought on the Italian peninsula. In 1522, at Bicocca, not far from Milan, a French army composed largely of Swiss mercenaries faced the Spanish army commanded by Prosper Colonna, who used the system that had been developed by Gonzalo de Cordoba. Colonna chose a defensive position, the front and flanks of which were well protected by ditches, and bolstered his flanks with well-placed artillery. As the Swiss pikemen attacked the

entrenched position, they met the fire of Colonna's arquebusiers head on and were caught in a vicious crossfire from the artillery on both flanks. The outcome of the Battle of Bicocca had a profound effect on the Swiss, whose morale was permanently lowered by the defeat. Recognizing at last that the formation that had served them for two centuries was an invitation to disaster in the face of the new weapons that gunpowder had produced, the Swiss lost some of their former audacity and confidence, although they continued to be used as mercenaries in many of the armies of western Europe.[41]

In 1525, Spanish arquebusiers departed from their normal pattern of defensive tactics and attacked French cavalry in

Gonzalo de Cordoba of Spain

the open. Combining surprise with a brilliant turning of the French flank, the mixture of pike and shot routed the French men-at-arms and captured the King, Francis I. The battle took place at Pavia, in Italy, and turned on the dominating fire-power of Spanish arquebusiers, who used walls and hedges for protection. When his own force became disorganized by the artillery fire of the French, the Spanish commander rallied his troops to withstand a premature French cavalry charge and gained the upper hand with the disciplined fire of his steady infantry, which was armed with hand weapons.[42]

Men of the Spanish armies fought battles as far away as Germany, Africa, and even the forests of the New World. As the Spanish Empire grew rapidly after 1500, the cost of the army grew as well. Spanish expansion in Europe was not only keyed to the growth of her political and economic power, but was also driven by a single-minded determination to defend the Catholic faith and to stamp out Protestantism. Charles I (1516–1556) founded the Hapsburg dynasty in Spain, but, since he had been educated in Flanders and had brought a sizable Flemish following with him to Spain, he was heartily disliked by the Spaniards. His son, Philip II (1556–1598), who inherited Spain and the Netherlands when Charles abdicated, cultivated a better relationship with his Spanish subjects. But Philip's zealous persecution of Protestants involved him in constant meddling in European affairs, many costly wars, and an increasingly hostile and explosive situation with the dissatisfied and fearful populace of the Netherlands. Open revolt broke out in the Netherlands in 1568, followed by

Spanish reprisals and a proclamation of independence from Spain in 1579. The steady success of the Dutch Revolt finally brought England into the conflict against Spain, when Maurice of Nassau, at the age of 17, succeeded his father as the head of the Dutch provinces in 1584. The English defeat of the Spanish Armada in 1588 helped to sustain the Dutch Revolt, which finally brought independence to the Republic of the United Provinces with the Peace of Westphalia in 1648. Maurice led the Dutch Revolt from 1584 until 1625, and during that time he produced profound military reforms, which are explained in a later chapter. At the same time, the Spanish were painfully aware of the fact that bloody campaigns and devastating battles were becoming too expensive, even if won.

The necessity to wage war more economically and the recognized value of the arquebus or other suitable hand weapon when used in combination with the pike encouraged the Spanish to develop a new type of fighting formation. Gonzalo de Cordoba had already experimented with companies of infantry in his army and had even grouped several of the companies into combinations of 400 or 500 men, called "battles," which could include cavalry, infantry, and guns. By 1534, the experimental system became standardized in Spanish units, and the grouping of several battles was designated a *tercio*. Essentially, the *tercio* was a defensive unit, composed of pikemen and arquebusiers in equal proportions and numbering anywhere from 1,000 to 3,000 men. Not yet were the arquebusiers able to stand alone and fight without the support and protection of the pike element. But the pike-

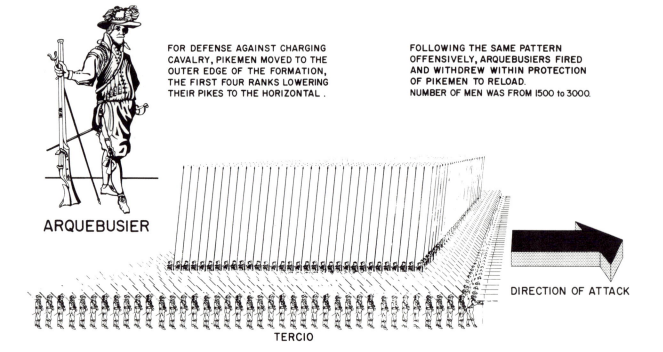

ARQUEBUSIER

FOR DEFENSE AGAINST CHARGING CAVALRY, PIKEMEN MOVED TO THE OUTER EDGE OF THE FORMATION, THE FIRST FOUR RANKS LOWERING THEIR PIKES TO THE HORIZONTAL.

FOLLOWING THE SAME PATTERN OFFENSIVELY, ARQUEBUSIERS FIRED AND WITHDREW WITHIN PROTECTION OF PIKEMEN TO RELOAD. NUMBER OF MEN WAS FROM 1500 to 3000.

DIRECTION OF ATTACK

TERCIO

The Spanish *Tercio* of the Sixteenth Century

men also gave a primarily defensive formation the power to deal an offensive blow when needed—it could, in other words, drive infantry and cavalry from the field. As long as the Spanish *tercio* could retain the integrity of its formation, it could repel the most formidable attack and, when operating under the right conditions, undertake offensive maneuvers.

Gradually the companies or similar groupings within the formation disappeared, and the organization of the *tercio* developed into the basic unit of the Spanish Army, inspiring copyists in other European nations to adopt the same system.[43] One known countermeasure to the *tercio* lurked over the horizon: mobile field artillery and the rain of shot that could tear huge gaps in the solid mass of men. As yet, however, field artillery was neither sufficiently mobile nor effective to seriously challenge the Spanish method of warfare. A later era and another master of warfare, Gustavus Adolphus, would build on the reforms of Maurice of Nassau and produce the combination that would signal the decline of the Spanish mass of pike and shot. In the meantime, the *tercio* represented the best use of firepower and hand weapons available to the infantry. At the same time, as long as the Spanish system proved less costly, budget-minded monarchs willingly accepted the slower-moving and less flexible mass of men.

Notes

[1] C. W. C. Oman, *A History of the Art of War in the Middle Ages*, 2nd revised edition (2 vols.; New York, 1924), I, 112-117; Oliver L. Spaulding, Hoffman Nickerson and John W. Wright, *Warfare: A Study of Military Methods from the Earliest Times* (New York, 1925), pp. 370-371.

[2] Oman, *A History of the Art of War in the Middle Ages*, II, 84-100.

[3] Richard A. Preston and Sydney F. Wise, *Men in Arms: A History of Warfare and Its Interrelationships with Western Society*, 2nd revised edition (New York, 1970), pp. 80-85; James Westfall Thompson and Edgar Nathaniel Johnson, *An Introduction to Medieval Europe* (New York, 1937), pp. 863-878; James Westfall Thompson, *An Economic and Social History of the Middle Ages (300–1300)* (New York, 1928), pp. 656, 794-806; John F. C. Fuller, *A Military History of the Western World* (3 vols.; New York, 1954), I, 437-442.

[4] Oman, *A History of the Art of War in the Middle Ages*, I, 240-241.

[5] The account of the Battle of Mortgarten is based on Oman's description; *Ibid.*, 233-241.

[6] *Ibid.*, 242.

[7] C. W. C. Oman, *The Art of War in the Middle Ages, A.D. 378–1515*, edited and revised by John H. Beeler (Ithaca, N.Y., 1953), pp. 89-92; Spaulding, *Warfare*, pp. 399-401.

[8] Oman, *Art of War in the Middle Ages*, pp. 92-95; George T. Denison, *A History of Cavalry from the Earliest Times with Lessons for the Future* (London, 1913), p. 173; Oman, *A History of the Art of War in the Middle Ages*, II, 262-263.

[9] Oman, *Art of War in the Middle Ages*, pp. 95-96.

[10] *Ibid.*, pp. 96-104; Lynn Montross, *War Through the Ages*, 3rd revised edition (New York, 1960), pp. 202-204; Spaulding, *Warfare*, pp. 403-404.

[11] Fuller, *Military History*, I, 446.

[12] Edouard Perroy, *The Hundred Years War* (Bloomington, IN, 1959), pp. 44-49, 54-57, 60-68, 92-93; Fuller, *Military History*, I, 442, 444-450, 454-459.

[13] Perroy, *The Hundred Years War*, pp. 69-76, 86-100; Alfred H. Burne, *The Crecy War* (London, 1955), pp. 17-25.

[14] Montross, *War Through the Ages*, pp. 168-169; Spaulding, *Warfare*, p. 372; Oman, *A History of the Art of War in the Middle Ages*, II, 60-61; Oman, *Art of War in the Middle Ages*, pp. 118-120, 126, 128.

[15] Spaulding, *Warfare*, pp. 374-375; Oman, *A History of the Art of War in the Middle Ages*, II, 127-131.

[16] Oman, *A History of the Art of War in the Middle Ages*, II, 126, 131-133.

[17] Spaulding, *Warfare*, pp. 375-376.

[18] *Ibid.*, pp. 376-377.

[19] Oman, *A History of the Art of War in the Middle Ages*, II, 134-138.

[20] Spaulding, *Warfare*, pp. 377-379; Burne, *The Crecy War*, pp. 176-183.

[21] Montross, *War Through the Ages*, p. 171.

[22] Oman, *A History of the Art of War in the Middle Ages*, II, 160-162.

[23] Spaulding, *Warfare*, pp. 382-89; Oman, *A History of the Art of War in the Middle Ages*, II, 163-174.

[24] Perroy, *The Hundred Years War*, pp. 138-140.

[25] Spaulding, *Warfare*, pp. 405-407; Lynn White, Jr., *Medieval Technology and Social Change* (Oxford, 1962), pp. 94-97.

[26] Montross, *War Through the Ages*, pp. 207-208; Spaulding, *Warfare*, pp. 406-407; Albert Manucy, *Artillery Through the Ages* (Washington, 1949), pp. 3-5.

[27] Preston and Wise, *Men in Arms*, pp. 102, 104, 106; Spaulding, *Warfare*, p. 416.

[28] Edward Mead Earle (ed.), *Makers of Modern Strategy: Military Thought from Machiavelli to Hitler* (Princeton, 1941), pp. 7-9; Spaulding, *Warfare*, pp. 416-421.

[29] Chapter XII, in *The Prince and the Discourses by Niccolo Machiavelli*, intro. by Max Lerner (New York, 1940), p. 44.

[30] Leslie J. Walker (ed.), *The Discourses of Niccolo Machiavelli* (2 vols.; New Haven, CT, 1950), I, 83.

[31] Lerner, in *The Prince and the Discourses*, p. xxxiii.

[32] *Discourses*, Chapters 17 and 18, in Walker, *The Discourses of Niccolo Machiavelli*, I, 403-413.

[33] Earle, *Makers of Modern Strategy*, p. 22.

[34] Sidney Toy, *A History of Fortification from 3000 B.C. to A.D. 1700* (New York, 1955), pp. 231-239; Spaulding, *Warfare*, pp. 429-433.

[35] Toy, *History of Fortification*, pp. 236-237, 243.

[36] *Ibid.*, pp. 245-247.

[37] B. L. Montgomery, *A History of Warfare* (London, 1968), p. 216.

[38] J. R. Hale in *The New Cambridge Modern History* (14 vols.; Cambridge, 1957-1971), I, 279, 285; Montgomery, *A History of Warfare*, pp. 216-217; Montross, *War Through the Ages*, pp. 205-206; Spaulding, *Warfare*, pp. 421-423; Preston and Wise, *Men in Arms*, p. 105.

[39] Spaulding, *Warfare*, pp. 425-426.

[40] *Ibid.*, p. 426; Montgomery, *A History of Warfare*, pp. 218-220.

[41] Spaulding, *Warfare*, pp. 439-440.

[42] Montross, *War Through the Ages*, pp. 210-211; Spaulding, *Warfare*, pp. 440-442.

[43] Spaulding, *Warfare*, p. 447; Montross, *War Through the Ages*, pp. 211-214.

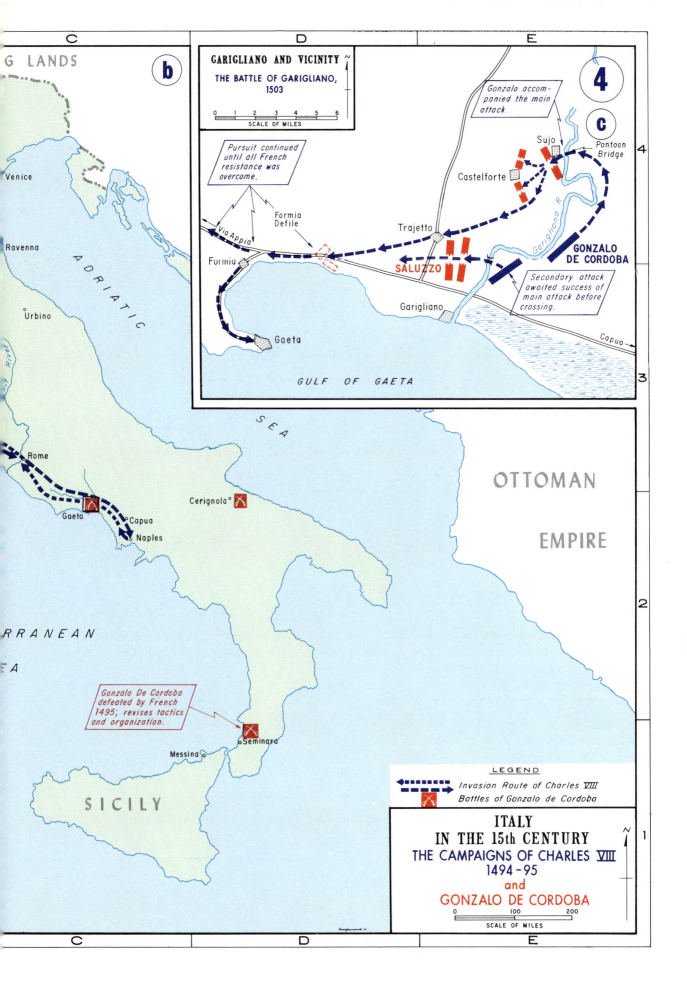

b

GARIGLIANO AND VICINITY
THE BATTLE OF GARIGLIANO, 1503

SCALE OF MILES
0 1 2 3 4 5 6

4

c

Gonzalo accompanied the main attack.

Pursuit continued until all French resistance was overcome.

Sujo

Pontoon Bridge

Castelforte

Formia Defile

Via Appia

Garigliano R.

Trajetto

GONZALO DE CORDOBA

Formia

SALUZZO

Gaeta

Gariglano

Secondary attack awaited success of main attack before crossing.

Capua

GULF OF GAETA

ADRIATIC

Venice

Ravenna

Urbino

SEA

OTTOMAN

EMPIRE

Rome

Cerignola

Gaeta

Capua

Naples

Gonzalo De Cordoba defeated by French 1495; revises tactics and organization.

Seminara

Messina

SICILY

RRANEAN

SEA

LEGEND
- Invasion Route of Charles VIII
- Battles of Gonzalo de Cordoba

ITALY
IN THE 15th CENTURY
THE CAMPAIGNS OF CHARLES VIII
1494-95
and
GONZALO DE CORDOBA

SCALE OF MILES
0 100 200

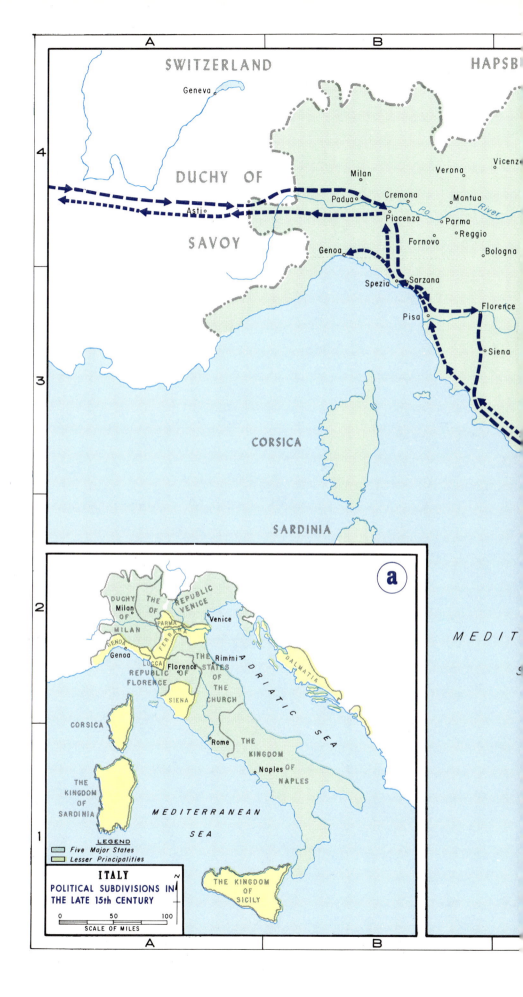

SWITZERLAND

Geneva

HAPSB

DUCHY OF

Milan
Verona
Vicenza

Cremona
Mantua

Padua
Po
Parma

Asti
Piacenza
River

SAVOY
Reggio

Fornovo
Bologna

Genoa
Sarzana

Spezia
Florence

Pisa

Siena

CORSICA

SARDINIA

MEDIT

a

DUCHY
THE
REPUBLIC
OF
Milan
OF
VENICE

MILAN
PARMA
Venice

GENOA
FERRARA

Genoa
LUCCA
THE
Rimini

REPUBLIC
Florence
STATES
DALMATIA

OF
OF
A
D
R
I
A
T
I
C

FLORENCE
THE

SIENA
CHURCH

CORSICA

Rome
THE
S
E
A

KINGDOM

Naples
OF

THE
NAPLES

KINGDOM
MEDITERRANEAN

OF
SEA

SARDINIA

LEGEND
THE KINGDOM

Five Major States
OF

Lesser Principalities
SICILY

ITALY
POLITICAL SUBDIVISIONS IN
THE LATE 15th CENTURY

0   50   100
SCALE OF MILES

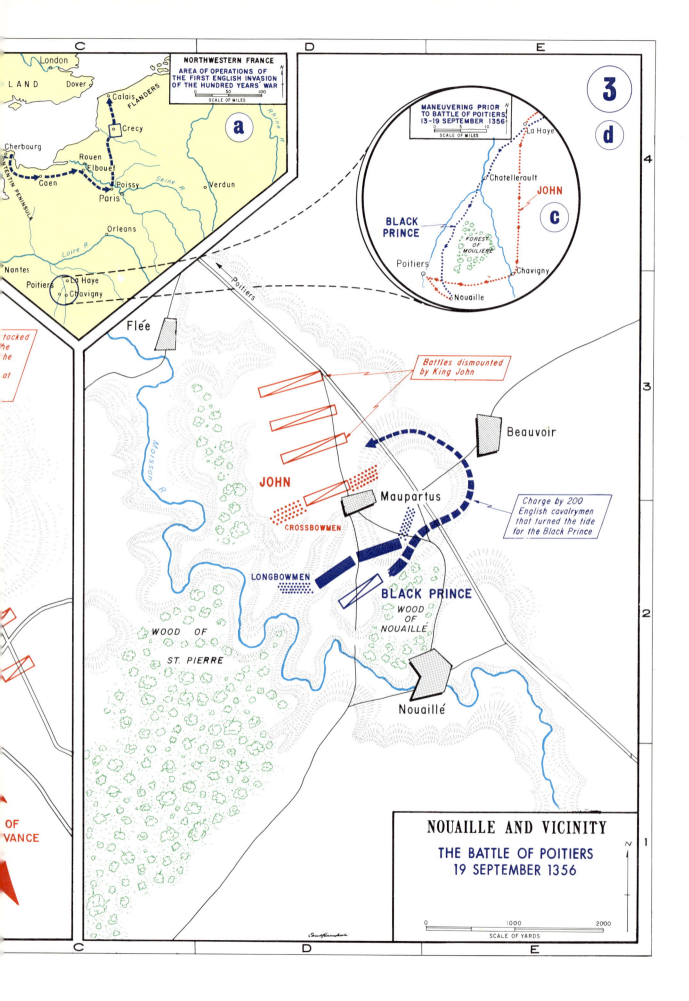

NORTHWESTERN FRANCE
AREA OF OPERATIONS OF
THE FIRST ENGLISH INVASION
OF THE HUNDRED YEARS' WAR
SCALE OF MILES
0   50   100

a

LAND

London
Dover
Calais
FLANDERS
Crecy
Rhine R.
Cherbourg
Rouen
Elbouef
Caen
Poissy
Seine R.
Verdun
COTENTIN PENINSULA
Paris
Orleans
Loire R.
Nantes
Poitiers
La Haye
Chavigny

**MANEUVERING PRIOR
TO BATTLE OF POITIERS,
13-19 SEPTEMBER 1356**
SCALE OF MILES
0   5   10

c

La Haye
Chatellerault
JOHN
**BLACK
PRINCE**
FOREST
OF
MOULIERE
Poitiers
Chavigny
Nouaille

4

3

Poitiers

Flée

Battles dismounted
by King John

Beauvoir

Moisson R.

JOHN

CROSSBOWMEN

Maupartus

Charge by 200
English cavalrymen
that turned the tide
for the Black Prince

LONGBOWMEN

BLACK PRINCE

WOOD
OF
NOUAILLE

WOOD OF

ST. PIERRE

Nouaillé

tacked
he
he
at

OF
VANCE

NOUAILLE AND VICINITY

**THE BATTLE OF POITIERS
19 SEPTEMBER 1356**

N

SCALE OF YARDS
0   1000   2000

2

1

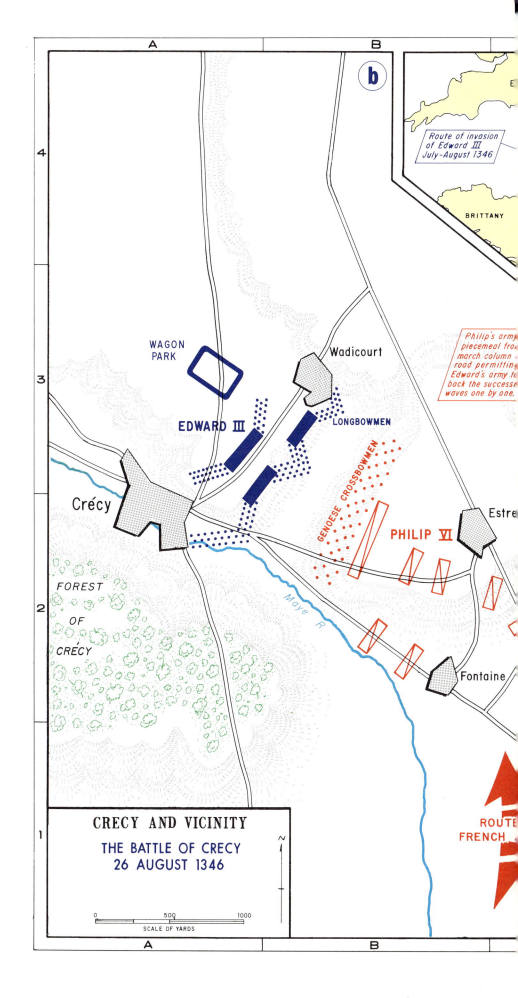

b

Route of invasion
of Edward III
July-August 1346

BRITTANY

WAGON
PARK

Wadicourt

EDWARD III

LONGBOWMEN

GENOESE CROSSBOWMEN

Crécy

Estre

PHILIP VI

Philip's army
piecemeal fro
march column
road permitting
Edward's army t
back the success
waves one by one.

FOREST

OF

CRÉCY

Maye R.

Fontaine

ROUTE
FRENCH

CRECY AND VICINITY

THE BATTLE OF CRECY
26 AUGUST 1346

N

0   500   1000
SCALE OF YARDS

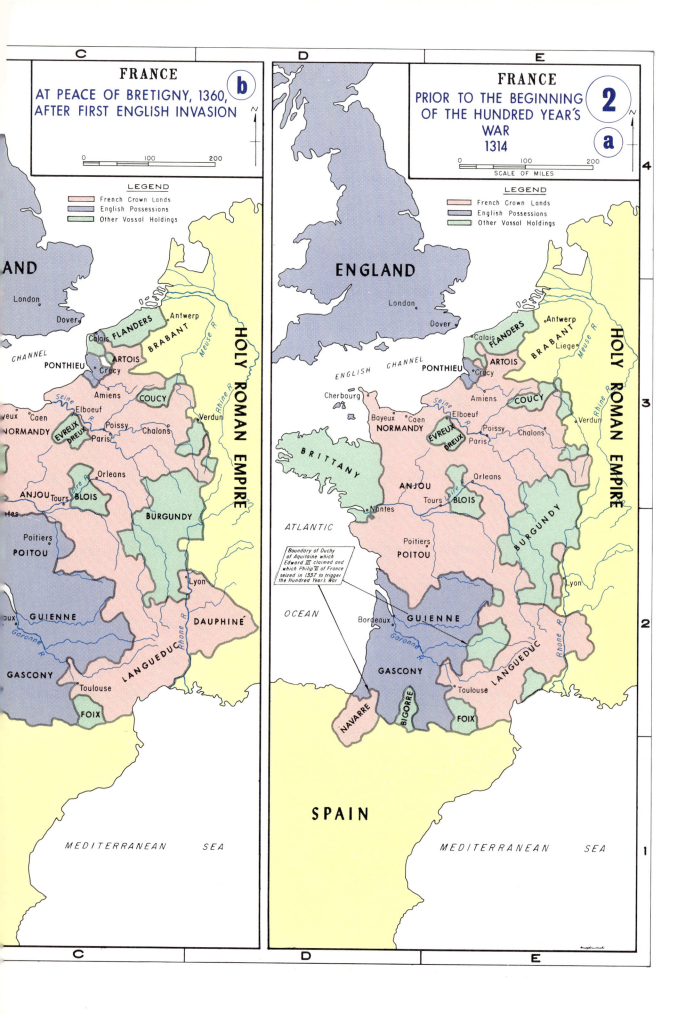

FRANCE
AT PEACE OF BRETIGNY, 1360, AFTER FIRST ENGLISH INVASION — **b**

0   100   200

LEGEND
French Crown Lands
English Possessions
Other Vassal Holdings

London
Dover
CHANNEL
PONTHIEU
Calais FLANDERS Antwerp
ARTOIS BRABANT
Crecy
Amiens COUCY
Meuse R.
Seine R.
Elboeuf Verdun
veux Caen
NORMANDY EVREUX Poissy
DREUX Chalons
Paris
Orleans
ANJOU Tours BLOIS
tes BURGUNDY
Poitiers
POITOU
Lyon
GUIENNE Rhone R.
aux DAUPHINE
Garonne R. LANGUEDUC
GASCONY
Toulouse
FOIX
HOLY ROMAN EMPIRE
MEDITERRANEAN SEA

FRANCE
PRIOR TO THE BEGINNING OF THE HUNDRED YEAR'S WAR 1314 — **2** **a**

0   100   200
SCALE OF MILES

LEGEND
French Crown Lands
English Possessions
Other Vassal Holdings

ENGLAND
London
Dover
ENGLISH CHANNEL
PONTHIEU
Calais FLANDERS Antwerp
ARTOIS Liege BRABANT
Crecy
Amiens COUCY
Meuse R.
Cherbourg
Bayeux Caen Elboeuf Verdun
NORMANDY Seine R. Poissy
EVREUX DREUX Chalons
Paris
BRITTANY
Orleans
Nantes ANJOU Tours BLOIS
BURGUNDY
ATLANTIC
Poitiers
POITOU
Boundary of Duchy
of Aquitaine which
Edward III claimed and
which Philip VI of France
seized in 1337 to trigger
the Hundred Years War
OCEAN
Bordeaux GUIENNE
Garonne R. Rhone R.
Lyon
GASCONY LANGUEDUC
Toulouse
NAVARRE BIGORRE FOIX
HOLY ROMAN EMPIRE
SPAIN
MEDITERRANEAN SEA

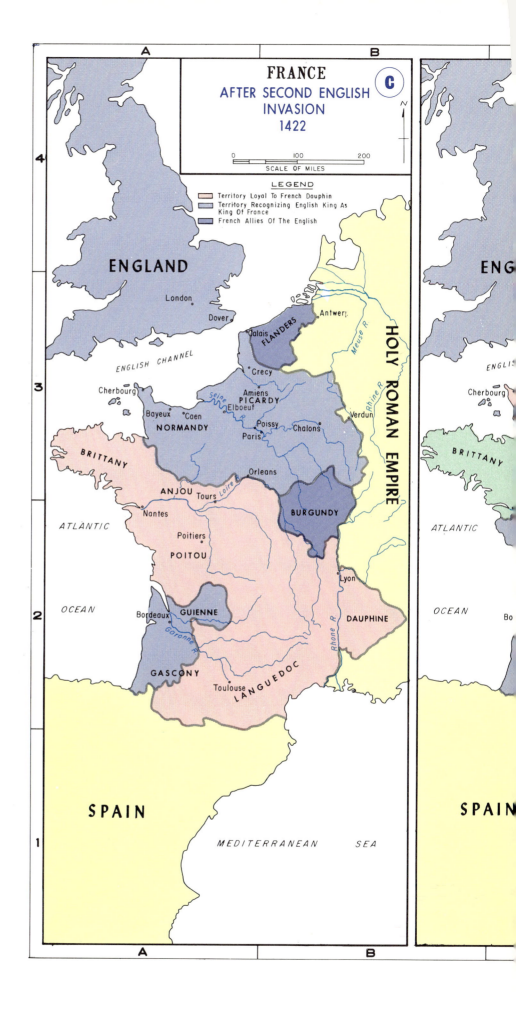

FRANCE
AFTER SECOND ENGLISH
INVASION
1422

C

SCALE OF MILES
0   100   200

LEGEND
Territory Loyal To French Dauphin
Territory Recognizing English King As
King Of France
French Allies Of The English

ENGLAND

London

Dover

ENGLISH CHANNEL

HOLY ROMAN EMPIRE

Antwerp

Calais
FLANDERS

Crecy

Meuse R.

Rhine R.

Cherbourg

Seine R.

Amiens
PICARDY
Elboeuf

Verdun

Bayeux   Caen

NORMANDY

Poissy

Paris   Chalons

BRITTANY

Orleans

ANJOU Tours

Loire R.

BURGUNDY

Nantes

ATLANTIC

Poitiers

POITOU

OCEAN

Lyon

Bordeaux   GUIENNE

Garonne R.

Rhone R.

DAUPHINE

GASCONY

Toulouse LANGUEDOC

SPAIN

MEDITERRANEAN   SEA

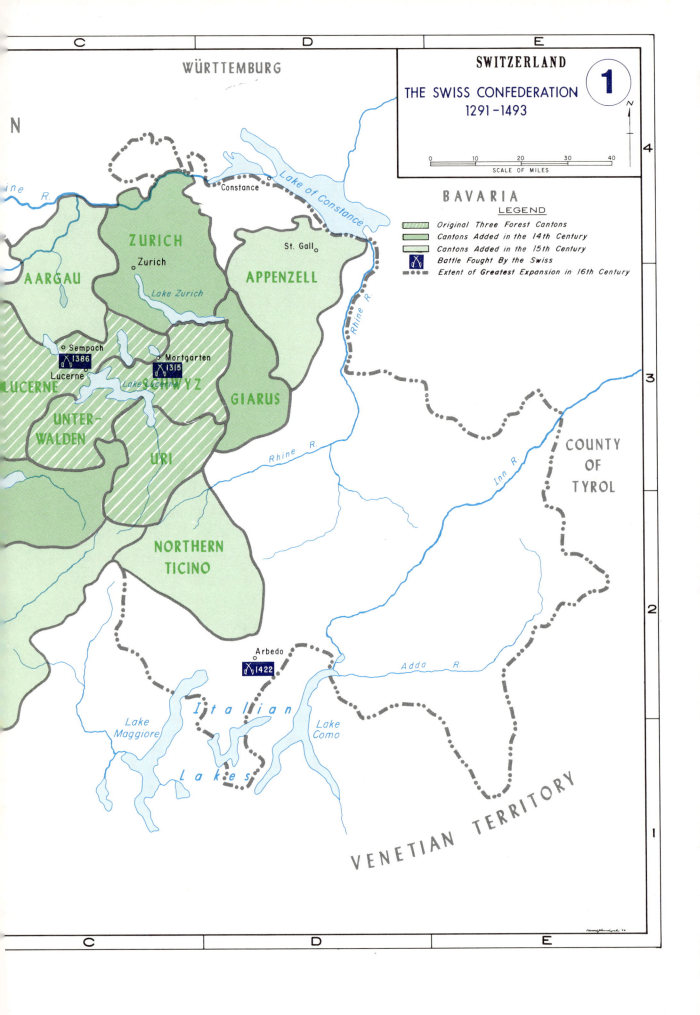

WÜRTTEMBURG

N

SWITZERLAND

THE SWISS CONFEDERATION
1291-1493

1

N

0   10   20   30   40
SCALE OF MILES

BAVARIA

LEGEND
Original Three Forest Cantons
Cantons Added in the 14th Century
Cantons Added in the 15th Century
Battle Fought By the Swiss
Extent of Greatest Expansion in 16th Century

Constance
Lake of Constance

ZURICH
Zurich
Lake Zurich

St. Gall
APPENZELL

AARGAU

Rhine R.

Sempach
1386
Lucerne
Mortgarten
1315
LUCERNE
SCHWYZ
Lake Lucerne
GIARUS
UNTER-
WALDEN
URI

NORTHERN
TICINO

Rhine R.

Inn R.

COUNTY
OF
TYROL

Arbedo
1422

Adda R.

Italian

Lake
Maggiore

Lake
Como

Lakes

VENETIAN TERRITORY

C   D   E

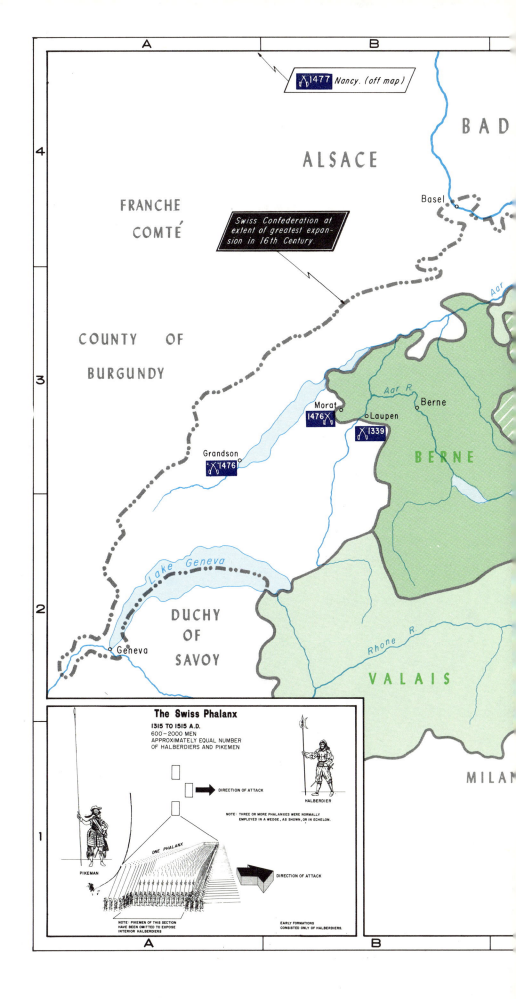

A · · · · · · · · · B · · · · · · ·

4

ALSACE

FRANCHE
COMTÉ

BAD

Basel

Swiss Confederation at
extent of greatest expan-
sion in 16th Century.

3

COUNTY   OF

BURGUNDY

Aar

Aar R.

Berne

Morat
⚔1476

Laupen
⚔1339

BERNE

Grandson
⚔1476

2

Lake Geneva

DUCHY

OF

SAVOY

Rhone R.

Geneva

VALAIS

⚔1477 Nancy. (off map)

MILAN

1

A   B

Early Developments in Naval Warfare

As Europe emerged from the Dark Ages and entered the Renaissance, the seaport cities of Italy became prosperous centers of commerce. Controlling the Mediterranean trade routes, the seagoing people inhabiting these cities carried the riches of the Orient from the western terminus of the overland caravan routes to the ports of Europe. Gradually, with the expansion of colonial empires and the shift of the center of commercial power from the Mediterranean to the Atlantic, a relocation of military power came about, accompanied by economic and political reorientations. At the same time, naval warfare experienced major changes, both evolutionary and revolutionary in nature. As the age of the galley passed, the age of sail emerged.

The age of galley warfare is generally considered to have spanned the bimillenium from 480 B.C. to A.D. 1571—Salamis to Lepanto having been the first and last great encounters in which the galley was the principal craft. But galleys did not immediately disappear from the sea; indeed, they were integral parts of fleets well into the age of sail. The transition of naval warfare into the age of sail is said to have occurred near the end of the sixteenth century. For the convenience of defining it by historical milestones, the age of sail extends from the cruise of the Spanish Armada (1588) to the Battle of Trafalgar (1805).

Regardless of the vehicle in which naval power is manifested, the mission of naval power, as an element of seapower, remains unchanged. Seapower, as a concept, also does not change, although its scope, its expression, and the effect of its execution may vary considerably. More inclusive as a term than naval power, seapower embodies the sum of a state's military, commercial, economic, and imperialistic interests in the ocean. Just as military strategy is but one element of national strategy, naval power is but one facet of seapower. Its mission is to control the sea—that is, to insure free access to seaborne lines of communication for oneself and, if desired, to prevent one's enemy from gaining that access. Seldom does a situation exist wherein a war can be won at sea, but examples abound to illustrate how a war can be lost at sea. Only in a rare instance wherein the conflict is purely commercial or economic, can the destruction of an enemy's seapower be decisive in forcing him to relinquish the advantage of commerce or a source of wealth. Most wars in history have involved territorial aspirations or political impositions, in which case a decision depends upon territorial conquest, the destruction of ground forces, and perhaps occupation. Such wars can be, and many such have been, lost at sea—either by the loss of logistical support necessary to continue the decisive land campaign, or by the failure to interdict the enemy's sea lines of communication.

The Age of Galley Warfare Passes

During the sixteenth century, the expansion of the Ottoman Empire became a threat to the prosperity and well-being of western Europe. After the fall of Constantinople in 1453, the situation steadily worsened. The Ottomans had expanded their domination along the Mediterranean coast of Africa and into the Balkans. Particularly following the accession of Suleiman I (the Magnificent) in 1520, a combination of shrewd diplomacy and military might on land and sea extended the Islamic domains from the Atlas Mountains of Morocco eastward beyond Baghdad, and from Buda on the Danube in Hungary south to Aden on the Persian Gulf.* Encouraged by the reluctance of Venice and other Christian states to risk a naval engagement when the Isle of Rhodes was besieged and taken, Suleiman continued to strengthen his fleet. The great commercial cities were in a quandary. With the Turks astride the

*Refer to Map 1 throughout this chapter.

trade routes from the East, the Italians had to reach some sort of accord to maintain their livelihood, but they were also committed to oppose aggression and the spread of Islam. Only the payment of tribute and the acceptance of unfavorable treaties could insure immunity from attacks by Turkish naval vessels and Mediterranean pirates. Decades of contention came to a climax in 1570 with the Turkish seizure of Cyprus, which had been a possession of the Republic of Venice for nearly a century.[1]

Pope Pius V, recognizing the threat that Ottoman expansion posed to Christendom, had already formed the Holy League to stem the Moslem tide, but the League lacked coordination. Control of the sea had been lost. Fear of attack on the high seas, slaughter, or enslavement in the Turkish galleys, haunted those who continued to venture upon the sea. The atrocities committed in the attack on Cyprus motivated the Pope to begin his campaign, and Venice eagerly joined in the venture.[2]

Cooperation between the Italian cities could not be assumed, because the cities themselves—Genoa, Milan, Florence, Venice—had warred for decades over territory, influence, and trading rights. The monarchies disliked and envied the Republic of Venice because she dominated commerce and had a lucrative trade with the East. But the Pope persisted, being a man of commanding presence and sound strategic sense. In urging that the Holy League engage Turks in a naval battle, Pius realized that gaining control of the Mediterranean would bisect the Ottoman Empire, separating the Levant from North Africa and checking the ability of the Ottomans to mass for further expansion into Europe.

Philip II, who had succeeded his father Charles V as King of Spain (but not as Holy Roman Emperor), was gradually brought into the Pope's plan. His Most Catholic Majesty was always willing to defend the faith, and as King of Naples and Sicily, Philip had much at stake in the war at sea. Despite his desire to see Venice's power diminished, he realized that the permanent loss of Cyprus would further constrain freedom of European movement in the Mediterranean. Spain's attention to her empire in the New World had weakened her hold on North Africa; Tunis and Algeria, in the western Mediterranean, swarmed with Moorish pirates. With the proviso that his half-brother, Don John of Austria, be named commander in chief, he offered his galleys to the combined fleet. Additionally, the majority of troops embarked in the fleet were to be Spaniards.

In September of 1571, the allied fleet set out in an easterly direction, destined to fight a decisive naval battle with the Turks at Lepanto. Although Don John's command consisted of the fleets of only the three allies—Spain, Venice, and the Papal States—there were also ships sent by noblemen, officials, and families of several other states, including Florence, Malta, and Savoy. The Holy Roman Empire, Portugal, England,

Don John of Austria

and France were not formally represented for various political reasons; but individuals from England, France, and nearly every Christian European country were to be found among the crews.[3] The motivating spirit of Pius V had clearly transcended the rising spirit of nationalism in this endeavor.

The Moslem commander, Ali Pasha, was aware of the approach of the allied fleet, and its composition was known, if somewhat underestimated. He was confident of the superiority of his forces. Although his force was approximately equal in manpower to that of the allies, his fleet was numerically superior,[4] and he was favored with the psychological advantage of prestige since the Turkish fleets and armies struck terror in European hearts. Superiority in combat power is measured in many ways, however; in weapons capability, tactical dexterity, and the immeasureable but decisive factor of moral resolve, the odds did not favor the Turks.

The Galley as a Warship

The galleys that sailed to do battle with the Turkish fleet only differed from those of earlier times in that they were larger. A single-decked vessel displacing some 170 tons, the typical galley was about 130 feet long at the waterline and 170 to 180 feet overall, including the "spur" at the bow. Unlike the underwater ram of earlier galleys, the spur occupied the place of the bowsprit of a sailing vessel. In a collision it would shear the oars from the enemy ship, and if the angle of attack were sufficient, it would seriously damage or sink the enemy craft. Besides its practical function as a foothold for tending the rigging, the spur could be used as a boarding platform, similar to the *corvus* on earlier Roman ships.

A beam of about 20 feet and a hold with a depth of 7 feet

The Spanish Flagship *Royal* at Lepanto

allowed adequate space in the lower compartments for provisions, ammunition, and equipment. The limiting factor in range of operation was water; carried in casks on deck, it was normally sufficient for about 20 days, while the provisions stored below deck were adequate for twice that period.

Propelled by sail, oars, or both when in transit, the galley was always rowed into battle, making as much as six or seven knots for short periods—perhaps 20 minutes—before the rowers were exhausted. The medieval galley was somewhat slower than that of ancient warfare, having fewer rowers per ton of displacements. A typical galley in 1571 had 75 oars on each side, the rowers sitting three abreast. Various configurations of fewer oars with more men per oar were common. Troops and other crewmen increased the ship's complement. The stroke on the 35-foot, 125-pound oar was a slow one, 26 per minute at maximum speed. It was a long stroke, described as "rise and fall." The rower would rise from his bench and push the handle of his oar as far aft as possible; he would then brace his inboard foot on the next bench and, dipping the oar, fall back with all his weight.[5]

The most significant difference between sixteenth century naval battles and earlier ones resulted from the introduction of ordnance on board ship. Still primarily an infantry engagement at sea, the sixteenth century naval battle was, nevertheless, well into the transition period that preceded the artillery battles of the age of sail. Indeed, the concept of the broadside battery had emerged decades earlier. At Lepanto, the Christian galleys mounted five guns on the bow, the Turks three. The larger guns, 36-pounders with a range of 1,800 yards, would be fired only once or twice as the fleets closed, but the smaller cannon—many Christian galleys had several in broadside also—would be fired as long as circumstances permitted. Not only did Don John's ships have more guns, but nearly all his troops were armed with the arquebus, while the Turks still relied upon archers.[6]

Don John's fleet also included a number of ungainly galleons, the major sailing warships of the period, but they were of little tactical significance at Lepanto. However, in an attempt to combine the greater firepower that the galleon did possess with the superior maneuverability of the galley, the galleass had been developed. Outfitted with artillery and as many as 500 infantrymen armed with the arquebus, it could deliver a heavy concentration of fire. Unlike the galley, it had a deck above the rowers which protected them from the weather and enemy missiles. The galleass was soon to pass from the scene as a result of improved sailing techniques, for it could neither deliver the firepower of a galleon nor compete with the oar power of the galley.

There had been little change in naval tactics during the centuries of Mediterranean naval warfare. Ships were deployed in line abreast; they then moved head-on into the enemy, collided, and sent troops to board and capture.

The Battle of Lepanto

Approaching the scene of battle with the wind veering west in his favor, Don John deployed his fleet in four divisions, each in single line abreast. With 63 galleys under his direct command in the center, he flanked his flagship on the starboard side with that of the Roman nobleman, Colonna, commander of the Papal squadron; to port, he placed the flagship of Sebastian Veneiro, the 75-year-old Doge of Venice. Commanding the left division of 63 galleys was the Venetian, Agustino Barbarigo. On the right, with 64 ships, was Giovanni Doria; and astern of the center, in reserve, the Spanish Marquis of Santa Cruz commanded 35. Finding it necessary to use galleys to tow the ungainly galleasses into position, Don John stationed them 1,000 yards in the van of the main battleline, forming a gauntlet of heavy artillery fire that the Turks would have to endure as they closed to engage. Barbarigo was ordered

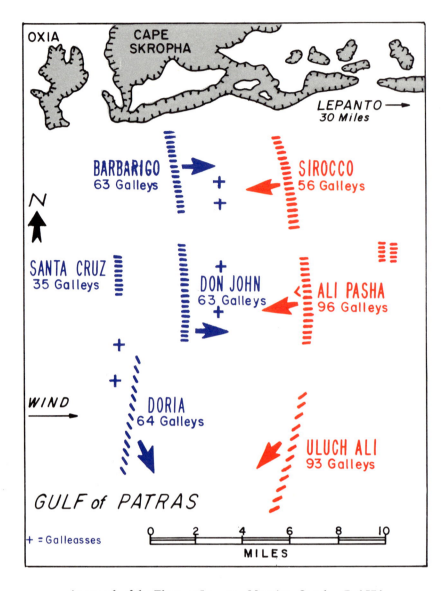

Approach of the Fleets at Lepanto, Morning, October 7, 1571

to remain as close inshore as possible to prevent an envelopment of the left flank, and Santa Cruz' instructions were to be alert for any portion of the line's giving way.

When the Turkish fleet appeared, it was in the form of a great crescent; but before battle was joined, the line straightened and formed into four divisions, practically identical in organization to that of the allied fleet. Because of his familiarity with the rocks and shoals of the local waters, Mohammed Sirocco, Viceroy of Egypt, had been given the right division of 56 galleys, close inshore. Ali Pasha himself commanded the 96 ships in the center, and Uluch Ali, a daring Barbary pirate, commanded the left, with 93 galleys.

Taking considerable losses from the heavily armed galleasses, Ali Pasha broke his line to pass them and then reformed.

The first contact between the major vessels came at the northern end of the line, where Barbarigo had crept ahead of

the rest of the fleet. Both because the galleasses had forced Sirocco's ships closer to the shoreline, and because his pilots were confident of their knowledge of the shallows, the Turkish right attempted to envelop Barbarigo's left, just as Don John had feared. With the same perception that was to inspire Lord Nelson on the Nile more than two centuries later, Barbarigo reasoned that if there was adequate water for a Turkish ship, there was also room for a Venetian ship, and he boldly altered course to port to engage. With Marco Quirini wheeling the right of Barbarigo's division to take the Turks in flank, and the inboard galleasses brought about so that their guns bore on their rear, the Turks were forced against the shore. In the ensuing melee of crashing ships, pointblank cannon fire, and swarming infantry engaged in hand-to-hand combat, the destruction of the Turkish right was complete. Barbarigo was killed by a Turk's arrow, and Sirocco, mortally wounded, was taken prisoner. The Turks who escaped to dry land were pursued and annihilated; not a single Turkish vessel of the northern flank escaped.

A half hour after the northern end of the line had engaged in battle, the centers clashed, creating an incredibly confused struggle of scores of individual contests, centering on the two flagships. Each commander had flanked his flagship with supporting ships from which fresh troops could be drawn, so they closed upon one another in closely grouped flotillas of nine ships each. A moment before they met, each flagship had fired its bow guns into the other. The Turks sustained the greater damage because Don John had removed his spur to give his gunners a clearer field of fire; when the collision came, amidst the smoke of the artillery, the long spur of the Moslem galley crushed into the bow of Don John's flagship, the *Royal*, and the vessels were grappled together. For an hour and a half, the fray raged indecisively. Boarders of Don John's flagship were repelled by the crew of Veneiro's ship, which, while undermanned, was attacked by another Turkish vessel; this in turn was sunk by gunfire from Santa Cruz, who was effectively dispatching his reserve. The tide turned in favor of the allies when Colonna succeeded in clearing one of the galleys alongside of Ali Pasha and penetrated his ram deep into the flagship, his arquebusiers clearing its topsides with a hail of shot. The resistance of the Turks was finally overcome, and the battle in the center of the fleets ended soon after Ali Pasha was slain.

In the encounter to the south, the actions of the third sections of the two fleets reflected the personalities of the two division commanders. Uluch Ali was a confident, skilled tactician, always ready to innovate or to react to a fluid situation. Doria, the Genoese, was distrusted by the other allied commanders because of the long-time animosity between Genoa and Venice. Additionally, he was known to be hesitant and somewhat lacking in imagination. As the battle opened, Doria observed that Uluch Ali was edging to the south. Fearing an envelopment of his right, Doria, whose galleasses were not yet in position to cover him, responded with a course alteration in that direction, opening a gap between his division and Don John's. Uluch Ali, with a 3 to 2 advantage in ships, was presented with several tactical alternatives. He could continue his apparent intention of enveloping Doria's right; he could envelop both wings of the separated division; or he could penetrate the gap and attack both Doria and the rear of the center force. The best course of action became apparent when 15 of Doria's vessels, on Doria's own left, abandoned him and headed for the center. This they did for two reasons: they feared being led into a trap by the Genoese, and they recognized the dire situation surrounding the fleet flagship. Uluch Ali raced for the gap and pounced upon the wayward vessels, easily overcoming them. With a revengeful Doria

swinging left into his rear, Uluch Ali continued toward the center. Too late to affect the decision in the center, Uluch Ali found both Santa Cruz and Don John maneuvering to intercept him. Seeing the folly of continuing alone against the combined Christian fleet, Uluch Ali sped on to the north. With many of his ships sunk or driven ashore by their pursuers, he disappeared over the horizon. Six hours after the opening gun had been fired, the Battle of Lepanto was over.[7]

Tactically, Lepanto was a stunning victory for the Holy League, but the allies did not exploit the strategic advantage it created—secure sea lines of communication. Because they failed to launch a subsequent land campaign, much of the significance of the victory was lost. Victory at sea can only set the stage; consummation almost always must involve the seizure of tenable territory.

So passed the age of the galley. It should be remembered, however, that nonmilitary sailing vessels had been plying the waters of the globe for centuries before the galley fell into disuse. Even in warfare, as early as 1217, King John's fleet of 500 sail—small merchant vessels of less than 100 tons—had established a tradition that was to last for 600 years by scoring the first English victory over a French fleet. Rather than the evolution of naval warfare in terms of propulsion (oars v. sail), it is, perhaps, more accurate to define it in terms of tactical employment of the ship, examining the transition from an infantry platform to an artillery platform. In order to trace the origins of the fighting sailing ship in this way, it is necessary to go back in time well before the Battle of Lepanto.

Developments in Ships and Guns

Sailing vessels were adapted to military use in the Atlantic earlier than in the Mediterranean because the galley, with its low freeboard, was not seaworthy in the open ocean. Until the introduction of gunfire, however, sailing warships were primarily transports. If an engagement did take place at sea, it was a hand-to-hand duel, with the ships being grappled together.

Military adaptations and concepts in ship construction went hand in hand with the development of the ships themselves. In the earliest conflicts between sailing ships, such as those that occurred during the Hundred Years' War, the round ship (usually single-masted) was modified to carry towers, or "castles," fore and aft, to be used as platforms for archers. Significant changes emerged as that war entered the fifteenth century, and as mariners ventured ever farther onto the unknown expanse of the high seas.

Thirteenth Century Round Ship

Early Ordnance

Sometime during the fourteenth century, the first installation of a cannon on board a ship took place. By 1412, as recorded in contemporary documents, breech-loading guns with removable chambers were to be found on English ships. Some authorities claim that the French had installed cannon aboard ships as early as 1356. However, throughout the Hundred Years' War, the potential for such a gun platform was not realized, or at least not exploited, by either the French or the English.

In order to satisfy requirements for portability and manageable dimensions, developers of naval guns could not greatly profit from the designs of the immense weapons used in siegecraft. The installation of arms in vessels had to conform to the nature of the ship's architecture and to its tactical deployment. In the Mediterranean, where the oar-propelled galley ruled the sea, guns were placed in the bow, to fire ahead in preparation for a ramming maneuver; later, smaller calibers were placed to fire abeam, to repel boarders. The larger sailing vessels in the Atlantic, unable to count on an end-on attack, had to be armed to fight on any bearing; their castles bristled with scores of pieces.

The Vessel Evolves

A significant change in the design of warships took place during the Hundred Years' War. For many years, the standard Atlantic merchant vessel, virtually unchanged when adapted to military use, had been the round ship, its single mast supporting one sail. (In the Mediterranean, the trading vessel was the similar nef.) Gradually, a mizzen mast (a mast to the aft) was added, and later a foremast, each also with a single sail.[8] It was thought that the additional sails, so placed, would make the ships easier to steer; but mariners soon realized that more sail area materially increased speed. For commercial purposes, this was an obvious advantage, and led to trial and error with various rigs. The principal type upon which most shipwrights settled was the caravel, a Portuguese vessel that had been developed for exploratory voyages along the west African coast. Shallow of draft, the caravel carried three masts. The foremast and mainmast were sometimes square rigged (a square sail oriented athwartships); usually all three masts were lateen rigged (triangular sails oriented fore and aft).

Subsequently, northern European traders noticed a new type of merchant vessel in Mediterranean waters. The carrack, as it was called, had a higher freeboard than the earlier hulls, and its forecastle and aftercastle were integral parts of the ship's design. Solidly walled, they did not resemble the hastily constructed vessels that had preceded them. (Merchant vessels, as well as warships, carried the high castles because one never knew when a cruising pirate might attack and attempt to board. If the waist of the ship were overrun, the defenders would retreat into the castles, from whence they would fire upon the boarders and, hopefully, repel them.) Longer and more easily handled than the caravel, the carrack was more suitable for adaptation as a warship, and made possible the

The Caravel (Square Rigged)

The Carrack

use of revolutionary tactics in naval engagements. The main-mast carried two sails, and the mizzen carried a triangular lateen; the rigging for tending the foresail gave the vessel maneuverability upwind that was superior to that of the caravel, and unprecedented for a ship of its size. A vessel suitable for carrying cannon in broadside had finally appeared, the forerunner of the "Great Ship" of more than a century later; even so, no artillery contests between carracks occurred during the Hundred Years' War. In 1415, when Henry V's forces captured Harfleur and cleared the way for the over-whelming English victory at Agincourt, both fleet commanders ignored the potential of their artillery, handling their carracks as though they were galleys. Riding swiftly before the wind,

the English entered Harfleur harbor and rammed the French vessels at anchor with a resounding crash, wrecking the forecastles on many of their own ships. The ships were then quickly bound together, and the hand-to-hand struggle that ensued lasted for nearly a day.

As the carrack evolved into the Great Ship of the Tudor period, the professional interest of Henry VIII in the development of arms spurred a variety of improvements. Born in the Palace at Greenwich and raised near the busy River Thames, the English king acquired an early interest in ships and an appreciation of seapower. As he laid the foundations of Britain's later supremacy on the seas, the youthful Henry turned his efforts toward supremacy in all types of arms and armor. Dissatisfied that most of his ordnance had to be imported, he brought experts to England from the Continent; Englishmen were then subsidized to learn their techniques. Foundries and shipyards were built. Experimentation resulted in a myriad of weapons of various dimensions, calibers, and weights.[9] Because of the continuous changes made, and the fact that names were not changed when a class of gun underwent alterations, any attempt to tabulate the various types is almost impossible. Generally, the pieces developed in the sixteenth century can be categorized in four groups: cannon, culverins, periers, and mortars. The cannons were of the largest caliber, 7 or 8 inches, with a barrel length of only 16 to 18 calibers. The culverin was lighter and smaller in caliber (4 or 5 inches), but had a longer barrel of some 30 calibers, giving it greater range. (Compare the diameter/length ratio of these guns with the 8″/55 heavy cruiser gun and the 5″/38 of the modern destroyer.) The perier, a smaller, lighter piece, was an ancestor of the howitzer.

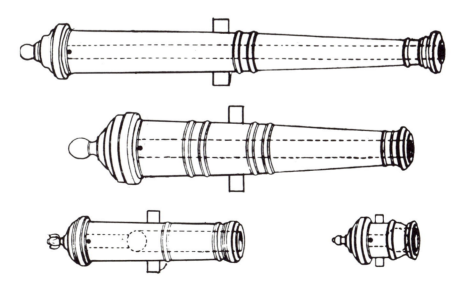

Sixteenth Century Naval Guns: Culverin, Cannon, Perier, Mortar

As metallurgical skills improved, brass became the metal most widely used for casting naval guns. Less brittle than cast iron, it was considerably more expensive. The truck carriage on which the gun was mounted for use aboard ship was an obvious solution to the problems of recoil and portability.[10]

During the reign of Henry VIII, heavily armed sailing vessels proliferated, their primary weapon being the "serpentine" cannon which were mounted in broadside on the uppermost full deck. Smaller guns continued to crowd the castles, for use against both the personnel and rigging of an enemy ship. The early breech loaders had universally given way to the muzzle loading piece. Not only was the insecure connection between chamber and barrel of the breech loader nearly as hazardous to the gun crew as to the enemy, but the threads joining the chamber to the barrel could not be unscrewed when the gun was hot.[11] In the midst of a close-range engagement, with the enemy swarming aboard, hardly a gunner was disposed to wait for his gun to cool before reloading.

The crowning achievement in warship construction under Henry VIII was the monstrously large *Henri Grâce à Dieu*, which was of nearly 1,500 tons displacement, its castles rising to dizzy heights fore and aft, and its four masts supporting a great expanse of sails. During an interlude in Henry's wars with Francis I of France, the *Great Harry*, as the ship was commonly known, was elaborately furbished to carry the English king across the channel to meet Francis on the Field of the Cloth of Gold. King Henry did not enjoy his voyage across the channel; exceedingly topheavy with so much ordnance in its superstructure, the *Great Harry* came perilously close to capsizing. Upon his return to England (in a different vessel, of less grandeur but more stability), the King and his naval architects went to work on the problem. The solution was so obvious that it seems incredible that it was so long in coming; by cutting portholes in the sides, they were able to place the guns on lower decks. *Henri Grâce à Dieu* was rebuilt, with four of its six decks bearing guns.[12] In its first action after the conversion, *Great Harry* demonstrated that its guns were effective against the timbers of enemy vessels, as well as against their personnel. No longer was it necessary to close and board. The broadside warship was to rule the sea until the age of the ironclad.

During the sixteenth century, another type of vessel appeared on the scene in increasing numbers. Probably evolved from the carrack, the galleon was more seaworthy, and with time continued to assume greater dimensions. The galleon

Henri Grâce à Dieu

Spanish Galleon

was narrower in beam-to-length ratio than the carrack, and rather than being blunt and rounded, the forecastle and poop extended far out over the hull. Although somewhat awkward to handle, the galleon was the largest and most dependable vessel that had yet been known. It was designed with three or four masts; the fore and main mounted square sails, while the mizzens, whether one or two, were lateen rigged. Often identified today as the "Spanish galleon" because of its extensive use by the Spanish in trade with their overseas empire, the galleon was in fact used by other major powers before Spain acquired one.

It is apparent that the age of sail had its genesis long before the age of galley warfare drew to a close. All the developments just recounted took place before Don John's rendezvous with history at Lepanto; but as the principal instrument of seapower, it was not until that date that the sailing ship was ready to claim its inheritance.

The Age of Exploration

During the fifteenth century, the Atlantic powers (Portugal, Spain, the Netherlands, England, and France) carved out the great overseas commercial empires, superseding the Italian seaports and the German cities of the Hanseatic League. This shift in focus from the East (the Mediterranean terminus of the trade routes to the Orient) to the West (through the Strait of Gibraltar) followed the fall of Constantinople. The opening of a sea route to the East made it possible to avoid the high cost of overland transportation to Mediterranean ports. Moreover, the age of exploration created an impetus for the construction of larger and faster vessels, as expanding empires competed with each other. The charting of open ocean sea routes was, in turn, the result of progress in the techniques of navigation, which made distant voyages possible.

The Art of Navigation

For centuries, sailors had recognized that the altitude of Polaris above the horizon was very nearly equal to the observer's latitude north of the equator; but on a rolling, pitching ship, such a measurement with the astrolabe was inaccurate, at best. Mathematicians and astronomers had devised the theory of celestial navigation, but the crucial roadblock to its practice, which was not to be satisfactorily solved until the appearance of chronometers late in the eighteenth century, was the inability to accurately measure time. Without such a measure of time, there was no way to determine longitude. (The simplest way to define longitude is to observe the passage of LAN—local apparent noon. In the northern oceans, at noon, the sun is due south of a point on the meridian that defines the time zone—0°, 15°, 30°, etc. The instant that the sun passes 180° in azimuth, then, is a function of angular distance from the observer to the time zone meridian. From the altitude of the sun above the horizon at this instant, one can also calculate latitude.)

The magnetic compass, brought to Europe during the crusades, gave an approximation of direction of advance, and various calculations of time of transit over courses of known length resulted in a rough method for estimating speed. The willingness of the great explorers to venture immense distances on the unknown seas, depending almost entirely on dead reckoning, is incredible; their success in finding their way (and back) is even more so.

Portugal and Spain

The person who was most influential in motivating the age of exploration was Prince Henry, son of a king of Portugal and brother of the next two kings. Known to history as Prince Henry the Navigator, he established at Cape St. Vincent, in 1415, a college for mariners, astronomers, mathematicians, and cartographers. Devoting his life to progress in the science of navigation—as well as to the establishment of a Portuguese empire—Prince Henry sponsored pathfinding voyages of Portuguese mariners, each voyage longer than the previous one. These seamen extended their explorations down the west coast of Africa, around the Cape of Good Hope, and eventually on to India and the East Indies. In less than a century, Portugal rose from an insignificant Iberian state to master of a far-flung empire, with colonies in Africa, Asia, South America, and the Atlantic, Pacific and Indian Oceans. The effect on the contest between the Christian and Islamic worlds was profound, for the Turks no longer controlled the lines of communication to the Orient. Lisbon became the leading commercial city of the world.[13] Portugal gradually weakened because of incompetent and greedy management under the rule of a succession of weak kings. Her decline was complete in 1580 when Portugal was annexed by Philip II of Spain.

Spain began its ascendancy as a seapower in 1469, with the unifying marriage of Isabella of Castile and Ferdinand of Aragon. Occupied for several years with ejecting the Moors from Iberia, Ferdinand and Isabella achieved dominance in 1492, with the conquest of the Moorish fortress of Granada, ending eight centuries of Moslem occupation. During the next century, Spanish explorers vied with, and eventually surpassed, the Portuguese. In an effort to avoid an inevitable clash between the two powers, Pope Alexander VI (patriarch of the infamous Borgia family) intervened, dividing the New World into Spanish and Portuguese spheres. The resulting Treaty of Tordesillas awarded to Portugal all territories discovered east of a line passing 300 miles west of the Cape Verde Islands, and to Spain all territories west of that line.[14] As it turned out, the line of demarcation—the great circle, longitude 46° W–134° E.—placed Brazil, Africa, Asia, and the East Indies in Portugal's sector, and the remainder of North and South America and the area from the Pacific to the Philippines in Spain's sphere.

When the King of Portugal died in 1580 without an heir, Philip II of Spain claimed the crown for himself. (A member of the Portuguese royal family on his mother's side, he was both nephew and son-in-law to the previous king.) Spain seemed strong beyond challenge. *(See Map 1.)* Philip ruled Spain, Portugal, the Netherlands, Franche-Comté, Milan, Naples, Sicily, Sardinia, part of North Africa, and an immense colonial empire; treasure fleets from the lands of the Aztec and the Inca poured wealth into his coffers. His forthcoming challenge to Elizabeth of England was to expose the myth of Spain's invincibility.

The Age of Sail Matures

The Armada: Background

Philip II had reason to be confident of his eminent position

among the crowned heads of Europe. In the 1580s, he ruled more people and owned more territory than any other. Yet, since Lepanto, two situations had arisen to cast shadows on his reign: the Netherlands were in revolt, and English vessels were raiding his treasure ships from America with annoying frequency. Both his Dutch subjects and the Protestant "usurper" of the Catholic throne of England would have to be taught a lesson.

In 1579, the northern provinces of the Netherlands had formed a Protestant confederation, and two years later had dared to proclaim their independence from Spain. To oppose the Dutch leader, William of Orange, Philip had sent Don John of Austria; subsequently, William had been assassinated and Don John had died in his camp at Namur. As Philip prepared for war with England, the Duke of Parma was in command of the Spanish forces, opposing William's son, Maurice of Nassau. Parma was successful in holding the southern, Catholic provinces (modern Belgium), but increasing aid to the Dutch from Queen Elizabeth was further straining the already precarious relationship between Spain and England.[15]

In the 30 years since her accession, Elizabeth I had greatly strengthened her shaky throne. Elizabeth's predecessor, Mary I, had been the second wife of Philip, and during the marriage he had held the title King of England, but without the right of succession. When Mary died, two years after Philip had become King of Spain, the succession of her half-sister

Philip II of Spain

Elizabeth I of England

An English Man-of-War in 1558

Elizabeth was opposed by Catholic Europe. A formidable pretender existed in the person of Mary Stuart of Scotland, cousin of Elizabeth. In order to secure her position in the face of intrigue and threatened assassination, Elizabeth had reluctantly assented to the execution of Mary Queen of Scots. This act, compounded by English assistance to the Dutch and by the attacks on Spanish ships of commerce by Francis Drake and others whose adventures were legitimatized by Letters of Reprisal from the Queen, so infuriated Philip that he put his plans for an invasion of England into motion.[16] He determined to claim the English crown for himself, based on his earlier marriage and on his descent from Edward III; but more significantly in the political concepts of the times, he would advance the fact that Mary Stuart had willed to him her own claim to the throne.

Only in recent years, as the Spanish threat became ominous, had the English Navy begun to regain the position of strength to which Henry VIII had guided it. Naval commanders John Hawkins and Francis Drake had modernized and rebuilt much of the fleet. Although smaller than the Spanish Navy, it was infinitely more proficient. Philip could rightfully claim that his *tercios* were the world's best troops, but the professionalism of his sailors left much to be desired.

Basically a galleon, the English man-of-war had evolved into a longer and narrower, low-freeboard ship, with less dominant castles. Hawkins favored maneuver, gunfire, and the stand-off artillery battle to the ancient tactic of boarding

and capturing; his concept was manifested in the increased proportion of long-range guns that had been installed. The English reduced the number of 32-pound shot cannon with its range of 2,000 yards and the 24-pound perier of 1,500 yards; the principal armament became the culverin, which fired a 17-pound ball 2,500 yards.

Drake's voice rang loudest among those who urged stopping the expected Spanish invasion before it could be launched. With less than enthusiastic support from the Queen, he put to sea to reconnoiter the Spanish coast. Learning that the harbor of Cadiz was the assembly point for much of

Sir Francis Drake

Philip's fleet, Drake carried out an overwhelmingly successful surprise attack on that port. As a result of this attack, and others that were less spectacular, Philip's operation had to be delayed for a year, until 1588.[17]

Philip's strategy involved the employment of forces from both Spain and the Netherlands. The Duke of Parma was to produce transports and move 17,000 troops from Dunkirk to Calais. The Armada would, if only by its presence, secure command of the channel, provide Parma with 6,000 additional troops, and then cover the invasion force as it crossed the Strait of Dover. If possible, naval action would be avoided until the forces had concentrated. The Pope had pledged a

fortune to defray the cost of the operation, payable when the first Spanish soldier landed on English soil.[18]

The Armada: The Encounter

On May 25, 1588, Philip's Grand Armada sortied from Portuguese and Spanish ports. One hundred and thirty-seven ships, many of them large galleons bearing the heaviest guns that could be fitted, carried a total of some 30,000 men, two-thirds of whom were troops. Still influenced by their success at Lepanto, the Spanish adhered to the Mediterranean concept of naval warfare; their fleet included only four galleys and

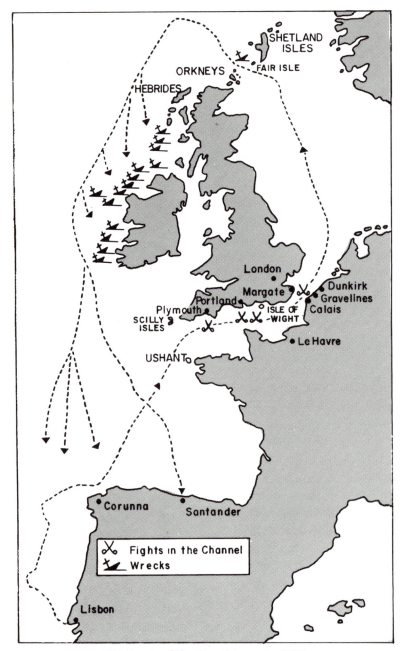

The Route of the Grand Armada, 1588

One of the Clashes Between the English Fleet and the Spanish Armada, 1588

four galleasses, but tactically they envisioned gunfire at short range, followed by boarding and capturing. Heavy weather delayed the movement for two months, but the Grand Armada resumed its northward voyage late in July.

Santa Cruz, one of the key personalities at Lepanto, had been in command of the fleet during its preparations. Following that leader's sudden death in 1588, Philip appointed the wealthy, staunchly religious Duke of Medina-Sidonia to command. Having absolutely no knowledge of ships, seamanship, or naval warfare, Medina protested—in vain. The King had made his choice.

The sequence of events that followed can be separated into several phases: the meeting engagement in the Channel, the run up the Channel to Calais, the night attack at Calais, the next day's battle at Gravelines, and finally the circuitous homeward voyage of the Spanish.

On July 30, Medina failed to take advantage of an opportunity to attack the English fleet—an opportunity that, if exploited, most likely would have drastically changed the course of events. As that fleet, commanded by the Lord High Admiral Charles Howard, put to sea from Plymouth against an unfavorable wind, Medina continued up the Channel to his rendezvous at Calais. The plan was to avoid battle at this time, but by holding to the letter of his orders Medina let pass a great tactical opportunity. By the next morning, the English had cleared restricted waters and had gained the

weather gauge* astern of the Spanish. In accordance with their concept of naval warfare, the English had no troops aboard their ships; they would depend solely on their guns.

Although the English had only 34 warships in commission, the fleet of armed merchantmen that were available, and other volunteers who joined, brought the total number of vessels to 197. Many were small, but they were maneuverable, manageable, and manned by gunners who were trained to fire accurately and rapidly.

Inconclusive English attacks on the flank of the crescent-shaped Spanish formation marked the first encounter. Drake clashed with Spanish vessels near Plymouth on the thirty-first, but the English had to remain out of range of the heavier Spanish guns. A close fight was to be absolutely avoided, because the castles of the Spanish ships loomed high over the English vessels, and it would be impossible to prevent Spanish troops from storming down on their decks if they came close enough to grapple. The first Spanish losses were due to collision and fires in the crowded Channel.

Dawn on August 2 found the fleets off Portland Bill, with the wind shifted to the northeast and the English therefore on the leeward gauge. Howard moved inshore in an attempt to pass around the Spanish left and gain the wind. Medina saw

---

*A position to the windward of another ship that affords an advantage in maneuvering.

the opportunity to hit him in flank and to close near enough to take advantage of his heavy guns, but the English broadsides held the Spanish off.[19] Both sides fired furiously, but little damage was done, and supplies of both powder and shot began to run perilously short. By nightfall, the wind had again backed to the west, tactically favoring the English, but the Spaniards had resumed their steady progress toward the scheduled rendezvous with Parma's troops.

On the fourth, a violent but again indecisive engagement of several hours' duration raged off the Isle of Wight. The light wind permitted little maneuvering, and Spanish attempts to attack with their oared galleasses were easily repelled. Morale on both sides was high; the English had been successful in keeping the formidable Armada at bay, and the Spanish, with practically no losses, had apparently achieved their first objective of reaching the Flemish coast. The Spanish fleet anchored on August 6 at Calais. The Duke of Parma and his *tercios* were not there.

The Spanish, in reacting to every feint and harassment by Howard's ships, had run critically short of ammunition. Their only source of supplies was the Netherlands, but an unexpected force had been at work—Parma was solidly blockaded by a Dutch and English fleet. Even if he were able to join Medina by an overland march, there would be insufficient craft to launch an invasion of England.

The two fleets had fired nearly 200,000 rounds during the week of activity in the Channel. Little major damage had been done, the Spanish shot having fallen short of its targets, and the 17-pound culverin having been too light to damage the stout Spanish ships at extreme range. The English could resupply from their home ground, or so the Spanish assumed.[20] Actually, the English ships, also practically void of ammunition, were meagerly resupplied. So occurred one of the most successful bluffs in history.

A dramatic event took place on the night of August 7, when eight fireships were sent drifting into Calais, each manned by a single helmsman who was to escape at the last possible moment in a small boat. The pandemonium in Calais harbor was disproportionate to the danger. As the Spanish frantically cut their anchor cables and groped to reach open water, the fireships continued harmlessly through gaps among the Spanish vessels. Their anchors lost, the Spanish ships had no choice but to beat their disorderly way into a contrary wind, and sail out to sea. Morning found them scattered along the Flemish coast near the port of Gravelines, midway between Calais and Dunkirk. Their attempts to avoid grounding had resulted in every ship maneuvering for itself and in the loss of all semblance of order. Gambling on the Spaniards' shortage of ammunition and favored with the weather gauge, Drake led his squadron in for a close range attack. The battle off Gravelines proved to be the costliest of the campaign to the

Spanish,[21] as their inability to return fire forced them to continue past Dunkirk. Standing on the quay at Dunkirk, the Duke of Parma watched the sails of the fleet that was to have borne him triumphant to England pass him by, as it retreated into the North Sea. Although losses had again been light, several Spanish ships had been badly mauled, and heavy personnel casualties had been taken.

Aboard the English fleet, all powder and shot had been expended. Nothing prevented the Spanish from turning about and passing through their pursuer, back to Dunkirk, to Spain, or even to England—but the Spanish were unaware of this. Not daring to attempt to run the Channel again and dismissing the alternative of wintering in northern Europe for fear of leaving Spain uncovered, Medina-Sidonia saw the long voyage north and west of the British Isles as his only option. Short on rations and water, damaged and leaking, and manned by demoralized crews, the Armada continued. Of the 137 ships that had set out, about a dozen had been lost in battle; only half would survive the dreadful voyage through surf and storm that lay ahead, and those that would return would be manned by far fewer souls than had embarked.

The Armada: Retrospection

It is generally accepted that the defeat of the Spanish Armada was a decisive event. Its significance, however, is often lost in the overstatement that it ended Spain's international supremacy and signaled the rise of English seapower, thus bringing a new empire into being. In fact, the disaster more accurately marks the birth than the death of the Spanish Navy, for Philip was made to understand the vital truth that naval power does not equate with seapower. The fact that Spain's decline accelerated after 1588 can be attributed to factors other than the failure of the Armada; the Navy increased in effectiveness as a result of lessons learned, although history records no battles to bear this out.

The withdrawal of the Armada did not end the war between England and Spain. Not until both Philip and Elizabeth were dead and the son of the ill-fated Mary Stuart was on the throne as James I was peace established—an inconclusive peace that profited neither side.

As for England, it may be said that she was saved from invasion, for the success of the Armada would most certainly have resulted in one. Even that is overstating the case, however, if it is accepted that the Medina-Parma mission was foredoomed. Considering the participation of the Dutch, the resolve of the English—including English Catholics—to resist, lack of generalship in the Armada, Spain's inability to support her fleet logistically, and the distance over which subsequent exploitation would have had to have been carried out, it is quite improbable that any but the most unlikely turn of events could have permitted the venture to succeed. Strategy had been ruled by emotion.

The immense significance of the defeat of the Spanish Armada lies elsewhere. First, although Europe was not thoroughly convinced, it demonstrated that the Counter Reformation was not going to succeed. Protestantism, like Communism in the twentieth century, was an institution that was going to remain firmly entrenched, even though another generation would have to endure a devastating war of thirty years before its coexistence with Catholicism would be established.

The rise of England and the decline of Spain followed in due course, but this occurred as a corollary of circumstances engendered by the Armada's defeat, rather than in response to that defeat. The Dutch, winning *de facto* independence from Spain under the leadership of Maurice of Nassau, built a fleet that the commercial-minded administration could employ in competition with the best. England, under James I, abandoned aid to the Netherlands, fomenting the sentiment that would be exacerbated by competition until it provoked a series of naval wars. In the Anglo-Dutch Wars, the age of sail would perfect its style of warfare.

As the Armada was enduring its frightful homeward voyage, a power struggle in France reached its climax. The following year saw the end of the House of Valois and the accession of the first Bourbon king. The balance of power on the Continent began to shift, much of Spain's lost prestige being reaped by Henry IV.

Finally, the art of warfare had undergone a test that validated certain concepts and put others to rest. Neither an exclusive dependence upon maneuver nor firepower was sufficient. Guns could not damage a vessel unless brought within reasonable range, and to do so required a ship that responded quickly and nimbly. Merchant vessels, designed for volume to carry cargo, were not suitable for conversion to warships; a ship had to be built with characteristics that enhanced deft tactical seamanship. Additionally, with the theater of warfare expanding to encompass a worldwide area, bases remote from the mother country were essential to maintain a viable claim to command of the sea. It had become a mercantile world in which command of the sea was vital; the future belonged to that nation which best grasped the ramifications of Philip's misfortune.

The Age of Sail in Action

As it became accepted that the sailing warship armed with artillery was to be the vehicle for naval warfare, centuries of tradition and deeply engrained assumptions had to be discarded. Analogy still existed between a land battle and one fought at sea, but adjustments had to be made in drawing parallels. For example, in a galley fleet, just as in a line of infantry, the direction of advance toward the enemy was the direction in which the units fired. With guns now mounted in broadside, the direction of fire had to be *at right angles to* the line of advance. An oar-driven warship can maneuver in any direction. Even the best vessels of the age of sail could sail only about six points into the wind.*

Following the Thirty Years' War (1618–1648), England fought three wars with Holland between 1652 and 1674, followed by seven consecutive wars with France between 1689 and 1815. In the first of these wars, fleet tactics were developed and doctrine was formulated.

The first question to be answered concerned the formation in which ships would sail. Positioning upwind and massing fire on the nearest ships of the enemy were seen as logical moves, but order had to be maintained or friendly ships would foul each other's range. The line ahead, or column, was the obvious disposition to maximize flexibility in gunfire with minimum risk to one's own fleet, while keeping friendly ships within supporting distance. The length of the line discouraged the enemy from attempting to pass ahead, where raking fire could be discharged from an angle on which one's own ships could not bear—that is, "crossing the T." During the Dutch wars, the merit of the line ahead was universally recognized, but differences of opinion were expressed regarding actions to be taken after the fleets were engaged. As a result of further unresolved questions, two concepts were advanced, which became known as the Formal School and the Melee School. The ideas of the two schools differ in degree of centralized control, application of the principles of mass and maneuver, and considerations of defensive action.

It is as true on sea as on land that an enemy is more easily overcome by massing combat power against part of his force while holding the remainder in check with economy-of-force tactics. The line ahead violated this principle by deploying force equally along the line. The line ahead, however, lent itself to orderly control by the fleet commander. With a system of visual signals that transmitted maneuver orders, he could effectively maintain control of all ships. This would be especially important as a defensive measure, since the English always sought to gain the weather gauge, from which escape upwind would be difficult. (The French, on the other hand, traditionally chose to fight from the leeward gauge. Unwilling

*There are 32 "points" in the compass; a point therefore corresponds to 11¼ degrees of arc. Sailing ships could not approach within 60 degrees of the direction from which the wind was blowing. A modern racing sailboat can sail almost, but not quite, into the wind; that feat will ever be contrary to the laws of physics.

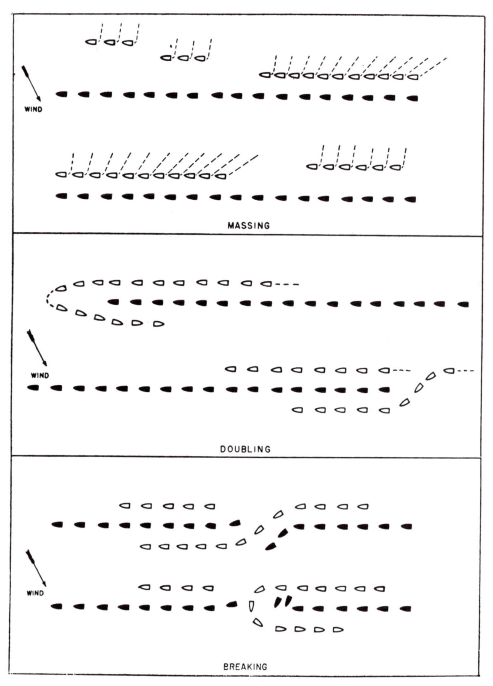

MASSING

DOUBLING

BREAKING

Melee Tactics

to risk destruction of their fleet, they wanted to keep the downwind avenue of escape open should the battle turn against them. This difference in preference between the two was convenient, inasmuch as they fought each other for 126 years.)

As devices for massing firepower against the enemy line, the Melee School proposed the tactics of massing, doubling, and breaking. Doubling and breaking also prevent an enemy from escaping to leeward. Massing meant simply decreasing the interval between some ships in the line, to bring more guns to bear on a portion of the enemy line. Because massing alone could easily be evaded unless the enemy were caught

between two lines, doubling and breaking tactics were employed. As the diagram shows, breaking is a penetration of the line. Since the "flanks" of a line ahead are in the van and the rear, rather than on the beam as with land forces (or with ships in line abreast), doubling is the nautical version of an envelopment. It can be seen that a cannon shot that missed the enemy vessel might well hit one's own, but the tactical advantage of outgunning the enemy was well worth the risk.

The meleeists had solved the problem of bringing superior combat power to bear upon a part of the enemy's fleet, but they had no solution for the holding mission of the economy-

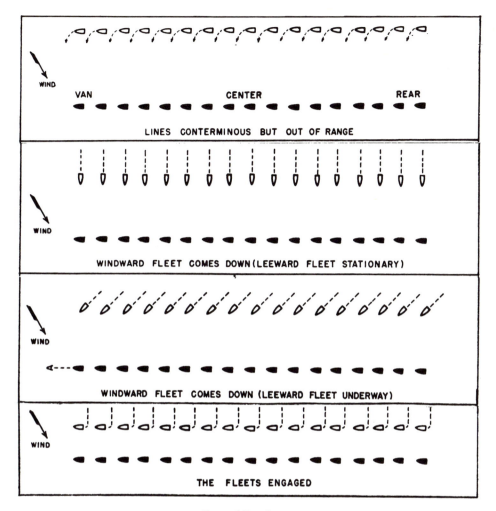

VAN   CENTER   REAR

LINES CONTERMINOUS BUT OUT OF RANGE

WINDWARD FLEET COMES DOWN (LEEWARD FLEET STATIONARY)

WINDWARD FLEET COMES DOWN (LEEWARD FLEET UNDERWAY)

THE FLEETS ENGAGED

Formal Tactics

of-force measure. With no rivers, defiles, forests, cliffs, or towns against which an enemy could be kept in check, a massing maneuver could be countered by a similar maneuver against the weakened portion of one's own line.

During the Dutch wars and the earlier French wars, the ideas of the Melee School were predominant. In the quarter century of peace following the War of the Spanish Succession, however, an element of conservatism influenced the Royal Navy. When hostilities resumed, this factor, coupled with the failure of melee tactics to cope with the problem of enemy countermoves, led to the ascendancy of the formal tactics that were to characterize fleet actions for much of the eighteenth century. The disadvantages of the Formal School of tactics were that initiative on the part of subordinate commanders was constrained, and success depended on gunnery expertise and the staying power of individual ships. Additionally, this deployment (analogous to a frontal attack) subjected ships to raking fire as they closed within range, and there was no way to prevent the enemy from simply shifting course and opening the range if he chose not to fight.

To implement the formal tactics, the fleet commander would form his line to windward of the enemy line, adjusting its length so that van was opposite van, center opposite center, and rear opposite rear, while still out of gun range. He would then close the enemy line, turning parallel when within range, and engage. Unfortunately, against the French, this maneuver was often costly. As has been mentioned, the French habitually sought the leeward gauge and the British the weather gauge. This was because the British considered their navy to be a tactical offensive weapon, its mission to destroy the enemy's armed force. The French considered their fleet a strategic weapon, and preferred the option of the downwind escape, placing them on the tactical defensive. With experience, the British learned that the French had a point. Moving a line of sailing ships into range was not the smartly executed maneuver that it is with a line of modern destroyers. The helmsmen could not all put their rudders over simultaneously, all ships could not close at the same speed, and all could not keep precise station. As a result, when the British line began to close the French would back their sails, killing headway,

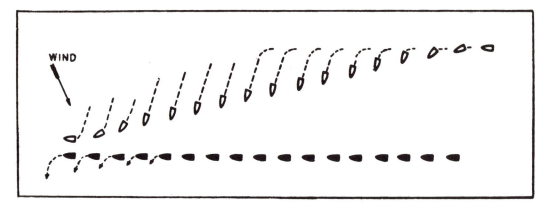

Closing Under Actual Conditions

and forcing the British to close head on into their line. *(See Diagram above.)* Not only did this situation present the opportunity to rake the English vessels with gunfire, but since the English did not all come within range simultaneously, the French were automatically massed against them without having to maneuver.[22]

Each victory strengthened the arguments in favor of the tactics that had been used, and each defeat forced reconsideration of other concepts. Often, the outcome of a battle was caused by factors other than tactics—weather, human error, luck, or materiel failures—but these influences were largely overlooked as the search for an ideal naval engagement continued. By the mid-eighteenth century, the Royal Navy had sufficient experience in war at sea to practice an appropriate

blend of doctrine and initiative. As a generality, the major sea battles of the later years of the age of sail were characterized by formal tactics to gain position and melee tactics to fight the battle.

A balanced study of military history requires an awareness of the situation at sea when it relates to the campaign being studied—as it so frequently does. The art of war has many expressions, and seapower, or the lack of it, has often spoken loudly. From humble beginnings in the Mediterranean, seapower grew to exert a global influence. Increased in scope, modified by technology, demonstrated under superior leaders, and inexorable in its application, seapower, and its strong arm, naval power, became inescapable influences upon man's endeavors.

Artist's Rendering of the Formal Battleline

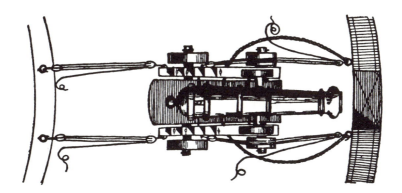

**Eighteenth Century Cannon, With Breeching to Restrict
the Recoil and Tackle for Return to Firing Position**

Seventeenth Century Ship-of-the-Line

Notes

[1] John Van Duyn Southworth, *The Ancient Fleets* (New York, 1968), p. 328.

[2] William Ledyard Rodgers, *Naval Warfare Under Oars* (Annapolis, 1939), p. 171.

[3] Southworth, *Ancient Fleets*, p. 330.

[4] John F. C. Fuller, *A Military History of the Western World* (3 vols.; New York, 1954), I, 570-571; Jacques Mordal, *Twenty-Five Centuries of Sea Warfare* (New York, 1965), p. 52.

[5] Fuller, *Military History*, I, 567; Rodgers, *Naval Warfare*, pp. 230-234; R. C. Anderson, *Oared Fighting Ships* (London, 1962).

[6] Fuller, *Military History*, I, 567; E. B. Potter and C. W. Nimitz, *Sea Power: A Naval History* (Englewood Cliffs, 1960), p. 16.

[7] Fuller, *Military History*, I, 570-576; Rodgers, *Naval Warfare*, pp. 196-210; Mordal, *Sea Warfare*, pp. 53-56; Potter and Nimitz, *Sea Power*, pp. 17-18; Lynn Montross, *War Through the Ages* (New York, 1960), pp. 229-230.

[8] E. B. Potter, unpublished manuscript, "Ships and Shipping in War and Peace," p.16.

[9] Frederick L. Robertson, *The Evolution of Naval Armament* (London, 1921), p. 72.

[10] O. F. G. Hogg, *English Artillery, 1326–1716* (London, 1963), pp. 38-39. See also Robertson, *Naval Armament*.

[11] Potter and Nimitz, *Sea Power*, p. 26.

[12] John Van Duyn Southworth, *The Age of Sails* (New York, 1968), p. 21; Potter and Nimitz, *Sea Power*, p. 26.

[13] Southworth, *The Age of Sails*, p. 51.

[14] William L. Langer, *An Encyclopedia of World History* (Boston, 1958), p. 390; Potter and Nimitz, *Sea Power*, p. 23.

[15] Southworth, *The Age of Sails*, p. 72; Montross, *War*, pp. 247-250.

[16] Southworth, *The Age of Sails*, p. 71.

[17] Garrett Mattingly, *The Armada* (Boston, 1959), pp. 82-90.

[18] *Ibid.*, p. 216.

[19] Mordal, *Sea Warfare*, p. 62; Mattingly, *Armada*, pp. 297-298; Michael Lewis, *The Spanish Armada* (New York, 1960), pp. 129-130.

[20] Lewis, *Armada*, pp. 148-162.

[21] Mattingly, *Armada*, p. 336.

[22] Potter and Nimitz, *Sea Power*, p. 39.

C   D   E

1

4

3

SWEDEN

BALTIC SEA

ARK

Niemen R.

LITHUANIA

POLAND

Vistula R.

Oder R.

Pripet R.

Dnieper R.

Dniester R.

SEA OF AZOV

Vienna

AUSTRIA

Danube R.

Budapest

HUNGARY

OTTOMAN

Danube R.

BLACK SEA

2

PAL TES

KINGDOM OF NAPLES

EMPIRE

Constantinople

NGDOM OF ICILY

MALTA

CORFU

Lepanto

RHODES

CYPRUS

CRETE (Venice)

SYRIA

MEDITERRANEAN SEA

1

EGYPT

C   D   E

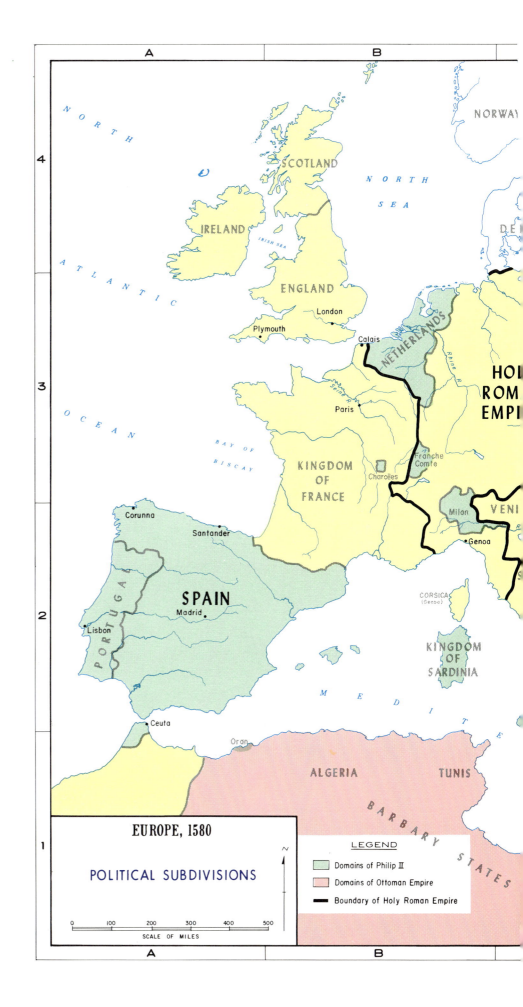

EUROPE, 1580

POLITICAL SUBDIVISIONS

LEGEND

Domains of Philip II

Domains of Ottoman Empire

Boundary of Holy Roman Empire

0   100   200   300   400   500
SCALE OF MILES

Gustavus Adolphus and the Swedish Renaissance in Warfare

Perhaps nothing else so symbolizes modern warfare as the rocket. Whether a missile to Mars, an intercontinental ballistic weapon, or an antitank device, rockets permeate the military thinking of our age. Although soldiers had used rockets in battle for centuries, they did not become satisfactory weapons of warfare until Germans, working at a remote site on the Baltic Coast called Peenemünde, developed missiles for Adolph Hitler. There was something quite poetic in the choice of that location, because three centuries earlier Peenemünde had witnessed the start of an adventure that did much to make possible the emergence of modern Germany, and in very large measure ushered in the era of modern warfare.

In that summer of 1630 the lamp of Protestantism was flickering low. Armies loosed by the Counter Reformation had swept to the shores of the Baltic. One state after another had succumbed to the forces of Ferdinand II, the Holy Roman Emperor. It appeared all but certain that the whole of the Germanic peoples would be brought into Vienna's orbit, reestablishing Catholic hegemony in central Europe. For Protestants it was the low point of the Thirty Years' War. Defeat was at hand.

Then, out of Sweden burst an army the likes of which had never been seen. At first the Swedes were only 13,000 strong, a ludicrously small force. Additionally, they had no allies. But they were, for their time, highly motivated and keenly professional. They were carefully trained, thoughtfully administered, well equipped, and splendidly led. Moreover, they were fighting for a cause.

Within two and a half years they had restored Protestantism to northern Germany, routed every force daring to oppose them in open battle, humbled the Emperor's best generals, marched to the Danube and beyond, and opened a new epoch in warfare. For two centuries afterwards, all armies would be profoundly influenced by the new system of fighting that the Swedes had introduced.

The primary force behind those brilliant successes was the

Gustavus Adolphus Vasa, King of Sweden
Pencil Sketch, 1632

superb leadership of the commander, the King of Sweden. Only 36 years old when he led his troops ashore at Peenemünde, the King was every inch a soldier. Tall, erect, broad-shouldered and unusually strong, he was inspirational in appearance as well as manner. Close-cropped hair and a golden, pointed beard framed burning eyes—eyes that radiated the drive, energy, restlessness, and ambition which welled up within him. He had spent his entire life preparing for that moment when he could finally dig his heel sharply into German soil. In just over two years he would reshape Europe, revolutionize warfare, earn enduring renown as one of the world's Great Captains—and die in battle. He was, of course, Gustavus Adolphus, "The Lion of the North."

Revolution in Warfare

To understand Gustavus Adolphus' contribution to the evolution of warfare, one must first examine the military reforms he effected prior to his campaigns in Germany. The proper starting point for this discussion is not Gustavus, but, instead, a contemporary military innovator, Maurice of Nassau.

Reform in the Netherlands

Maurice matured, lived, and died in a single setting: the long and bitter struggle of the Netherlands to win freedom from Spain. War was his background, avocation, and business. Only 17 when he became champion of the Dutch cause, Maurice was wise and capable far beyond his years. From 1584 to 1625 he served conspicuously as both political and military leader in the Dutch Revolt. Given the severe restrictions under which he operated, his campaigns were splendidly mounted; taken alone they would assure him an honored place in military history. However, it is for intellectual attainments as a military theorist that he is best remembered.

As noted earlier, in the sixteenth century Spain had developed the *tercio* to take advantage of new weapons.* A formation of definite size, combining pike and arquebus, the *tercio* was a great improvement over the Swiss column. It presented a small target to enemy gunners, had fewer ineffective men lost in its center, possessed organic firepower, and could be grouped with other *tercios* in tactical formations. Because of these advantages it was the supreme instrument of war in Europe for the greater part of a century. In general, everyone aped the Spanish system unquestioningly. Yet it retained serious disadvantages. The utilization of manpower

*See Chapter 1, p. 20.

Maurice of Nassau

was still extravagantly wasteful; of the 30 or 40 ranks of pikemen, no more than the first five or six could actually employ their weapons. Only a few of the arquebusiers could fire at any given time and, if more were added to the formation, the already serious problem of finding protection from cavalry inside the pike ranks became all but unsolvable. Nor did the *tercio*'s size help. Attempting a maneuver with 3,000 tightly packed men—later, versions of 1,500—was a risky business. If the solid wall of pikes was ever broken, the *tercio* was doomed. The formation was cumbrous. It was used on occasion to attack, but the circumstances had to be just so. Essentially, the *tercio* was an immobile, defensive organization. It lacked flexibility. It flourished for lack of competition, not because of any degree of inherent strength.

Sixteenth century cavalry was no better. Unwilling to charge at a gallop into the prickly face of a *tercio*, and enamored with the wheel-lock pistol, cavalrymen turned their backs on shock action to toy with missile tactics. The caracole came into being. In theory it would blow a breach in the *tercio*; in practice it was wholly futile. Basically, the horsemen would trot in stately formation to within yards of the enemy, swerve right while discharging left-handed pistols, swerve again to the left in order to fire their right-handed pistols, and then ride off to reload. Since a pistol could not pierce a breastplate at a range much beyond a pike's length, little harm was done. Even if a breach were made, there waited no riders with sabers drawn, ready to dash into the gap. Mounted men persisted in performing the caracole, foolish as it was, probably because as the *tercio* became more and more immobile the debility of the cavalry was not as noticeable.

Two other factors contributed to the atrophy of offensive warfare in the sixteenth century. Artillery was excessively heavy and could be moved only with extreme difficulty after a battle had opened. Second, engineers, after watching cannon batter down medieval walls, had begun to construct fortifications that were more or less impervious to anything short of a formal siege.

That, briefly, was the face of warfare that Maurice viewed. The art of war had petrified. A war of movement was unheard of; generals aimed at *avoiding* battle wherever possible. A siege could consume a campaign. Maurice's task was to restore mobility to the battlefield.

Maurice was able to pinpoint the central problem as a result of his actual experience on the battlefield. Then, for a solution, he turned to military history. Reading and rereading the theories and maxims of past philosophers—especially the ancient Romans—he gradually contrived an altogether new form of warfare. An effective system, it seemed to him, had to be based on three key factors: an efficient use of every man, flexibility, and a combination of arms. To obtain the greatest effect from a unit's firepower, he advocated the adoption of a more linear formation than the massive squares then in vogue. Smaller units would make a force more flexible. Underlying all of his theories was the basic concept that soldiers must be painstakingly drilled and trained. These ideas changed warfare. Linear tactics were born, a tactical form whose ultimate would be attained under Frederick the Great of Prussia. More immediately, Maurice called for shallower and longer formations of pike, with separate groups of musketeers flanking the pikemen rather than surrounding them, and a basic unit much reduced in size. His battalion, patterned somewhat after a Roman cohort, numbered 550 men. His system was vastly more flexible and maneuverable than that of the Spanish. A Spanish army of 12,000 troops normally was subdivided into four *tercios*; Maurice split the same number of men into 24 battalions. The Dutch soldier was setting the stage for another climactic battle between the phalanx and the legion.

Into other areas, too, his ideas breathed fresh air. In siegework, he advocated massing artillery barrages against limited points in the defense. He standardized the Dutch artillery. He used field fortifications and required his soldiers to dig. Military maps and telescopes became common in his armies. Discipline and training came to the fore. His troops were paid more regularly than any in Europe, and were more carefully administered.

But, for all that, Maurice did not complete the process of bringing forth a new form of warfare. He did nothing to improve cavalry, and not enough to make artillery truly mobile. Nor was he ever able to demonstrate the effectiveness of his system. Despite his theoretical espousal of the offensive, in practice he waged war defensively. His military reputation was gained largely as a master of siege warfare. He fought—and won—only one pitched battle, but victory did not spur him to greater attempts.

As a theorist, Maurice was ahead of his contemporaries; as a commander, he was a prisoner of his age. It was left to another to complete Maurice's reforms and to introduce to the world a revolution in warfare. Gustavus Adolphus was that person.

The Education of a Great Captain

Historians are fond of comparing Gustavus Adolphus to Alexander the Great. Both set out on military careers while still youths; there was a striking physical resemblance and a certain similarity of character; each opened a new epoch in warfare; each had a keen sense of exhilaration in battle which impelled him into the thick of the heaviest fighting; each died young, leaving behind unfinished work too grand in concept to be completed by his successors. Yet there was a most substantial difference. Alexander inherited from his father a trained and experienced military organization. All he had to do was wield it. Gustavus started with nothing, and constructed his own army.

Only days after reaching his seventeenth birthday, Gustavus Adolphus Vasa became King of Sweden. The time was January 1612. Surveying his new kingdom proved to be anything but a pleasant or promising experience. Political dissension prevailed throughout Sweden, and it was not in the least soothed by severe economic difficulties. Abroad, Denmark, Russia, and Poland each had long-standing quarrels with the Scandinavian nation. Warfare around the Baltic was endemic. Worse, Sweden's small, poorly trained, inadequately organized army was utterly incapable of coping with any of its major antagonists. All told, a more inauspicious moment to assume the mantle of leadership can hardly be imagined. But the young man on the throne was not an ordinary monarch; fortunately for Sweden, he was one of those rare individuals for whom the word genius was coined.

From birth, Gustavus was groomed for kingship. A precocious and spirited child, he was placed in the hands of a learned tutor to receive a rigorous academic education. Latin and Greek classics, history, political science, theology, and law constituted his theoretical courses. The lad was fascinated by history; he later wrote a history of his own times. In the field of languages, the young prince was especially gifted. Bilingual from childhood in Swedish and German, he could converse clearly in eight other tongues by the time his schooling was over. Mathematics, optics, and mechanics came next. Then began his professional military training. He pored over the history of the military art from the Roman era right up to his own day. Xenophon, Livy, Aelian, Leo VI, Frontinius, Vegetius, Polybius, Machiavelli, and Lipsius were some of the more significant authors on his reading list. Long periods of discussion and reflection were evoked by the innovations of Maurice of Nassau. Those concepts originated by the famous Dutch leader implanted themselves deeply in the perceptive student's mind. Instruction by and conversations with officers who had fought under Maurice helped to clarify the new ideas, which seemed so logical to Gustavus but which none of Europe's established armies was eager to accept. The intellectual stimulation Gustavus received was wholly matched by his own intellectual curiosity.

By no means, however, was the practical side of his education neglected. At the age of 10 he began attending council meetings. In the next few years he heard complaints from subjects, received foreign ambassadors, and actually performed the myriad of other tasks required of a king. But, at heart, he was a soldier. He implored his father for an independent command when he was just 15. That request was denied, but a year later he did see action in the Danish War. Upon becoming king, therefore, Gustavus was ready for the responsibility, despite his youth.

In the winter of 1612, the most immediate danger to Sweden came from Denmark. The bad feelings between the two countries were rooted in sovereignty claims in the Arctic, and in Danish resentment of Sweden's success in gaining independence a century earlier. Gustavus' father had elected war rather than negotiation, and King Christian IV of Denmark

Gustavus Adolphus

was only too happy to oblige him. Having inherited a war that was going poorly for Sweden, the youthful new ruler left for the front the day· he became king, determined to bring hostilities to an end—by fighting or negotiation. Displaying an offensive spirit, Gustavus at once initiated raiding operations designed to harass and confuse his foe. Fighting was generally inconsequential during this short winter campaign, but in at least one instance the King had a close call. Forced to flee when Danish cavalry scattered his guard, Gustavus escaped by spurring his horse over the thin ice of a nearby lake, only to find himself submerged in the frigid waters. There would be numerous other brushes with death in the next 20 years.

The pace of the war quickened with the coming of summer and the initiation by Christian of a two-pronged advance. Although Gustavus was too weak to seek a decisive battle with his stronger enemy and was therefore anxious to negotiate a peace, he was forced to react. Parrying the uncoordinated Danish thrusts separately, Gustavus showed skill in maneuvering and an ability to take advantage of his enemy's strategic lapse. The Danes were checked on land, but Christian tried once more—at sea—to defeat Sweden. Failing in this endeavor, he acceded to Gustavus' earlier request for negotiation, and the war ended with Christian gaining the greatest benefit from the peace settlement.

Gustavus now shifted his attention to Russia, where Sweden had also been involved in a long-standing clash of interest. Worried by Poland's growing dominance over Russia and determined to control the Gulf of Finland, the Swedes were maneuvering to influence the selection of a new tsar. Ultimately, Gustavus led a force into Narva to reinforce his army there and to carve out Swedish claims by conquest. The King was sorely hampered by the weakness of Sweden; his resources and manpower reserves were small, his people were weary of war, and the armistice with Poland in yet another clash of interests was tenuous. Nonetheless, he persevered, carrying the fight to the Russians rather than standing on the defensive. Although disease ravaged his camps, his sieges went poorly, and stubborn Russian garrisons minimized his gains, the King slowly achieved his ends. In 1617, two years after negotiations had begun and in the same month that Gustavus celebrated his fifth anniversary on the throne of Sweden, diplomats signed the Treaty of Stolbova. By its terms, Sweden gained complete control of the Gulf of Finland, cutting Russia off from the Baltic. By thus excluding Moscow from Europe, Gustavus set Russia back almost a century, profoundly affecting future events in Europe.* Just 22 years of age, the King was already gaining some renown as a soldier, and was leaving his imprint on the face of Europe.

*Michael Roberts, *Gustavus Adolphus: A History of Sweden; 1611–1632* (London, 1953), Vol. I, p. 89.

Although Swedish internal affairs cried for Gustavus' attention, there was one more unfriendly ruler with whom he had to deal—his cousin, Sigismund of Poland. As in the cases of the Danish and Russian wars, Gustavus inherited the Polish problem. It centered on Sigismund's claim to the Swedish crown and attendant Swedish fears of a Polish invasion, competition for influence in Estonia—indeed, the entire Baltic—and Polish efforts to dominate Russia. The two-year truce between Sweden and Poland had expired in the fall of 1616, and, even as he sought then without much hope to negotiate a permanent peace, Gustavus was readying a force to invade Lithuania in the event that it became necessary. Such being the case, in 1617 the King took a small force into Kurland. There he had initial success, the bulk of Sigismund's forces being occupied elsewhere. As a result, another truce was signed a year later; but Gustavus had a foothold, which he exploited in 1621 with the seizure of the important port and fortified city of Riga.

Although there would be another truce with Poland, followed by a subsequent renewal of operations which would drag on in varying degrees of intensity, the capture of Riga marked an important point. With his performance there, Gustavus emerged from his apprenticeship and attracted the serious attention of western Europe. He had drunk deeply from the well of wisdom and eaten heartily from the table of experience; from both he had benefited. Theoretical aspects of warfare were always lurking in his mind, even as he mastered by practice all the technical details of generalship. His intellectual depth had permitted him to comprehend and assimilate lessons encountered in the campaigns since 1612.

As he returned to Stockholm, he was keenly aware of the need to remold Sweden's entire military organization—from the individual soldier to the national system that provided and supported the Army. Too often had Gustavus been obliged to see his hopes fade because his army was an imperfect instrument. When next he fought it would be with *his* army trained *his* way and responsive to *him*.

Gustavus' Reforms

An army is inevitably a reflection of the state it represents. Understanding that, Gustavus turned, as the first step in strengthening his army, to the rejuvenation of Sweden. Working hand-in-glove with his great minister and alter ego, Axel Oxenstierna, the King planned and implemented social and economic reforms that dramatically changed his little nation. Commercial interests were expanded, natural resources rapidly developed, and new manufacturing techniques introduced; ministers labored to streamline the fiscal system, overhaul the tax base, and prepare Sweden's first true budget; education, religion, and law received attention. Sweden soon hummed with new-found vitality. Gustavus may have developed the state only as a result of his mobilization for war, but the impact of his civil reforms was real and lasting.

Militarily, Gustavus began where Maurice had left off. Indeed, he quite openly acknowledged Maurice as his mentor. As a student, he had been well versed in Maurician theory; as a young commander, he had acquired a firm, practical foundation in the realities of war. Now he was ready to integrate his knowledge. First, however, he checked once more

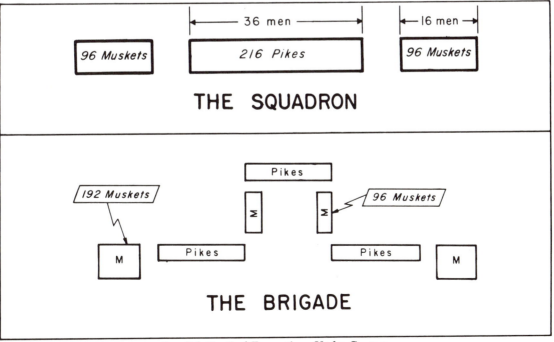

Swedish Tactical Formations Under Gustavus

with the Dutch—holding extended discussions in 1620 with Maurice's cousin, John of Nassau—to gain the benefit of their latest thinking. He firmly believed that a military education should be continued throughout one's lifetime. It is neither experience nor years that make a brave soldier, he proclaimed, but continual meditation on the practice of war. He strictly followed his own advice.

The basic fighting unit in Gustavus' army was the squadron, a body of pike and shot containing 408 men. Similar to though smaller than Maurice's battalion, the squadron was suited for both offensive and defensive action. Contrary to a widely held belief, Gustavus did not reduce the proportion of pike to shot; he increased it (216 pikes to 192 musketeers in the Swedish squadron, compared with 250 to 240 in the larger Dutch battalion). This provides valuable insight into Gustavus' thinking, for such a formation derived its offensive punch from "push of pike." Three or four squadrons were grouped together to form a brigade. In actual battle, each squadron might receive a supplement of shot, but in other operations those musketeers were employed on outposts, for reconnaissance or with cavalry. Gustavus thus retained Maurice's linear concept, but made it even more flexible and mobile while further stressing the combined arms aspect.

Of all the cavalry in Europe, only the Polish horsemen had not adopted the caracole. Gustavus contrasted their crashing charges with lance and saber to the pistol-popping tactics used elsewhere; it did not take him long to decide which was better. Henceforth, his cavalry attacked in three ranks, only the first firing pistols at close range as all three, sabers drawn, closed at the gallop. Pistols could be used in the melee, but the primary weapon was the saber. To increase mobility, the King stripped his troops of much of their body armor; to provide them with more protection, he attached infantry and artillery elements. Through his changes in cavalry tactics, Gustavus restored shock action to the battlefield. It was long overdue.

Perhaps the King's greatest single contribution to the art of warfare was in the realm of field artillery. In his mind, an artillery piece was more than a mere machine used to blast holes in a hostile wall—more than a bulky tube used to engage the opposing line at battle's start. Gustavus felt that artillery should be a flexible method of delivering fire wherever and whenever the commander wanted it. From the Dutch, he copied methods of salvo fire,* creeping barrages against defensive works, and massive fire on a single point.

In Gustavus' early campaigns, moving a single large cannon required 30 or 40 horses. He soon reduced the weight of his pieces and, by 1630, had limited gunmakers to three sizes: 24-pound, 12-pound, and 3-pound. By 1625, he had the lightest and most mobile field artillery in Europe. Even so, to operate and support 36 guns required 220 wagons and 1,116 horses. The King was not satisfied. When he landed in Germany in 1630, he had about 80 field pieces, but needed only 100 wagons and 1,000 horses. The most revolutionary development was the regimental piece, a 3-pounder that could be moved easily with one horse or by three men.† By assigning a regimental gun to at least one platoon in each squadron, Gustavus provided artillery support right down to the smallest combat unit. Some guns also went to the cavalry. So mobile was the small weapon that it could be—and was—used in all types of operations, not excluding reconnaissance.

In short, Gustavus Adolphus injected into both infantry and cavalry an offensive spirit and an offensive capability; he magnified the firepower of all arms, while also increasing their mobility; and in building his new organizations, he never lost sight of the combined arms concept.

Gustavus did not stop with tactical reform alone. The best organization is no better than the worst unless it is comprised of men able and willing to make it work. Pay the men promptly, he insisted. Clothe them warmly. Feed them as well as circumstances permit. Recruit among Swedes insofar as possible; then hire only the best of mercenaries to fill the ranks. Train troops diligently and educate officers thoroughly. Provide religious services. Prohibit prostitutes from entering the camps. Retire elderly officers and replace them with young and eager men. Finally, weld everything together with a disciplinary system that, though just, is hard and uncompromising. In the twentieth century these ideas do not seem at all strange. But early in the seventeenth century, they were uncommon indeed. Although he was never able to adhere to all of them all of the time, Gustavus' administrative reforms, like his tactical ones, contributed to the creation of an army that had no peer.

The Thirty Years' War

Someone once compared the Thirty Years' War (1618–1648) to a vicious whirlpool, caused by irresistible surface and subsurface currents, that pulled Germany down to drown in its own blood and misery. The analogy is apt. It was terrible and inhumane, virtually beyond comprehension. When it was over, Germany lay prostrate; some 10,000,000 people had

---

*Several guns firing their rounds in unison at the same target are said to be firing in salvo.

†At first, this gun was constructed by tightly wrapping a very thin copper barrel with rope and covering it snugly with leather. This was the famous "leather gun." However, by 1630 all Gustavus' 3-pounders were fashioned entirely from metal.

been killed* and all Europe gasped in exhaustion. Religious differences in an intolerant age ignited it and continued to feed the flames, but there were other major causes: the territorial ambitions of France and, later, Sweden; the political rivalry between Bourbon and Hapsburg; and, not least, the fragmented condition of Germany, which led the various Germanic states alternately to band together or to cut one another's throats. The impact of the confluence of these crosscurrents can be seen in the awkward alliance they spawned. Throughout, shifts in coalitions were frequent and sometimes dramatic. For instance, France, directed by a cardinal of the Catholic Church, united itself in the latter half of the war with Protestant Sweden to fight against Catholic Spain and Austria. The Pope sided with France.

Confusing though it was, one must grasp at least a simplified conception of the Thirty Years' War, for it was the setting in which Gustavus Adolphus achieved greatness and in which France began her climb to the pinnacle of power in Europe. But for this war and the threat it brought to Swedish interests in the Baltic—as well as the religious threat—Gustavus might have continued campaigning in Poland.

Early in the seventeenth century, particularism and Protestantism threatened not only the Hapsburg hold on the Bohemian crown, but the very existence of the Holy Roman Empire. The fiery Bohemian Calvinists became incensed in 1617 when the Emperor, the childless Matthias, intimidated the Protestant-dominated Bohemian Diet into electing as heir to the Bohemian throne his cousin, Ferdinand of Styria, a fanatical opponent of Protestantism. Resenting this violation of the Royal Charter (permitting free exercise of religion) and disavowment of a tradition that the crown was truly elective, the Bohemian Protestants revolted, summoned a Protestant Estate to Praguè, and in 1618 pointedly heaved two of Ferdinand's trusted officials from an upper story palace window. They then raised a motley Bohemian army, gained support from the Protestant Union, and successfully carried the fight to Imperial forces.

Early Catholic Victories

The problem might have been localized and arbitrated by the German princes had not Matthias died in March 1619, thus vacating the throne of the Holy Roman Empire and tempting other Hapsburg territories to flaunt the dynasty, as Bohemia had done. His hands full, Ferdinand repelled a Protestant invasion of Austria; then, in August 1619, he managed to be elected Emperor at Frankfurt, where he captured the votes of all seven Electors (three spiritual, four temporal). After ineffectual protests, the Protestant electors capitulated in order to make the vote unanimous. (The four temporal Electors were the rulers of Bohemia, the Palatinate, Brandenburg, and Saxony, the latter three being Protestant. *(See Map 1.)* Ferdinand claimed and voted the Bohemian Electorship. Meanwhile, the Bohemian Protestants, having earlier rejected Ferdinand, had convened a Diet, and just three days earlier had elected Frederick, the Elector Palatine, as their king. But the new king only learned of his election *after* Ferdinand's triumph at Frankfurt, a tragic height of ridiculousness. The young, inexperienced, and somewhat vain Frederick foolishly accepted the crown, which set him clearly at odds with the Emperor. Frederick had voted for Ferdinand at Frankfurt; now, in some circles, he seemed to be playing the role of a vassal revolting against his lord. Naturally the war intensified, as Ferdinand fought to regain the Electorship that was a prerequisite to his being Emperor. The idea that religious motives predominated above all others quickly disappeared. Frederick's Protestant friends largely abandoned him, with John George of Saxony displaying the most mischievous and self-seeking attitude of all.

In 1620, two Catholic armies converged on the Protestants. From the Spanish Netherlands marched 24,000 Spanish troops to trample the Palatinate; from Austria, the 25,000-man army of the Catholic League struck Bohemia. Led by a veteran mercenary general, Count Johan Tzerclaes Tilly, the latter force caught and defeated the poorly prepared Protestant army near Prague in November. *(See Map 2.)* This should have ended the war. The Emperor had won. But Ferdinand's appetite was unsatiated. Driven on by militant, crusading Jesuits, he darkly pronounced, "Better to rule over a desert than a country full of heretics." Unabated persecution drove desperate Protestants to further resistance. Rallying to the banner of Count Ernest von Mansfeld, a mercenary, they fought with little success. Meanwhile, Ferdinand made Maximilian of Bavaria the new Elector Palatine, a sharp political slap at all the Protestant states. They began to look outside Germany for help. The Thirty Years' War then escalated from a clash in Germany to a conflict in Europe.

In 1624, emissaries approached Gustavus Adolphus. He listened, and agreed to help—but only on his own terms. Foremost among those conditions was an ironclad commitment to place all Protestant forces under his sole command. He would not risk a campaign in Germany without a guarantee of unity of command. But the German rulers would not hear of it. They turned instead to Gustavus' old enemy, Christian of Denmark. Christian agreed to champion the Protestant cause.

In Vienna, Ferdinand was appalled. His Catholic League army was far too weak to do battle with the Danes, and he had no other allies willing to fight for him. Just then an

---

*From statistics, which are at best rough guesses, only 350,000 died by the sword. Famine, disease, and murder accounted for the other deaths.

answer strode into his palace in the person of one of the most fascinating characters in history, Count Albrecht von Wallenstein. A wealthy Czech businessman, Wallenstein proposed to make a business of war. He offered to raise an army of 50,000 and defeat the Danes—at no cost to Ferdinand. The only stipulations were that he, Wallenstein, be sole commander of the army and, of course, that any spoils of war be given to him. Quickly, Ferdinand accepted the proposal.

From 1625 to 1629, Wallenstein was every bit as good as his word. That first summer he promptly defeated Mansfeld while Tilly stopped Christian. Then, methodically, Wallenstein directed the clearing of Germany all the way to the Baltic, pushing the Danes back to their own territory. Gradually the size of his mercenary army increased until it reached a strength of over 100,000 men. Wallenstein had become the strongest man in Europe; even his allies began to cast worried glances in his direction.

Once more the Emperor had won. In June 1629, the warring parties signed a treaty, ending hostilities. But, again, Ferdinand's militant Catholicism got the better of him. To a defenseless Germany he promulgated the Edict of Restitution, an act restoring to the Church all ecclesiastical lands appropriated in the past three quarters of a century. By that stroke, Ferdinand infuriated the Protestants, spurring them on to even further resistance. He also thoroughly alarmed Cardinal Richelieu, the First Minister of France. Richelieu saw Ferdinand's moves as all-too-successful consolidations of Hapsburg power throughout Germany and the Rhine Valley. Such gains clashed directly with his own aspirations of extending French influence into lands along the Rhine. He glanced

around the map of Europe for a counterpoise—and saw the Lion of the North. This time, everyone was ready to receive Swedish help on Swedish terms.

Meanwhile, Ferdinand played into his enemies' hands. He wanted to attack the Dutch, but the German Electors balked. Moreover, the Electors wanted to be rid of Wallenstein, and pressured Ferdinand into agreeing to dismiss the mercenary leader. To everyone's surprise, Wallenstein quietly resigned upon learning that the Emperor no longer desired his services. Ferdinand heaved a great sigh of relief. But he relaxed prematurely. At that very moment, a Swedish army was streaming ashore at Peenemünde. The Thirty Years' War would continue for another 18 years.

The Swedish Invasion of Germany

Gustavus had not agreed to an invasion of Germany lightly, or on the spur of the moment. His entry into the war was the culmination of years of preparation.

During the 1620s, while the Thirty Years' War had occupied Europe's attention, Gustavus had energetically fashioned a new type of army. Once it was built, the King promptly proposed to submit it to the most rigorous of field tests: war. He had been prepared to intervene in Germany in 1625, but only on his own terms. When Denmark agreed to engage the Catholic League forces, Gustavus decided he could best support the cause of Protestantism—not to mention his own dynastic and territorial ambitions—by renewing the running war with his Catholic cousin, Sigismund of Poland.

Accordingly, early in the summer of 1626, a Swedish army sailed across the Baltic, landed in Prussia near Konigsberg, and assailed an astonished Poland. Prussia was then a part of Brandenburg, a state ruled by George William. A weak-willed individual, George William was nonetheless a Protestant, an Elector of the Empire, and the brother-in-law of Gustavus Adolphus. A Swedish attack had not been unexpected, but Sigismund and his advisers, thinking their western flank secure, had forecast an assault from the north. Gustavus' heavyhanded violation of neutral Prussia gave him the benefit of surprise and a fine base of operations, but it won few friends for him in Berlin.

Leading limited forces, and unsure of his new organization, Gustavus moved cautiously. He carefully carved out a secure rear area, besieged key fortresses, and fended off the much larger Polish army. In clash after clash, the superiority of his system became evident, particularly at Mewe in September. The cavalry was the only Swedish arm that did not prove a match for its Polish counterpart. Gustavus resolved to correct that. After a harsh winter in which disease and Polish partisans took a severe toll among the Swedes, war resumed.

Count Albrecht von Wallenstein

Attempting a surprise night crossing of the Vistula in May of 1627, Gustavus received a wound that forced him to retire, thus breaking off the action. As soon as he recovered he initiated another offensive. Near Dirschau, in August, he came up with the main Polish army. On the seventeenth, his improved cavalry clearly bested the Polish horse, marking another step in the creation of Sweden's fighting machine. The next day, in a general action, Gustavus was on the verge of a complete victory when a musketball ripped into his neck and shoulder. It was a grievous wound that bothered the King for the rest of his life. When he fell, the Swedish attack faltered and ground to a halt. Twice now his being put out of action had spoiled an entire operation. The lesson was plain. Subordinate commanders had to be trained to carry on without him. Determinedly he set about correcting that deficiency. Proof that he succeeded is to be found in his later campaigns in Germany—in no battle more so than his last one.

In 1628, Denmark was collapsing before the advances of Wallenstein and Tilly. Wallenstein, reaching the Baltic shores, stopped there only because he had no fleet. For Gustavus, the dynastic and religious motives of his struggle in Poland paled beside the new threats of economic penetration of the Baltic and military invasion of his homeland. That winter in Stockholm, Gustavus and his advisors concluded that it would be better to carry the fight to Germany than to await invasion by the Catholic armies. At once, the King sent a garrison to help the important port city of Stralsund resist a siege by Wallenstein's troops. The Polish War was relegated to a low priority in 1628 as the Protestant situation in Germany continued to crumble. In spring of the next year, Denmark signed a peace treaty with the Emperor's representatives.

Gustavus, however, could do nothing until the Polish War was terminated. Frantically, he plunged into Poland, seeking to bring his opponent to bay. But the Poles evaded his every move. Then, in September of 1629, Richelieu intervened. Arranging a six-year truce between Poland and Sweden, he freed Gustavus to enter Germany the following year. *(See Map 3.)*

At Peenemünde, Gustavus tripped when stepping off the narrow gangway, fell heavily, and injured his knee. The story soon spread that the Protestant savior had fallen to his knees in prayer as his first act in Germany. This anecdote illustrates two facets of Gustavus' invasion. First, whatever other motives possessed him, there is no denying his sincere belief in the religious cause. Second, his propaganda machine was quite active and effective. As a matter of fact, the King had been waging a campaign of psychological warfare long before his arrival, trying to induce a favorable reaction to the Swedish invasion. His efforts had so far not secured him a single ally, although several states were plainly pleased with his appearance. Prudently, they would see what he could do before committing themselves. Nevertheless, Protestants in general were overjoyed.

The first order of business was to carve out a secure base of operations. Like Alexander the Great, who won a base on the Mediterranean Sea before he plunged into Asia, Gustavus acquired Pomerania on the Baltic Sea before striking into Germany. Then, too, he had to build up his forces before engaging in a major campaign. His invasion force of 13,000 would be swallowed up just by holding the necessary fortifications in Pomerania. Gradually, throughout 1630, he enlarged his army. Reinforcements came from Sweden, troops transferred from the Polish front, England privately contributed 6,000 (most of whom promptly died of disease upon landing), and German and Scottish mercenaries flocked in. Soon native Swedes were in the minority. But every man and unit was carefully equipped, indoctrinated, and drilled in the Swedish method. By year's end, Gustavus was ready to begin the second phase of his invasion.

Actually, when Gustavus came ashore in 1630 he had not yet evolved an overall strategy. The situation in Germany was too uncertain. Beyond securing a base and gathering forces and supplies, his aims were not defined. He intended to attract allies, watch the enemy situation develop, and then act. Very generally, he wanted to engage Tilly in open battle, probably somewhere up the Oder River, but as yet he had no plan to force his opponent to fight. That winter, however, events beyond the King's control conspired to set the stage for his greatest battle.

The free city of Magdeburg, on the Elbe River, declared its support of Gustavus. Immediately, Imperial forces besieged it. The Swede, pushing up the Oder toward Frankfort-on-Oder, grew concerned as spring approached and the enemy persisted in the siege. *(See Map 3.)* To relieve his ally he would have to march across parts of Brandenburg and Saxony, neither of which had yet joined him. Both electors denied him permission to use their territory. Desperate to win them as allies, Gustavus declined to force his way. He was also inclined to stay on the Oder, where Tilly's main army was operating, in hopes of precipitating a battle. He had one chance in March 1631, but first called a council of war, which voted against risking battle. As a result, Tilly got away. That hesitation was one of the few military blunders Gustavus ever made. He put no more faith in councils of war. Having evaded his opponent, Tilly marched rapidly to the Elbe, where he assumed command of the investment of Magdeburg. Gustavus, still stymied by his potential allies, took a more forceful course. He marched to Berlin and, at cannon point, "convinced" his brother-in-law to join a coalition. But John George of Saxony remained adamant. He would have nothing to do with the Swedes. At that juncture, on May 20, Magdeburg fell.

Then occurred the greatest single tragedy of the Thirty

Years' War. Tilly's troops, starving and enraged after their long period in the scorched lands around Magdeburg, brutally sacked the city. Most of the town was then burned—probably by accident, for Tilly needed it as a base. Between the sacking and the conflagration, at least 20,000 inhabitants were slaughtered; some accounts go as high as 40,000. For weeks, mutilated, charred corpses floated down the Elbe to the North Sea.

As Swedish propaganda agencies energetically spread the word of Magdeburg's horrible fate, a wave of revulsion swept Germany. Previously neutral Protestants began to waver or to join the Swedes. Tilly, deprived of a base at Magdeburg, made a bold decision to strike at Gustavus, whose troops just then were not massed for battle. But the King was well aware of the need for security. His forces, wherever they stopped, habitually constructed field fortifications. In late July, Tilly made a futile thrust near Werben. Repulsed, he retired. That first clash between the two famous leaders redounded to Gustavus' favor. More allies appeared. Then, angered by Tilly's callous disregard of his lands, John George brought Saxony into the Protestant coalition. At last, Gustavus was able to launch an unhindered effort to corner the enemy army. Tilly fell back toward Leipzig, with Gustavus eagerly pressing him.

Count Johan Tzerclaes Tilly

The Siege of Magdeburg, 1631

The Battle of Breitenfeld

On September 15, 1631, the day Leipzig fell to Tilly, some 18,000 Saxons joined the Swedes at Düben, 25 miles north of Leipzig. That reinforcement, which gave Gustavus a numerical superiority over Tilly of 42,000 to 35,000, sealed the latter's fate. Gustavus was determined to do battle, and Tilly could no longer elude him. The experienced campaigner—Tilly was then 72 years old—seems to have recognized that fact and was on the point of barricading himself in Leipzig until help could arrive, but events passed him by. Count Pappenheim, the fiery and able cavalry commander, thought Tilly senile. Early on the sixteenth, he rode out with a reconnaissance party and ran into the Swedes. Holding his ground, he arrogantly informed Tilly that he was unable to break contact to return to Leipzig and must be supported where he stood. It apparently never crossed his mind that a battle could have any outcome other than a Catholic victory. Never before had he lost. He anticipated riding roughshod over the barbaric Swedes, just as he had done to every other foe. Tilly, trapped and loudly lamenting the fact, marched north, much against his better judgment.

About four miles from Leipzig, and a mile from the Swedish army, Tilly selected a piece of ground near the village of Breitenfeld. He chose well: the prevailing wind could be expected to whip dust and smoke towards the Swedes and Saxons, and since Tilly was astride a slight rise, the gentle incline of the ground to his front would give him a marked advantage over Gustavus. In the center of his single line, Tilly formed at least 15 and possibly as many as 18 massive *tercios*. Cavalry covered each wing, with Pappenheim on the left. His entire front was two miles long. Artillery stood forward in the center. Thus arrayed, the Imperialists awaited a Swedish attack. *(See Map 4a.)*

"As the larke begunne to peepe . . . the trumpets sound to horse, the drummers calling to march . . . we marched forwards in God's name." So recalled Robert Monro, a Scot in Swedish service. Gustavus approached to within half a mile of the prepared foe and, unmolested by Tilly, crossed a stream en route to his final position. In full view of the enemy, he then methodically arranged his army parallel to that of Tilly. Swedes hustled into positions on the center and right, with Saxons to the left. Of the Saxon formation, little is known. John George massed all his infantry in the center in clumps of 1,000 men each, creating a pyramid-like formation. Cavalry was posted on each flank and artillery stationed in front. The Swedes, though, quickly formed in a manner strange and surprising to Imperialist generals and Saxon allies alike. In the center, covering the infantry, was heavy artillery under Leonard Torstensson, a most brilliant gunner. Or-

ganized in brigades, infantry held the center, the cavalry flanking it. But, unlike Tilly's single line, there was great depth in the Swedish formation. Moreover, regimental pieces were with every brigade, cavalry was integrated into the infantry-strong center, and attached musketeers, in groups of 50, were interspersed among the cavalry brigade for support. Flexibility and the combined arms concept were evident throughout.

The battle opened about midday with a conventional cannonade. The close-range slugfest was terribly galling to both sides, but Gustavus' superior artillery, firing three times as fast and with far greater accuracy, quickly gained the upper hand. Robert Monro's terse tale paints a firsthand picture: ". . . the enemy [artillery] was thundering amongst us, with the noise and roaring whistling of cannon-bullets; where you may imagine the hurt was great; the sound of such musick being scarce worth the hearing . . . then our cannon begunne to roare, great and small, paying the enemy with the like coyne, which thundering continued alike on both sides for two hours and a half. . . ."

Pappenheim, chafing under the heavy pounding, and unable to endure it any longer, opened the actual fighting by leading his 5,000 cavalrymen in a rash and unauthorized charge—if one can describe the caracole as a "charge"—at the Swedish right. *(See Map 4b.)* Marshal John Baner, able to adjust quickly with his small, mobile formations, refused his flank. Heavy and accurate musket fire from the pockets of attached musketeers combined with blasts of grapeshot from the regimental guns to stop Pappenheim's charge dead. Furiously, he flung his horsemen again and again at Baner's unwavering flank. As the Imperialist cavalrymen streamed back after their seventh bloody repulse, Marshal Baner committed his fresh reserve, scattering the weary Catholic troopers and driving Pappenheim entirely off the battlefield and out of the battle.

Meanwhile, on Gustavus' left flank the Saxons had been faring poorly. Having seen Pappenheim advance on the left, Tilly's right-flank cavalry, not 3,000 in all, had bravely charged John George and his 18,000 Saxons. Although a professional intriguer, John George was strictly an amateur soldier. One glimpse of an attack coming his way was enough. Fear-stricken, he whirled his horse and sprinted away. His army promptly followed his example, pausing only long enough in their frantic retreat to loot the Swedish trains. Suddenly, Gustavus found himself alone and outnumbered, with one flank entirely open and the other being severely tested.

Tilly saw the opportunity. *(See Map 4c.)* Victory lay within his grasp. Quickly he issued orders to deliver the coup de grâce. The *tercios* were to incline to the right, march obliquely

Count Pappenheim

to overlap the Swedish left, execute a left wheel, and smash into that unprotected flank. At the same time, Tilly's right wing cavalry, fresh from routing the Saxons, would reform and strike the Swedish rear. Tilly now envisioned a battle of annihilation.

Against any other army it might have been just that. The lumbering *tercios* would have completed their maneuver and fallen upon a similarly organized enemy line before it could have reacted. But the King had purposefully forged flexibility and mobility into his army to meet just such an emergency as this. Marshal Gustavus Horn rapidly executed a maneuver considered in that age virtually impossible: he changed front to the left in face of an enemy attack. Still the situation was critical. Bearing down in lockstep on Horn's 4,000-man force were over 20,000 of Tilly's veterans, their bristling pikes glinting fearsomely. Unhesitatingly, the marshal attacked them with every man he could muster. His gallant charge checked the enemy advance. At the same time, Gustavus sent two brigades from the second line of his center to reinforce Horn's left. The light regimental pieces, moving and wheeling right along with their parent units, continued to pour deadly volleys of grape into the dense *tercios*, while Tilly's artillery, immobile and unmaneuverable, was quickly left behind. The Imperial forces were thrown back in considerable disorder. At that moment, on the other flank, Pappenheim's last charge was disintegrating.

Now it was Gustavus' turn. Riding from one end of the smoke-covered battlefield to the other, the King had inspired first one wing, then the other. Shouting, committing reserves, soaked in sweat, he had seemed to be everywhere. Just then

the wind changed, blowing blinding smoke and dust into the eyes of Tilly's struggling troops. In a flash, when other men could hardly see 50 paces through the muck of battle, Gustavus saw—perhaps "sensed" is a better word—the decisive point. *(See Map 4d.)* He sent Marshal Baner racing down the front of the Swedish infantry to hammer the Catholic left. Then, his voice too hoarse to be heard and his features so grimy as to be almost unrecognizable, the King personally led a cavalry charge straight up the slope to seize the stationary enemy guns. After dispatching a contingent of cannoneers with orders to blast Tilly's reserve cavalry, he continued around to strike the rear of the reeling foe. Torstensson, meanwhile, was exerting all efforts to wheel every available gun into position to fire at the Imperialists. Soldiers in the *tercios*—their formations broken and their pikes snagging on one another, their ranks too compressed to resist, their eyes filled by the swirling dust, and their ranks decimated by merciless Swedish cannon fire—were methodically herded into a tighter and tighter ring. What followed was more murder than war. An observer wrote that the Swedes "fell to and basted the enemy's hide so briskly that at last he had no choice but to yield." The pitiable remnants of Tilly's once-proud army threw down weapons and surrendered or stampeded as night fell. Swedish cavalry chased fleeing survivors late into the night, ruthlessly sabering all they could locate.

Morning's light revealed 7,600 dead Imperialists on the field of battle. Another 5,000 or so had been slain in the wild retreat. There were 6,000 prisoners, mostly wounded. Later, 3,000 more fugitives were captured. Tilly, himself sorely wounded, had lost altogether at least 21,000 men. Gustavus' casualties were just one-tenth that many, and most of those had been suffered during the opening cannonade.

Throughout that long, dusty day, the Swedish infantry in the center had stood firm, forming a staunch link between the two wings, but otherwise remaining spectators to the battle. Gustavus had defeated the entire Catholic army with slightly more than half the Swedish force! Once more the legion had vanquished the phalanx.

Breitenfeld was important both militarily and politically. It changed the thrust of warfare, altered the course of the Thirty Years' War, and saved northern Europe from Jesuit and Hapsburg domination. Moreover, it established Gustavus Adolphus as that generation's greatest warrior.

To the Danube and Back

Brilliant as Breitenfeld had been, Gustavus erred in not following it with a relentless pursuit to destroy every last vestige of the enemy army. His cavalry did give chase to the survivors for a while, inflicting no little harm, but that was all. Within a week Tilly had gathered 13,000 of his dispersed men. He would fight again.

At the moment, though, it hardly seemed to matter. Recruits flocked to the Swedish colors, with previously standoffish German princes making haste to join Gustavus. As army and allies grew, so too did ideas. Previously, Gustavus had followed no clear strategy, other than a plan to meet and defeat the Emperor's army. He had done that. Germany now lay at his feet. The path to Vienna was undefended. He could, if he chose, sweep through Bohemia and winter in Emperor Ferdinand's palace. Many at the time urged him to do so; many since have criticized him for failing to grasp the opportunity.

But Gustavus had too much strategic sense to violate so basic a principle of war as the objective. Vienna was an enemy capital in name only. Its fall would not have ended the war—indeed, it would have had very slight political impact. Ferdinand's power base was not Austria, but the Catholic states along the upper Danube and the Rhine. Bavaria, for instance, had provided the bulk of his soldiers. The straight road to Vienna was mountainous and poor. If the Swedes had reached Vienna, they would have done very little damage to their enemy and would have found themselves in a most overextended and vulnerable position. The temptation to construe a hostile capital as a proper military objective without an appreciation for its significance to the country has led not a few generals to disaster. Gustavus was not about to fall into that trap.

Instead, the King selected the indirect approach. *(See Map 3.)* Gustavus decided to swing his own army in a wide arc from Breitenfeld to the Rhine, and from there down the Danube to Vienna. By taking that route he would be able to conquer one by one the states supporting Ferdinand, base himself on the Protestant Palatinate, protect his flank and rear by closing the Alpine passes (which would also sever Spain's overland link with the Emperor), and leave the Emperor no refuge. Moreover, war had not touched those rich, fat lands, and Gustavus liked the thought of making the Catholic areas bear the burden of supporting armies for a change. The greatest advantage would be that the Swedes would actually grow stronger as they advanced, whereas the foe would become weaker. It was a strategy of breathtaking sweep, quite beyond the imagination of all but a few generals throughout history. Surely no other soldier of the seventeenth century would have even dreamed such a thing.

Wasting no time deliberating over his next course of action, Gustavus moved toward the Rhine. By Christmas 1631, he had conquered the entire Rhineland, forced Spanish troops back to the Netherlands, and occupied the Main River Valley. As far as ministers in Stockholm could tell, their monarch had literally disappeared deep into the heart of Europe.

Oxenstierna, the chancellor, was summoned to him there. Together they fashioned alliances and shaped a huge army for the final campaign in 1632.

During the winter, the King had hoped to raise the total strength of his seven separate armies to 210,000, of which he would have placed 170,000 in his main effort and 40,000 under John George in Bohemia. However, when he headed for the Danube he had only 120,000 with him, while John George had just 20,000. Another statistic is illuminating: in that huge "Swedish" force of 140,000 men, no more than 13,000 were native Swedes. Clearly, the King was not draining his own nation to fight the German War.

Because he had failed to destroy Tilly after Breitenfeld, Gustavus began his 1632 campaign before he was quite ready. That able old campaigner had returned to the fray with a refurbished army. Gustavus could not allow him to operate unhindered. He marched to bring his opponent to battle. The fury of the Swedish advance was too much for Tilly to face. He retreated. In late March, Gustavus crossed the Danube at Donauwörth and burst into Bavaria. Tilly took up a strong defensive position behind the River Lech, but Gustavus was not to be discouraged. After a personal reconnaissance to the far bank, he massed his artillery, laid down a smokescreen by burning wet straw, and crossed under the cover of that dense cloud of smoke and a hail of cannonballs. Across, he destroyed the last Imperialist force. Tilly himself was mortally wounded. At that moment it appeared that Gustavus was assured of success, and that the war was approaching an end.

But Ferdinand had one last card to play. Wallenstein, the brooding mercenary genius, was available with a 20,000-man private army. He had already agreed to fight Gustavus, but only on conditions that in effect subordinated everyone in the Holy Roman Empire, including the Emperor, to him. Now, with absolutely no other hope, Ferdinand gave in to the Czech's preposterous demands. Gustavus was to have a worthy opponent. *(See Map 5.)*

Shrewd general that he was, Wallenstein formed two simple precepts for dealing with his famous foe. First, avoid at all costs an open battle with the marvelous Swedish Army. Second, strike not at Gustavus, but at his notoriously weak ally, John George. By driving into Saxony, Wallenstein rightly reasoned, he could threaten Gustavus' lines of communication and oblige him to quit the Danube. Immediately attacking Saxon forces in Bohemia, Wallenstein sent John George scurrying back to Saxony. Shocked, Gustavus marched northward to deal with this new threat. With his columns strung out en route, he was attacked by Wallenstein near Nuremburg, but managed to recover when the Czech failed to push his advantage. Both threw up strong field fortifications, Gustavus to gather his strength and Wallenstein to wait out his adversary. For weeks the two stared at one another while their troops, having eaten the countryside clean, starved. Finally, in early September, Gustavus in desperation assaulted the formidable Imperial defenses. The attack was a costly failure.

Utterly frustrated, the King decided to march towards Vienna in the hopes of forcing Wallenstein out of his trenches. But the Czech would not be fooled. As soon as the Swedes disappeared, he decamped and marched north into Saxony. Unable to depend on John George, Gustavus hurried after his wily enemy, overtaking him near Leipzig. But by then it was November, and the campaigning season was over. Wallenstein had saved Vienna and the Empire by strategy alone.

Expecting Gustavus to go into winter quarters, Wallenstein made his own dispositions. He ordered most of his army into bivouac near Lützen, sending Pappenheim off to the west with a large detachment. But Gustavus wanted to fight. By violating an important principle of war, security, Wallenstein brought about the major battle he had striven all summer to avoid.

The Mists of Lützen

Learning of Pappenheim's departure, Gustavus concluded correctly that Wallenstein was unaware of his approach. Eagerly he pressed forward on November 15, hoping to catch his enemy in camp that very day. Unfortunately, an Imperialist cavalry detachment rode by accident across the Swedish advance, courageously delayed them in a defile, and sent word

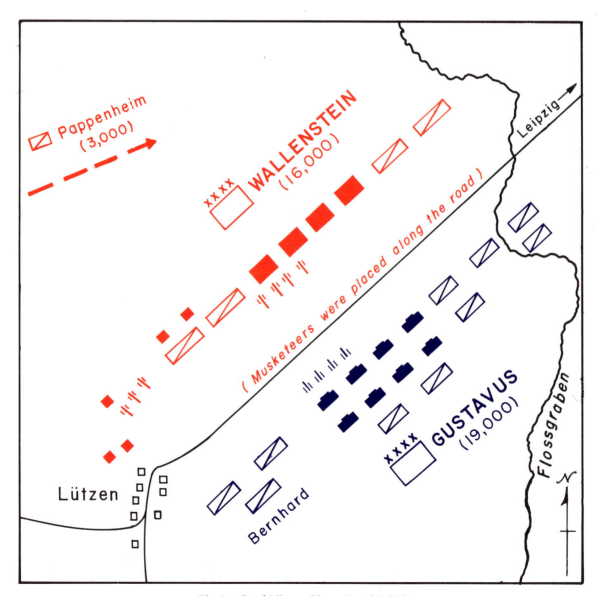

The Battle of Lützen, November 16, 1632

back to Wallenstein. That general, astounded and caught at severe disadvantage, sent couriers galloping after Pappenheim while urgently ordering his men to throw up hasty fortifications. Gustavus moved up to attack the first thing the next day.

The plain of Lützen was almost level, broken only by an elevated road running east from Lützen to Leipzig. Wallenstein formed his main line behind the road, placing musketeers along the road itself. His left tied into a small, fordable river; his right to the village of Lützen. In the center he posted four great *tercios*; cavalry covered both flanks. Near his center, and also on a slight hill behind Lützen, the Imperialist artillery stood ready. His line of communication ran along the road to Leipzig.

Gustavus formed two battlelines and held out a large cavalry reserve. In the center were eight infantry brigades, standing just behind and to the right of his artillery. On the left, Prince Bernhard of Weimar commanded a cavalry contingent, while Gustavus himself assumed command of the heavy right wing. His plan was to assail Wallenstein's left flank, driving him back toward Lützen and destruction. Wallenstein had approximately 16,000 men in ranks, not counting Pappenheim's 3,000. Gustavus was attacking with not more than 19,000, and did not have his best generals with him. Horn, Baner, and Torstensson were all elsewhere.

At about 8:00 a.m. on November 26, 1632, the Swedes moved forward only to be halted by an impenetrable mist which rolled in over the two armies. Gustavus used the delay to exhort his men. At about 11:00 a.m., the dense fog broke briefly. At once, the King sent his army forward. Crashing through the musketeers along the road, the Swedish right swept up to Wallenstein's left and broke it. The King wheeled his troops inward to begin rolling up the enemy line. Bernhard, meantime, was making no headway against the heavy concentration of artillery near Lützen, while in the center the Swedish infantry was slowly forcing the *tercios* back. With victory seemingly gained on his flank, Gustavus rode for his left flank to push it forward in hopes of achieving a battle of annihilation. At that moment, Pappenheim arrived. Wallenstein ordered him to counterattack the Swedish right. His charge caught the Swedes unawares, pushing them back, but a cannonball cut Pappenheim down. The loss of their leader caused the entire Imperialist left to panic. No one knows what really happened from then on, for the fog, thickened now by clouds of acrid smoke, descended solidly once again.

Wallenstein, unable to see the rout on his left and thinking Pappenheim was carrying the field, launched a furious attack along his line which pushed the Swedes back to the road. Gustavus, groping through the mist, rode into the melee. A ball smacked into his horse's neck. The startled animal bolted straight into a group of enemy horsemen. One fired a pistol into the King's back, dropping him from his saddle. With one foot caught in a stirrup, Gustavus was dragged some distance along the ground before managing to free himself. As he gasped for breath, face down in the mud, a shot in the head killed him.

When the King's horse returned bleeding and riderless, the news spread like wildfire among the Swedish ranks. Imperialists, hearing the news, raised a triumphant shout and surged forward. The swirling mists, however, slowed their advance, giving Bernhard of Weimar a chance to rally the Protestant army. Now in command, he resolved to attack again to avenge Gustavus' death. He assumed that his men would never fight harder, and he was right. Attacking in blind rage, tears streaming down many a face. Gustavus' soldiers paid him the ultimate compliment. Wallenstein's weary troops could not withstand that last savage onslaught. They broke and fled from the field, leaving perhaps 7,000 dead behind. Upwards of a third of the Swedish force died that day, too, but the one irreplaceable loss had been the King himself. The Swedish Army would never again be the same.

A summary of the impact of Gustavus Adolphus on the art of warfare is almost superfluous. He changed it during his own lifetime. The Thirty Years' War began as an old-style slugging match; it ended with every general doing his best to copy the methods of the great Swede. He restored mobility and strategy, demonstrated the effectiveness of combining arms, resurrected shock action, maximized firepower, maneuvered larger armies than had been seen before, and mobilized a nation and a people for war. He led superbly and fought with finesse. He was the giant of his age, a Great Captain, the father of modern warfare.

The leading historian of that period recently proclaimed that following the military revolution that was begun by Maurice and completed by Gustavus:

> The modern art of war had come to birth. Mass armies, strict discipline, absolute submergence of the individual, had already arrived; the conjoint ascendancy of financial power and applied science was already established in all its malignity; the use of propaganda, psychological warfare, and terrorism as military weapons was already familiar to theorists, as well as to commanders in the field; and the last remaining qualms as to the religious and ethical legitimacy of war seemed to have been stilled. The road lay open, broad and straight, to the abyss of the twentieth century.*

*Michael Roberts, *The Military Revolution, 1560–1660* (Belfast, 1956), p. 32.

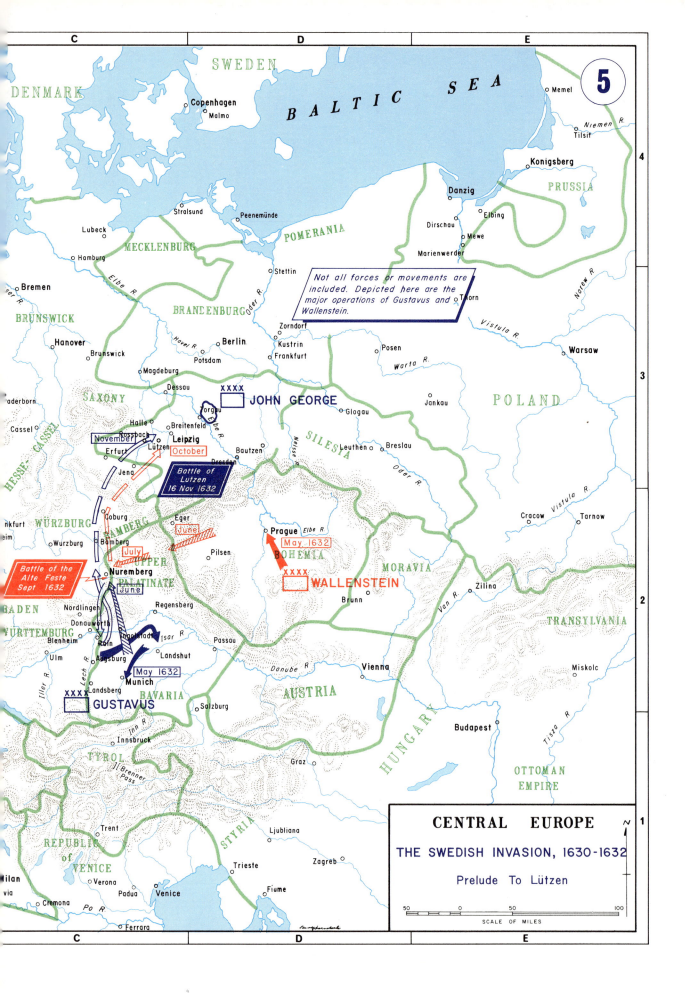

CENTRAL EUROPE

THE SWEDISH INVASION, 1630-1632

Prelude To Lützen

SCALE OF MILES
50   0   50   100

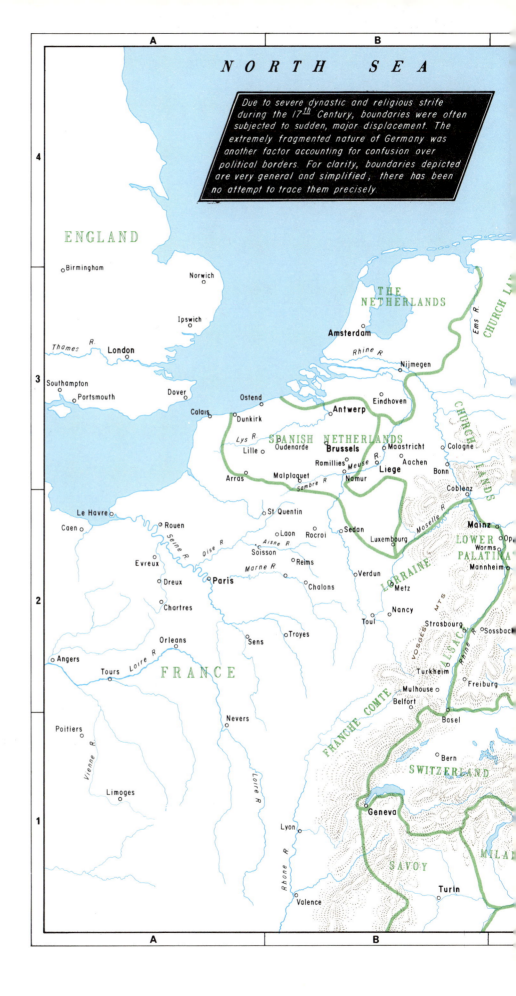

NORTH SEA

Due to severe dynastic and religious strife during the 17th Century, boundaries were often subjected to sudden, major displacement. The extremely fragmented nature of Germany was another factor accounting for confusion over political borders. For clarity, boundaries depicted are very general and simplified; there has been no attempt to trace them precisely.

ENGLAND

Birmingham

Norwich

Ipswich

Thames R. London

Southampton
Portsmouth

Dover

THE NETHERLANDS

Amsterdam

Rhine R

Nijmegen

Ems R.

CHURCH LANDS

Ostend

Eindhoven

Calais
Dunkirk

Antwerp

Lys R. SPANISH NETHERLANDS

Cologne

Lille Oudenarde Brussels Maastricht
Ramillies *Meuse R.* Aachen Bonn
Liege
Arras Malplaquet Namur
Sambre R. Coblenz

CHURCH LANDS

Le Havre

St Quentin

Caen

Rouen

Laon Rocroi

Sedan

Soisson *Aisne R.*

Seine R. *Oise R.*

Evreux

Reims

Luxembourg

Moselle R.

Mainz

LOWER
PALATINA

Op

Worms

Mannheim

Verdun

Dreux Paris *Marne R.* Chalons

Chartres

Metz

LORRAINE

Nancy

Troyes

Toul

Sens

Strasbourg

Sossbac

Orleans

Loire R.

Angers

Tours

FRANCE

VOSGES MTS

ALSACE

Rhine R

Turkheim

Mulhouse

Freiburg

Belfort

Nevers

FRANCHE COMTE

Basel

Poitiers

Loire R

Vienne R.

Bern

SWITZERLAND

Limoges

Geneva

1

Lyon

Rhone R.

SAVOY

MILAN

Turin

Valence

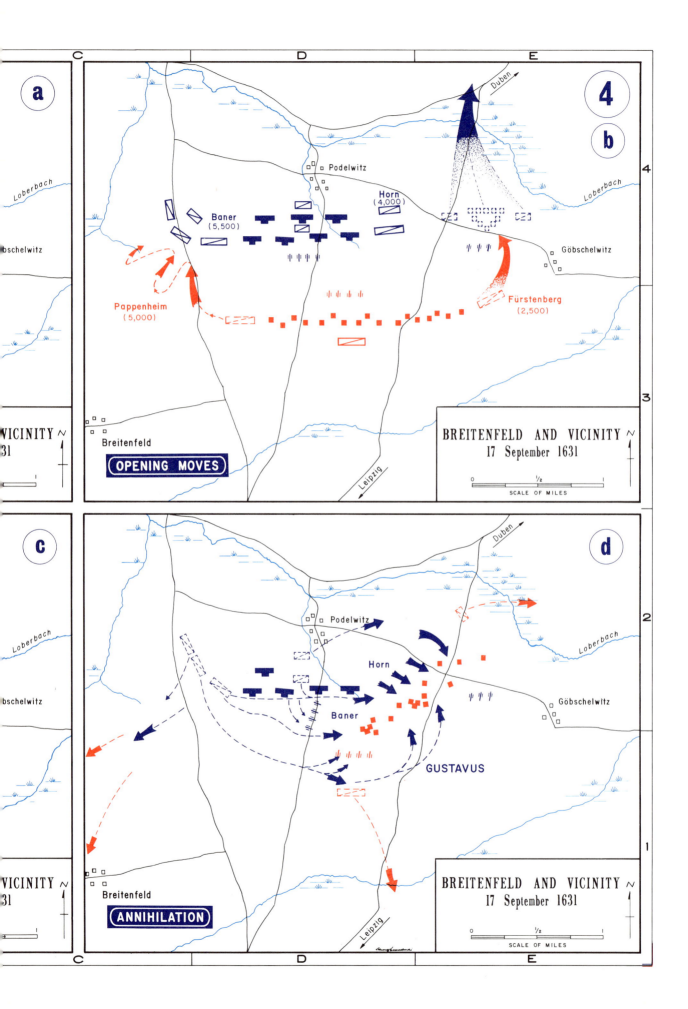

a

b

4

Loberbach

bschelwitz

Podelwitz

Duben

Loberbach

Horn
(4,000)

Baner
(5,500)

Göbschelwitz

Pappenheim
(5,000)

Fürstenberg
(2,500)

VICINITY ~
31

Breitenfeld

OPENING MOVES

Leipzig

BREITENFELD AND VICINITY ~
17 September 1631

0   ½   1
SCALE OF MILES

4

3

---

c

d

Loberbach

bschelwitz

Duben

Podelwitz

Loberbach

Horn

Göbschelwitz

Baner

GUSTAVUS

VICINITY ~
31

Breitenfeld

ANNIHILATION

Leipzig

BREITENFELD AND VICINITY ~
17 September 1631

0   ½   1
SCALE OF MILES

2

1

C   D   E

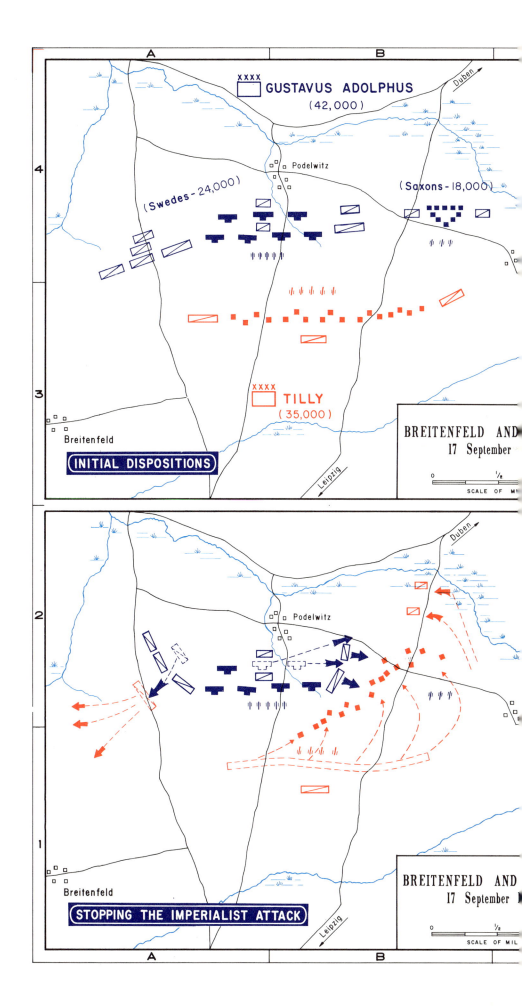

GUSTAVUS ADOLPHUS
(42,000)

Duben

Podelwitz

(Swedes–24,000)

(Saxons–18,000)

TILLY
(35,000)

Breitenfeld

INITIAL DISPOSITIONS

BREITENFELD AND
17 September

0   ½
SCALE OF M

Duben

Podelwitz

Breitenfeld

Leipzig

STOPPING THE IMPERIALIST ATTACK

BREITENFELD AND
17 September

0   ½
SCALE OF MIL

CENTRAL EUROPE

THE SWEDISH INVASION, 1630-1632

From the Baltic to the Danube

SCALE OF MILES
50   0   50   100

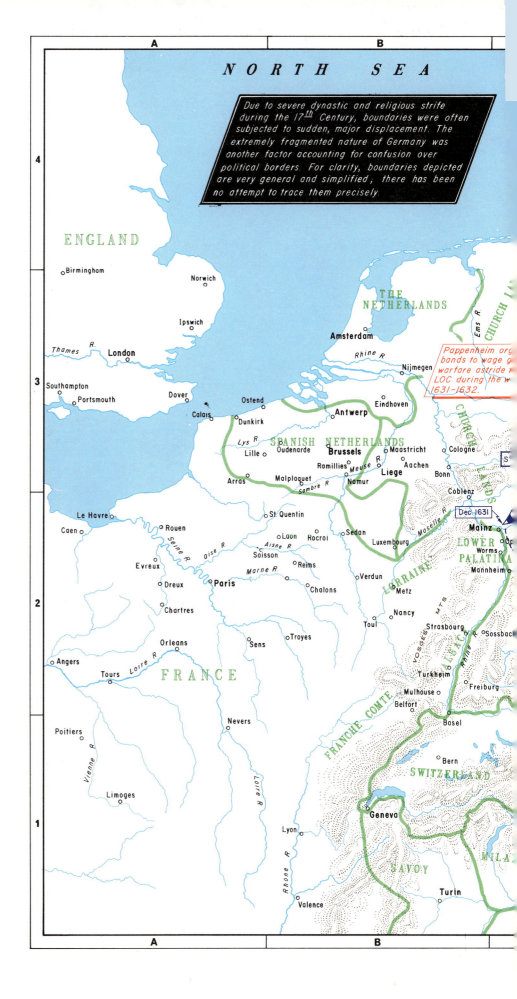

NORTH SEA

Due to severe dynastic and religious strife during the 17th Century, boundaries were often subjected to sudden, major displacement. The extremely fragmented nature of Germany was another factor accounting for confusion over political borders. For clarity, boundaries depicted are very general and simplified; there has been no attempt to trace them precisely.

ENGLAND

THE NETHERLANDS

Pappenheim org
bands to wage g
warfare astride
LOC during the w
1631-1632.

CHURCH

SPANISH NETHERLANDS

Dec. 1631

LOWER PALATIKA

LORRAINE

ALSAC

VOSGES MTS

FRANCHE-COMTE

FRANCE

SWITZERLAND

SAVOY

MILA

Birmingham
Norwich
Ipswich
Thames R.
London
Southampton
Portsmouth
Dover
Calais
Dunkirk
Ostend
Antwerp
Eindhoven
Amsterdam
Rhine R
Nijmegen
Ems R.
Cologne
Bonn
Aachen
Liege
Maastricht
Brussels
Lys R.
Lille
Oudenarde
Ramillies
Meuse R.
Namur
Malplaquet
Sambre R.
Arras
St. Quentin
Le Havre
Caen
Rouen
Seine R.
Oise R.
Laon
Rocroi
Sedan
Luxembourg
Coblenz
Moselle R.
Mainz
Worms
Mannheim
Evreux
Dreux
Paris
Aisne R.
Soisson
Marne R.
Reims
Chalons
Verdun
Metz
Nancy
Toul
Chartres
Orleans
Sens
Troyes
Strasbourg
Sossbach
Rhine R.
Angers
Tours
Loire R.
Turkheim
Freiburg
Mulhouse
Belfort
Basel
Poitiers
Nevers
Loire R.
Vienne R.
Limoges
Bern
Geneva
Lyon
Rhone R.
Valence
Turin

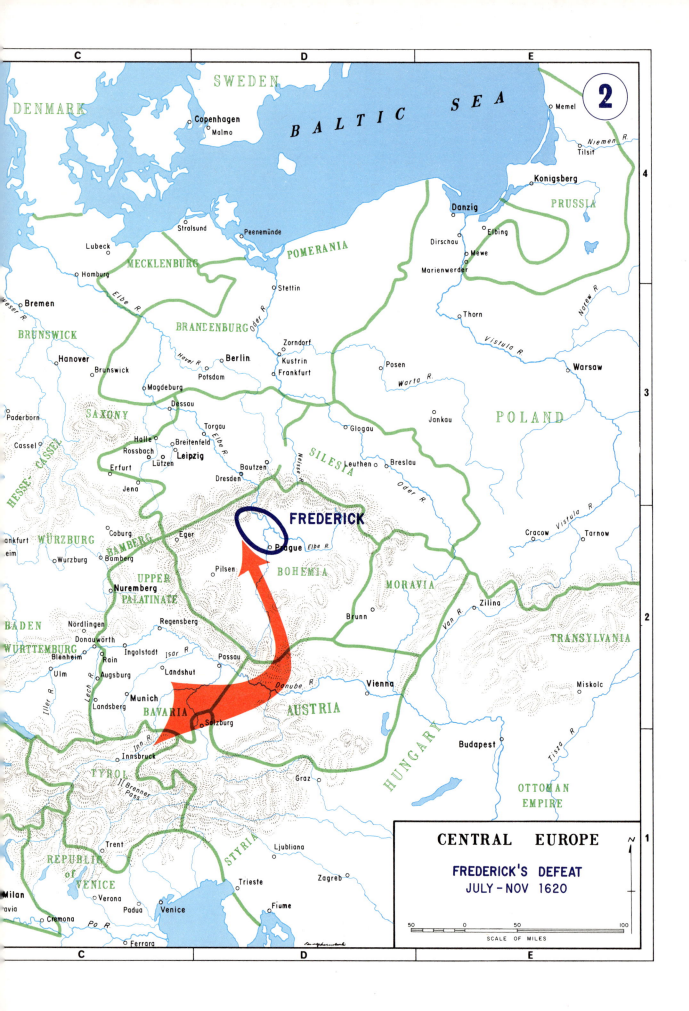

CENTRAL EUROPE

FREDERICK'S DEFEAT
JULY – NOV 1620

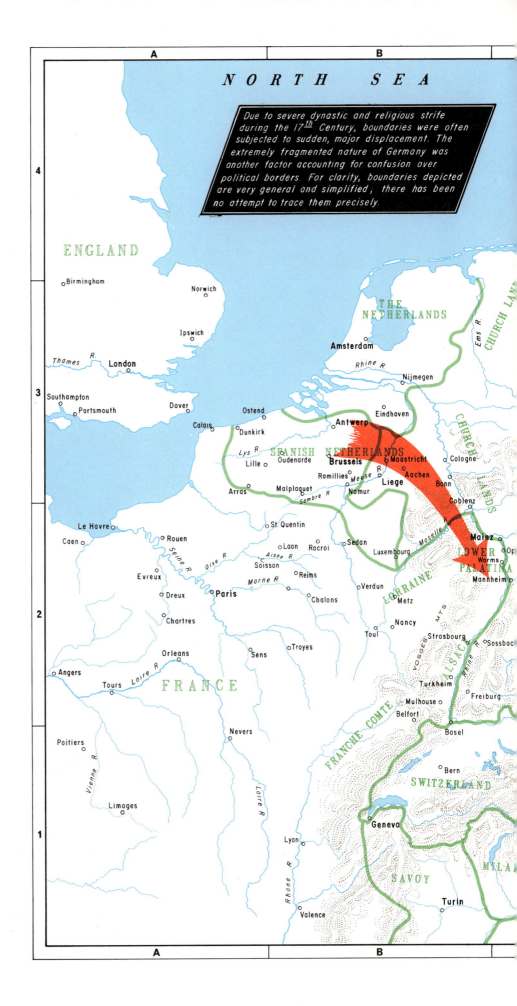

N O R T H   S E A

Due to severe dynastic and religious strife
during the 17ᵗʰ Century, boundaries were often
subjected to sudden, major displacement. The
extremely fragmented nature of Germany was
another factor accounting for confusion over
political borders. For clarity, boundaries depicted
are very general and simplified; there has been
no attempt to trace them precisely.

ENGLAND

○ Birmingham

Norwich ○

Ipswich ○

THE
NETHERLANDS

Amsterdam ●

CHURCH LAND

Thames R. **London**

Rhine R

Nijmegen ○

3

Southampton ○

Portsmouth ○

Dover ○

Ostend ○

Eindhoven ○

Antwerp ●

Cologne ○

Lys R.

SPANISH NETHERLANDS

Maastricht ●

CHURCH LANDS

Calais ○

Dunkirk ○

Brussels ●

Oudenarde ○

Aachen ○

Lille ○

Ramillies ○ *Meuse* R.

Liege ●

Bonn ○

Arras ○

Malplaquet ○

sambre R.

Namur ○

Coblenz ○

Le Havre ○

○ St. Quentin

Moselle R.

Mainz ●

Caen ○

Rouen ○

Laon ○

Rocroi ○

Sedan ○

Luxembourg ○

LOWER
PALATINA

Op○

Worms ○

Seine R.

Oise R.

Aisne R.

Verdun ○

Mannheim ●

Evreux ○

Reims ○

Marne R.

LORRAINE

Dreux ○

Paris ●

Chalons ○

Metz ○

MTS

2

Chartres ○

Nancy ○

Troyes ○

Toul ○

Strasbourg ○

Sossbac○

VOSGES

ALSAC

Rhine R.

Orleans ○

Sens ○

Turkheim ○

○ Freiburg

Angers ○

Loire R.

FRANCE

Tours ○

Mulhouse ○

FRANCHE COMTE

Belfort ○

Basel ○

Nevers ○

Poitiers ○

Vienne R.

○ Bern

SWITZERLAND

Loire R.

Limoges ○

Geneva ○

1

Lyon ○

Rhone R.

MILA

SAVOY

Turin ○

Valence ○

CENTRAL EUROPE

APPROXIMATE HOLY ROMAN EMPIRE
IN 1618

N O R T H   S E A

Due to severe dynastic and religious strife
during the 17th Century, boundaries were often
subjected to sudden, major displacement. The
extremely fragmented nature of Germany was
another factor accounting for confusion over
political borders. For clarity, boundaries depicted
are very general and simplified; there has been
no attempt to trace them precisely.

ENGLAND

4

THE
NETHERLANDS

CHURCH LAN

Birmingham

Norwich

Ipswich

Amsterdam

Ems R.

3

Thames   R. London

Rhine R.

Southampton

Nijmegen

Portsmouth

Dover

Ostend

Eindhoven

Calais

Dunkirk

Antwerp

CHURCH LAN

Lys R.

SPANISH NETHERLANDS

Maastricht

Cologne

Oudenarde Brussels

Lille

Aachen

Bonn

Ramillies

Meuse R.

Liege

Coblenz

Arras

Malplaquet

Namur

Sambre R.

St. Quentin

Le Havre

Sedan

Luxembourg

Moselle R.

Mainz

LOWER
PALATINA

Caen

Rouen

Laon Rocroi

Worms

Oise R.

Aisne R.

Verdun

LORRAINE

Mannheim

Evreux

Soisson

Reims

Marne R.

Metz

Dreux

Paris

Chalons

Nancy

VOSGES MTS

Chartres

Toul

Strasbourg

ALSACE

Rhine R.

Sossbach

Troyes

Orleans

Sens

2

Turkheim

Freiburg

Loire R.

FRANCE

Angers

Mulhouse

Tours

Belfort

FRANCHE COMTE

Basel

Nevers

Poitiers

Vienne R.

Bern

SWITZERLAND

Limoges

Loire R.

Geneva

1

Lyon

Rhone R.

SAVOY

MILA

Turin

Valence

= Electors

England
vs.
France

The Sun King and the Lord Protector

4

The longest standing rivalry in the western world was that between England and France. From the Middle Ages to the dawn of the twentieth century, London and Paris conducted a bitter, running feud which erupted time and again in war.

Actually, there were three basic conflicts between the two nations. First was the controversy over English ownership of territories on the Continent. France won that round by eventually ejecting the English from their possessions in northern France. Calais was the last stronghold to fall, succumbing in 1558. Second was the dispute over control of the English Channel, which in London was synonymous with prevention of French hegemony on the Continent. Competition for colonies and world trade was the third. It is the history of the second and third with which we are now concerned. Although originating earlier, both are central factors in the history of warfare from the Thirty Years' War through the Napoleonic Wars. Waterloo (1815) was the climactic battle of these wars, signalling ultimate victory for England. Diplomats created Belgium in 1831 as a neutral and independent state, settling the question of control over the Channel, while in 1904 the Entente Cordiale finally ended the squabbling over colonies.

Those accords were reached only after a series of clashes spanning two centuries. Europe, America, and the high seas provided the primary battlegrounds in all of them. Collectively, the major clashes were the wars of Louis XIV, the wars of Frederick the Great, the American Revolutionary War, and the Napoleonic Wars. The wars of Louis XIV began during the Thirty Years' War (1618–1648) and lasted through the War of the Spanish Succession (1701–1714). Frederick's wars commenced a quarter of a century later. From the viewpoint of a contest between England and France, the American Revolution and the Napoleonic Wars are part of the continuing story.

After Gustavus Adolphus was killed at Lützen in 1632, France was compelled to enter the Thirty Years' War as a full-fledged participant. There the story begins.

French Ascendancy; Spanish Decline

The young Frenchman scowled. Beyond a slight swale, atop a gentle ridge about 1,000 yards away and just south of the town of Rocroi, stood a forbidding line of precisely formed Spanish squares. Having invaded his country, the Spaniards seemed now to be mocking the French commander, daring him to attack. The 22-year-old Duke of Enghien wanted to oblige them; he was, in fact, bursting to charge. But he was inexperienced at war, and his older and more knowing generals had emphatically advised caution. Let the Spanish attack, they had said. Musing, Enghien recognized sound logic in their reasoning. After all, not only were Spanish soldiers reputed to be the best in Europe, but here they outnumbered

Prince Condé (Enghien)

the French, 27,000 men and 20 guns to 22,000 and 12. Still and all, the Duke's instinct shouted for an assault.

The May day wore on. Both lines stood under arms, nervously surveying one another, each hoping that the other would make the initial move. Melo, the Spanish commander, had organized his 8,000 crack Spanish infantrymen into several bristling *tercios*. Most European armies had long since shifted away from the *tercio* concept, adopting instead the flexible line introduced by Gustavus Adolphus. But not the Spanish. They had invented the *tercio* over a century before, had fought successfully with it, and saw no reason to change. Behind his veteran Spaniards, Melo placed a second line of similar size but comprised of less dependable Italian, German, and Walloon mercenaries. On his right flank waited some 3,000 cavalrymen; on the left, 5,000. Enghien, soon to become Prince Condé and later to be called the Great Condé, had arrayed his troops in a nearly identical manner, with cavalry split right and left, two infantry lines in the center, and a small cavalry reserve. But the French were organized according to the Swedish system, with smaller, more mobile units. There was one other important difference—the French commander was imbued with the offensive spirit. As the sun

set, Enghien ordered his army to sleep.

At 3 o'clock the next morning, blaring trumpets called the French camp to arms. The Duke, now wearing a hat with flowing white plumes, rode along his front. He would attack that day.

The entire French force advanced simultaneously. With his furiously charging right-wing cavalry, which he himself commanded, Enghien smashed the Spanish left, sending it reeling from the field. Dispatching a group of horsemen to pursue, the youthful commander next turned to strike the left wing of Melo's infantry. Meanwhile, the left-wing French cavalry had not fared as well; it had, indeed, been sharply beaten back. Having seen failure on their left, the French infantry had halted. Enghien at that critical moment gathered all his troopers to lead them on a reckless, streaming, saber-slashing charge through the two lines of hostile infantry to fall upon the rear of the enemy's right-wing cavalry. Those Spaniards surviving the onslaught raced off in rout. That bold act also discouraged Melo's infantry, sending his second line bolting from the battlefield.

Almost before anyone realized what had occurred, only the 8,000 Spanish veterans remained on the field to face over

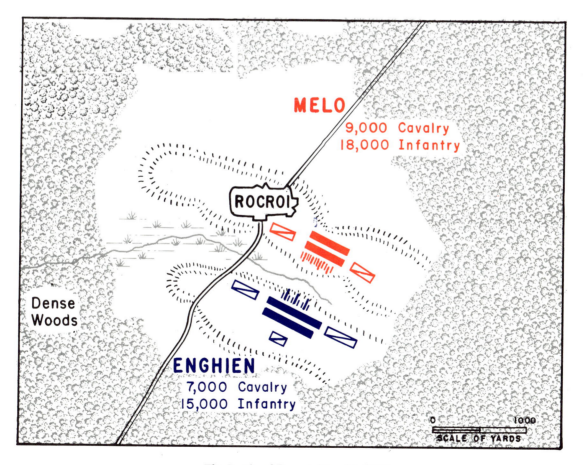

The Battle of Rocroi, May 19, 1643

Cavalry Clash at Rocroi

twice that many Frenchmen. But those staunch soldiers of the famed *tercios* were not to be easily dismissed. Assailed violently from all sides, they held. Again and again, Enghien ordered his men to charge, only to be repulsed each time. Finally, nearly out of ammunition and having suffered severe casualties, the Spanish officers offered to surrender. Riding forward to accept the capitulation, Enghien was fired upon by several confused Spanish infantrymen. Enraged at such "treachery," the French fell savagely upon their battered foe, giving no quarter. By nightfall, the pride of Spain's army lay hacked to pieces on the blood-soaked ridge of Rocroi.

That day's events put a final end to the long era of Spain's pretensions to world power. Henceforth, France would be the strongest power in Europe. The Battle of Rocroi, though not in itself responsible for the ruin of Spain or the rise of France, marked a watershed in European history. The year was 1643.

It was not for Louis XIII that Enghien and his men had won the great victory. That king had died three days before. The new French monarch, Louis XIV, was a 4-year-old child. No more auspicious event than Rocroi could conceivably have signalled the beginning of the long reign of the "Sun King." Meanwhile, in England, 1643 marked the emergence of an obscure country gentleman, Oliver Cromwell. Brilliant victories that year in the English Civil War elevated him into a position of power and prominence that would permit him to depose and behead the English king and to establish a military dictatorship with himself serving as "Lord Protector."

A fateful year, to be sure. It was also the twenty-fifth year of the Thirty Years' War. Gustavus Adolphus had been dead more than a decade.

The Thirty Years' War

After mourning Swedes had buried their great leader, they grimly continued the war. Bernhard of Weimar and Marshals Horn and Baner picked up the slack reins of military command, while Axel Oxenstierna assumed responsibility for foreign affairs. Wallenstein gathered his shattered forces to invade Silesia, but he soon became convinced that Germany's real interest lay in unity rather than a continuation of the war. His subsequent attempts to secure a workable peace among the German states ran contrary to the powerful Spanish faction at the Imperial Court—and led directly to his assassination. In September of 1634, Bernhard and Horn met a combined Imperial and Spanish army at Nördlingen, near the Danube citadel of Donauwörth. The Swedes, outnumbered more than 2 to 1 in infantry and almost as much in cavalry, aggressively, if foolishly, attacked the entrenched Catholics. In unfavorable terrain, without the guiding genius of Gustavus Adolphus and in the face of a greatly superior foe, the Swedes blundered badly. The slaughter was terrible; over half the Protestant force fell on that field. At Nördlingen, the marvelous army fashioned by Gustavus perished.

Only two individuals had possessed the vision, tolerance, ability, and position to terminate the long war—Gustavus Adolphus and Wallenstein. Both were dead. Only one army had been capable of winning a clear-cut, decisive victory—the Swedish. It had been cast away in an unwise battle. From 1635 to the end of the Thirty Years' War, there is little to be learned about the art of waging war, but much about the art (or lack thereof) of achieving peace.

Spring of 1635 saw John George lead Saxony and many other Protestant states over to the Catholic side. France at the same time declared war on Spain. Thenceforth it was all but impossible to draw any religious lines at all. As a matter of fact, it is tremendously confusing for the casual student even to keep straight who was fighting whom at any given time. Moreover, the principal characters began to change. Bernhard, Baner, Emperor Ferdinand II, George William of Brandenburg, and Richelieu were among those passing from the scene. Mazarin, another Catholic cardinal, replaced Richelieu. Torstensson, Gustavus' great gunner, succeeded to the command of Sweden's forces and proved to be a truly outstanding battle captain. Young Enghien earned lasting fame at Rocroi, but a fellow Frenchman, Turenne, emerged as the best commander produced by that nation during the war. Everyone wanted peace, but politicians were unable to agree on its form, while generals were equally unable to gain a military victory that would force one side or the other to submit.

Germany, long a battlefield, became a wasteland. Armies and armed bands marched and countermarched from one end to the other, gruesomely strewing in their wake devastation,

Leonard Torstensson

disease, and death. Discipline disappeared. Rape, pillage, arson, and murder became the norm. Historians have been virtually incapable of adequately describing the utter horror,

Foraging and Pillaging During the Thirty Years' War

Discipline in the Seventeenth Century

the depth of misery, the abject human debasement. Millions perished. Bohemia's population had been 2,000,000 in 1618; by 1648 it was 700,000. Perhaps half the homes and farms and villages went up in flames; sheep, oxen, cattle, and horses all but disappeared. Famine stalked the land; starvation was epidemic. Peasants revolted, preying like wild beasts on straggler and stranger alike. Barbarity vied with brutality. Only armies were safe; teeming hordes of women and children followed them, the destitute wife "half a prostitute and half a gypsy," the starving children scavenging behind the soldiers like packs of jackals. It was total war in its most evil sense. Europe would not soon forget it.

Rocroi in 1643, following a complete Dutch naval victory in 1639 at the Battle of the Downs, ended Spain's reign as a major power. Torstensson decisively defeated the Saxons at Jankau in 1645, driving Saxony out of the war. In 1646, Turenne led a French and Swedish force south of the Danube to raze Bavaria. The last year of the war saw Turenne at the Inn River and a Swedish force besieging Prague—the city where it had all begun 30 years earlier. Military successes and sheer exhaustion at last brought an end to the bitter war. The Treaty of Westphalia was signed in October 1648. Louis XIV was then 10 years old.

Louis XIV and the Ministerial System

Unlike Gustavus, whose victories had been the result of tactical innovation, Louis XIV accepted warfare as he found it.

Like the Swedish monarch, however, the Sun King brought domestic stability and governmental and military efficiency to his nation through centralization, albeit extreme in nature. That bureaucratic emphasis produced magnificent dividends at first, but proved eventually to be self-defeating.

It is true that an army quite reliably reflects the character of the nation fielding it. Seventeenth century France was moving by swift strides toward absolute monarchy, as power shifted from the aristocracy to the king. Cardinal Richelieu began the trend, Cardinal Mazarin continued it, and Louis XIV completed it. Every cord of control came to be pulled from a central location, effectively eliminating the previously powerful nobles from the conduct of government. Members of the aristocracy were expected to participate in the elaborate rituals of court, and were encouraged to lose themselves in that sensuous and shallow life of frills and facade, pomp and charade, and effeminate curly locks. They could with propriety engage in but one activity of state; men whose blood ran blue could spill it fighting for France. Everything else was done by monarch and ministers—economics, administration of government, foreign relations, control of the Army and Navy, and internal development. It is hardly surprising, therefore, that France's military forces were affected by the overall movement toward centralization and standardization.

Aristocrats could aspire to the throne, but men of humble birth could not. For that simple reason Richelieu, Mazarin, and Louis XIV all drew their ministers from among the middle classes, while most senior soldiers came from the lesser nobility. In the early part of his reign, Louis XIV was exceptionally fortunate in the talent available. Colbert, the finance minister, was a forceful and most able administrator; Le Tellier and later his son, Louvois, performed admirably in the position of war minister; Turenne and Condé (Enghien) proved to be two of the most outstanding soldiers of the age; and the incomparable Vauban became Europe's leading engineer.

Laboring for king and country rather than for personal advancement, the ministers and professional soldiers created a unity and efficiency that allowed Louis XIV to harness the latent strength of his populous and abundant land. France had three or four times as many people as England, Spain, or Austria, while she outnumbered smaller nations such as Sweden, Denmark, and the Dutch Republic by 6 or 8 to 1. Rich and varied soil, large mineral deposits, and access to two oceans provided a foundation on which a prosperous economy could be erected. Thus, seventeenth century France possessed all three of the basic ingredients necessary to create armed strength: people, resources, and organization. Moreover, France's foreign policy required her to raise and maintain a sizable military instrument, for the Sun King determined to extend the borders of his country to its "natural" frontiers—the Rhine, the Alps, and the Pyrenees. Such a policy was bound to bring him into conflict at one time or another with his neighbors. That, then, is the background and setting in which Colbert began to build a navy and Le Tellier and Louvois turned their talents to revitalizing and revamping the French Army.

It is roughly accurate to say that every single aspect of the Army was centralized in the war ministry, which was headed by a civilian loyal to and working directly for Louis XIV. Directives pertaining to organization, logistics, strategy, and even tactics emanated from that central office. Given the fragmented, almost anarchic system in use before, such centralization immediately bore significant results.

Units were brought to strength—and maintained there. Drill, organization, and equipment were improved and standardized. Discipline became harsh and uncompromising as rampaging armies were brought to heel. Engineers and artillerists became regular members of the Army. Hard-nosed inspectors strove to insure that standards were strictly maintained. (One, Inspector General Martinet, gave his name to the English language; the word, in French, now means cat-o'-nine-tails.) By improving recruiting methods and absorbing auxiliary forces into the standing army, Louvois greatly increased its numbers—200,000 to 300,000 became the normal size. Appointments and promotions came from Versailles, thus reducing favoritism and nepotism. Finally, Louvois altered the entire logistical system; contemporaries nicknamed him the "great victualler." The manufacture, transportation, and stockpiling of stores and equipment came under his close scrutiny. He established supply depots at strategic locations around the country, and kept them full.

Thanks to his ministerial system, Louis XIV could send into battle armies that were large, well trained, properly equipped, fully supplied, and responsive to his direction.

Unfortunately, neither the King nor his ministers showed the slightest indication of being blessed with any military talents whatsoever. The French armies were to perform as well as they did in spite of, and not because of, the incessant meddling of Louis and Louvois. This highlights the fatal flaw in any centralized system—a weakness at the center. By its very nature, concentrated control eliminates initiative at lower echelons, has a deadening effect on subordinate leaders, and fails to inculcate decisiveness and confidence among field commanders. Eventually, nothing functions without precise and timely guidance from the top. If the center remains strong and sure, the system works; if it becomes weak and uncertain, the entire structure crashes.

There is not space here to describe adequately the accomplishments of Vauban or to explain completely the role he had in the rise of France. At once a minister and a marshal, he was peerless both at building and besieging fortifications. Famed in his own lifetime, he profoundly influenced warfare for more than a century after his death in 1707.

After early cannon had battered down medieval walls about their defenders' ears, a natural reaction set in. Engineers promptly began to design fortresses to withstand artillery, and to mount cannon to return the fire of attackers. Eventually the pendulum swung back and fortifications became more or less impervious to attack. Starvation again served as the besieger's main weapon. This phase probably reached its peak during the time of Maurice of Nassau. When Vauban first studied the art of the military engineer, that was still the general situation. He changed it.

Vauban's method of besieging a fortress was first to surround and isolate it, and then gradually but irresistibly close in on a designated point without subjecting his men to counterfire. The entire object was to advance one's cannon close enough to the fortress to subdue the defender's guns and open a breach in the walls, all the while protecting the advancing guns and men against fires and sorties from the fortress. Vauban employed an intricate system of parallels and connecting trenches and shifting battery positions, all mathematically calculated and minutely designed to place his massed artillery and sappers at the precise location chosen for making the breach. Each parallel could support the one farther in, while the third was located adjacent to the hostile works. Victory became virtually inevitable. Practiced by professionals, Vauban's method was so certain that he could often predict the very hour a position would fall.*

---

*To appreciate the complexity of a contemporary siege, see page 67. While that sketch is not an example of Vauban's siege operations, the picture shows the intricacy of the Turkish trench system, the positions occupied by Turkish artillery, and the selective destruction of Hapsburg bastions during the siege of the Hofburg at Vienna in 1683. The sketch was drawn by Daniel Suttinger in 1683, and is here reproduced from *Vienna Gloriosa, id est peraccurata & ordinata Descriptio* (Vienna, 1703).

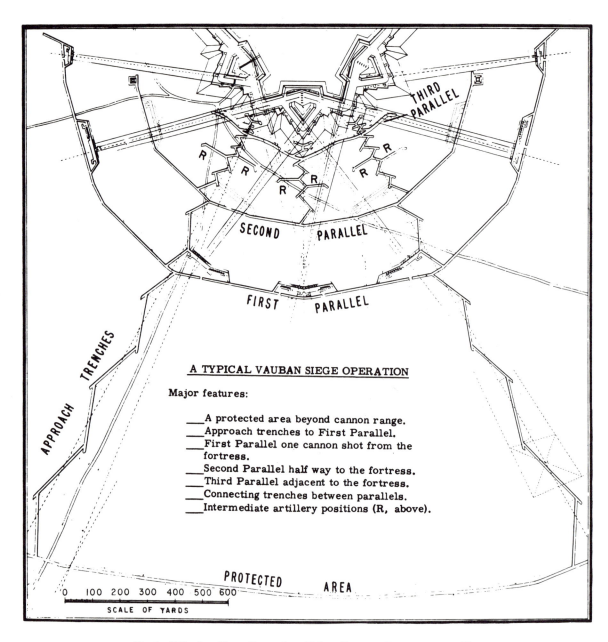

Typical Vauban Siege Operation, Taken From a Contemporary Plan

Vauban also vastly improved the construction of fortifications. The theory of bastioned fortifications—a method permitting flanking fire to converge along the wall faces—was not an invention of Vauban, but he used it so extensively that it almost became synonymous with his name. Details of his improvements in fortress construction are no longer important, but his concept—a highly flexible one—was to utilize to the maximum existing terrain advantages. Common sense, therefore, was as important as mathematical precision.* Once the trace of the defense was selected by terrain analysis, the

bastions were placed to provide mutual support and defense in depth. Strategically, he raised multiple chains of fortresses designed to provide defense in depth to the entire French nation. *(See Map 1.)* Ultimately, when Louis XIV's centralized system finally brought France to the brink of defeat, it was only Vauban's defenses that saved her. Moreover, those same defenses performed the same function nearly a century later. In fact, not until the advent of rifled artillery in the last half of the nineteenth century did Vauban's work become entirely obsolete.

It was said, without too much hyperbole, that "a town besieged by Vauban was a town captured—a town defended by Vauban was a town impregnable."

---

*Ironically, this point was not appreciated by disciples who, for a century or more, blindly erected "Vauban Fortresses" according to the *form* not the *substance* of his teachings. They ignored his essential ingredient of flexibility.

Turkish Siegeworks at the Hofburg, Vienna, 1683

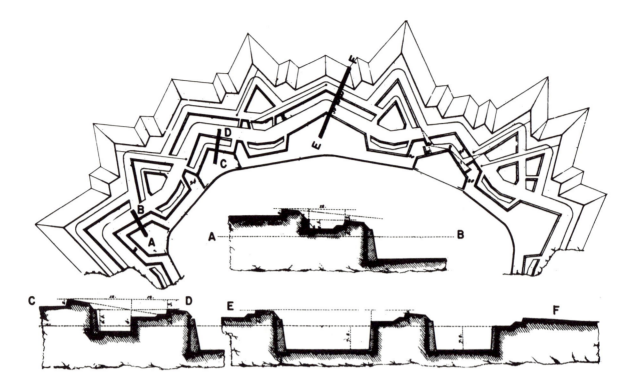

Profiles Showing the Construction of a Typical Vauban Fortress, Taken From a Contemporary Plan

Cromwell and the New Model

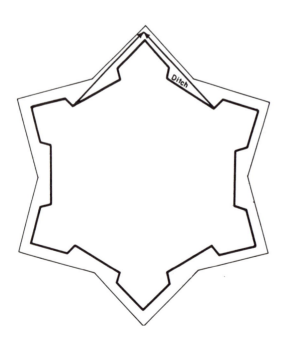

Schematic of a Bastioned Fort

Meanwhile, across the English Channel, more abrupt events were in progress—events significantly transforming the English Army and establishing the pattern it would generally follow until the twentieth century.

Almost from the moment he was crowned in 1625, Charles I had remained at odds with Parliament. To begin with, his aggressive foreign policies ran contrary to the then prevailing isolationist mood of his subjects. Parliament was extremely reluctant to grant funds to restore England's dilapidated military establishment or to support unpopular wars with Spain and France. Those wars—hostile disagreements is a better description—were terminated in 1630, the year Gustavus Adolphus invaded Germany; but Charles continued to have financial difficulties at home. Parliament and King grew further apart. Both became intransigent. Not even the massacre of 30,000 Protestants in Ulster in 1641 was enough to convince the representatives to give Charles an army. Finally, in 1642, the inevitable break occurred. Charles raised his standard at Nottingham; Parliament organized its own army. The Great Rebellion had begun.

England at that time possessed not even a vestige of a professional army. Traditionally, forces had been organized as the situation demanded—and disbanded the moment the

Oliver Cromwell

need abated. Therefore, both sides formed units from recruits and local militiamen, although the latter were unwilling to fight beyond the boundaries of their home county. Such experience and expertise as existed was found among veterans of the Thirty Years' War. Not surprisingly, the first major clash, the Battle of Edgehill, was a clumsy, brutal, bungled affair, ending in a bloody draw. One of the participants, a 43-year-old country gentleman without any previous military experience, sat down afterwards to analyze the battle. Certainly, he mused, there must be a more efficient way to wage war. To Oliver Cromwell the answer seemed evident: farmers are not fighters. Merely handing a lad a gun and calling him a soldier is not enough. Such an approach creates armed mobs, not armies. Intelligence, common sense, and historical experience all vividly reveal that truth.

Accordingly, during the winter of 1642–1643, Cromwell set out to recruit, organize, and train a professional cavalry regiment. Believing that "a few honest men are better than numbers," he was highly selective in his recruiting, thorough in his organization, and rigorous in his training. It became almost a passion with him to pay, feed, and clothe his men adequately. When spring of 1643 arrived, Oliver Cromwell led the finest unit in England. "I have a lovely company," he said, "they are honest, sober Christians: they expect to be used as men!" That statement is significant, for, although Cromwell insisted on fashioning a professional force, he carefully shied away from putting together a mercenary one. He clearly understood that the most truly professional army is one drawn from the broad populace, one that reflects the views and aspirations of the people for whom it fights, one that has a cause higher than money. He avoided the common

mistake of confusing "mercenary" with "professional."

Throughout that year, Cromwell's regiment gained fame and experience, becoming competent and confident. They were ready for the decisive battle of the Rebellion, Marston Moor.

On July 2, 1644, a Parliamentarian (Roundhead) army of about 25,000 men encountered some 18,000 Royalists (Cavaliers) at Marston Moor. Both formed for battle, infantry in center and cavalry on both flanks, but neither cared to attack. Finally, toward evening, Cromwell, whose regiment held the Roundhead left, charged the cavalry force on the Cavalier right. With that movement, both lines surged forward. The infantry fight in the center developed into a severe slugfest, with Royalists perhaps holding the edge; Royalists definitely won the cavalry duel on their left. Cromwell, however, soon smashed his opponent—Prince Rupert, whose splendid regiment of cavalry was previously undefeated—and, though wounded, led his men behind the enemy infantry to take in rear and crush the remaining Cavalier cavalry. Then Roundheads converged on the hapless Royalist infantry and destroyed it. Virtually single-handedly, Cromwell's cavalry (dubbed "Ironsides") had won the day.

Parliament took prompt notice of the value of military professionalism as evidenced in the Ironsides, authorizing an entire army to be organized along the same lines. That army, the New Model, was without equal in England. A national army required a national uniform. Scarlet was selected; the "redcoats" were born. Commanded by Sir Thomas Fairfax, the New Model Army met Charles, who had rebuilt his army, at Naseby on June 14, 1645. Prince Rupert, eager to avenge his defeat at Marston Moor, launched a fierce cavalry attack against Fairfax's left, driving it off the field. Cromwell, however, held the right. As Rupert savagely pursued the beaten left wing, Cromwell overwhelmed the enemy left and center. The victory was total. Charles surrendered. The first phase of the Great Rebellion was over, won by the side that had chosen to become more militarily professional.

But the matter was by no means settled. Fighting erupted again in 1648. This time Cromwell commanded the New Model Army, though now, by virtue of an ill-advised Parliamentary effort to disband it without pay, it was less an instrument of the government and more a tool of Cromwell. In a series of brilliant campaigns, Cromwell defeated all opponents. Charles, in the meantime, was beheaded. The Commonwealth, a republican form of government, was established in 1649, although Cromwell remained the real power. When all military enemies had been ground under by the New Model, Cromwell ousted his detractors in the Government. He served as Lord Protector, and virtual military dictator, from 1653 to his death in 1658.

England gained at least one national characteristic from

her revolutionary experience: a deep-seated, even irrational fear of a standing, professional army. (Paradoxically, the Great Rebellion also proved the superiority of a professional force over an amateur body.) That characteristic fear, inherited by colonists in America, was to play a significant role in future wars through modern times.

Limited Warfare

From the end of the Thirty Years' War to the beginning of the Napoleonic Wars—nearly a century and a half—European warfare was noted for its extreme limitations in every way but one—frequency. There were plenty of wars.

Many factors limited warfare. Among them, the horrible excesses of the Thirty Years' War were not the least; rulers had vivid evidence of what could happen when armies run amuck. Moreover, that entire period, called the Age of Reason, was marked by an almost slavish devotion to reason and logic, form and orderliness. It followed naturally that warfare, too, would be viewed in detached, analytical, rational terms. Just another affair of state, wars involved very few people—many citizens were unaware if their country was at war or peace, nor did they really care, as a rule.

It became increasingly important to maintain the economic strength of one's country, so armies were generally filled with the unproductive segments of society. Officers came from the idle aristocracy and soldiers from jails and gutters—the steeple and the mudsill of the social structure. Mercenaries came to be more highly valued than ever. A foreign hireling was worth three men: one soldier more under arms, one less for some potential enemy, and one native worker able to remain at his job and pay taxes.

Armies were large, and they remained in being year round. Equipping, training, and paying a soldier was not inexpensive; casualties, then, meant loss of capital. Tactics, too, impinged on the problem. After the Thirty Years' War, everyone converted to linear tactics. Firepower became all-important, especially when the flintlock musket replaced the matchlock, and the bayonet made the pike obsolete. To make a soldier really proficient in the evolutions required in battle consumed anywhere from two to five years. To the simple monetary loss when a soldier was killed was added the great delay in replacing him. When two forces collided in battle it was apt to be a devastating affair. They would line up facing each other, approach to within pointblank musket range, and blow each other to bits. A great victory could ruin a ruler whose finances were unable to recover from losses incurred. Maneuver, therefore, displaced battle. A good commander did not fight to win as much as he fought not to lose.

The proliferation of fortifications and the expanding knowledge of poliorcetics* had a hand also in greatly reducing the scope and scale of seventeenth and eighteenth century warfare. Even if an army did decide to invade enemy territory, it could not press into the interior without first reducing that country's frontier fortifications. Leaving them astride the line of communication would have been folly. But, the destruction of those strongholds normally consumed at least the first campaign, granting the opponent time to react. What's more, the new logistical system tied armies increasingly to magazines. To proceed far, a commander had to build, stock, and secure depots as he went. Those posts made possible his further progress and also provided a safe route of retreat, but they did not support a lightning advance. Roads remained primitive, of course, and the numbers of horses required to move an army remained high; rivers and forage were, therefore, prime logistical considerations—and key factors inhibiting mobility. Most wars, as a result, were confined to populated border areas, and consisted mainly of sieges.

In keeping with the times—and due in no small measure to the impact of Vauban—sieges became as extravagantly orchestrated as a stage production, and as formalized and standard as a parade ground maneuver. Since a siege was inevitably successful unless the defenders received outside help, it made very little sense to hold out to the last. It was rational, even respectable, to surrender in order to avoid needless bloodshed. Hence, mutually agreeable rules of conduct came into being to permit a defender to submit with honor at the proper moment. It was a rather complicated business, painstakingly learned by the military engineers of the day. Some soldiers complained, however, that schools taught "not the art of defending strong places, but that of surrendering them honorably after certain conventional formalities." Should a fortress commander be so boorish as to refuse to surrender when properly summoned, the attacking troops then had the right to put his garrison to the sword and pillage the city. That did not happen often. Horace Walpole, the Earl of Orford, lamented: "War has become so peaceful that when a city is besieged today and falls, the women inside can't even hope for the benefits of a good rape." Sieges were great shows, resplendent with pomp and color and ceremony, especially after engineers gained enough skill to predict the climactic moment. Louis XIV loved sieges, the bigger the better. Ladies were invited, servants spread a banquet on an overlooking hill, and final assaults were launched to the accompaniment of violins. Waltzes were preferred.

Finally, political leaders refused to grant field commanders more than a modicum of initiative. Restrictive orders, cen-

---

*Drawn from the Greek word *poliorketes* (taker of cities), poliorcetics is the science of siege warfare.

tralized control, and the actual presence of the ruler or a deputy severely crimped the general's ability to take advantage of unforeseen opportunities. Strategy did not die, but it assumed a rather queer, shrivelled character. No longer did the commander plan a campaign to destroy the enemy; the intent was to *avoid* him. It was a "strategy of evasion."

The Evolving Command and Staff System

Larger armies, greater supply problems, and expanding specialties such as artillery and engineering induced a gradual change in methods of supervision. No longer could a general exercise adequate command and control through a coterie of aides and general assistants; specific functions began to emerge. By the time of Louis XIV, most armies had similar staff organizations and concepts.

There was a single commander, of course. Under him were usually one or more lieutenant generals who would command various portions of the army in battle and on the march. Generally, the battalion or regiment was the largest organized unit; divisions and corps did not make their appearance for another century. Regiments, under their own commanders, would be combined in *ad hoc* fashion prior to each operation into a wing or a task force commanded by one of the generals. Normally, too, generals would be designated to head the cavalry, direct the artillery, and supervise the engineers. The general exercising overall command manipulated his force by adherence to a previously discussed plan, by use of galloping messengers and aides, and by personal action at decisive points. It was not at all uncommon for the general himself to lead the key charge, to rally a faltering line by personal example, or to emplace and fire artillery at a critical juncture. Command remained distinctly personal.

Staff functions were assuming forms still familiar today. Titles and responsibilities were not fixed, and they varied from country to country—for instance, staff officers in some forces also doubled as line commanders—but it is generally correct to say that the military staff was beginning to evolve. A chief of staff existed, though he might supervise other staff officers, or command the garrison in camp, or hold a command in battle, or do all of those things. Logistics were almost invariably handled by separate staff officers, called quartermasters or *maréchaux des logis*. In France, an inspector general was appointed for each arm to assure field compliance with directives. Supply, transportation, pay, medicine, and intelligence were also beginning to be considered as formal staff responsibilities. Many staff activities were duplicated at subordinate echelons, such as the cavalry or artillery headquarters.

Nevertheless, one must not presume that the modern staff had arrived full-blown. It obviously had not. Responsibilities remained somewhat nebulous, depending in large measure on the whims of various commanders. Staffs were small, their duties limited, and their areas of action ill defined. But, embryonic or not, the beginning of a military staff was definitely a part of the seventeenth century scene.

The Contest for Dominance in Europe

Three times after Cromwell's seizure of power, England and the Netherlands fought naval wars (1652–1654, 1665–1667, 1672–1674). Behind each war lurked the simple motive of money. As a British general admitted, "What we want is more of the trade which the Dutch have." At the end of the Thirty Years' War, the Netherlands had become far and away the leading maritime nation in Europe. The Lord Protector determined to usurp that position for the British Isles— England thus became an aggressor at sea just when France was nurturing expansionist policies on land. Cromwell's New Model Army was mostly discarded after his death, but his boost to English seapower and imperialism endured.

The results of the swirling clashes at sea are important. First, England did become the world's foremost sea power—a status she relinquished only when the United States overtook her in World War II. Second, England's position in North America grew apace. New Amsterdam became New York, thereby placing the entire eastern seaboard from Maine to northern Florida under the British flag. Fearing the loss of Baltic naval stores, Cromwell developed a burgeoning timber trade with the American colonies. Fleet and colonies thus became the foundation of Britannic power and prestige.

So was set the stage for future drama—the world's strongest sea power and the world's major land power were to be the central characters, while Europe and America were fated to provide scenery, supporting actors, and side plots.

French Aggression

Montgomery of Alamein, an English soldier turned historian, recently wrote, "Of the various individuals who have set out to dominate Europe, none ever made a more long-standing nuisance of himself than Louis XIV." In search of *gloire* for himself and France, the Sun King engaged in continual intrigue and encroachment. He also waged four major wars:

the War of Devolution, 1667–1668; the Dutch War, 1672–1678; the War of the League of Augsburg, 1688–1697; and the War of the Spanish Succession, 1701–1713.

In the first of these, Louis aimed purely at territorial aggrandizement, attempting to wrest the Spanish Netherlands (Belgium) from Spain. Turenne overran much of Flanders and Hainault, while Condé conquered Franche-Comté. Spain was too weak to offer much resistance. Frightened, the United Provinces hastily formed a coalition with England and Sweden to induce Louis to cease his aggression. Reluctantly, he did so, returning Franche-Comté, but retaining a series of fortified towns along the border between France and the Spanish Netherlands.

Angry at the Dutch, and still eyeing the wealthy areas to the northeast of France, Louis plotted carefully to deprive the Netherlands of allies. After France had signed treaties with England, Sweden, and several German states, Louis struck again in 1672, this time directly against Holland. The Dutch, involved in a sea war with England, divided politically at home, and owning a sadly neglected army, were no match for the massive force Louis flung at them. With Turenne, Condé, and the King himself heading invading columns, success seemed certain. Such resistance as was mustered was mostly ineffectual. Indeed, observers referred to the invasion as "a military promenade."

Then, in that moment of crisis, the Dutch people turned to 22-year-old William III of Orange. The family that had produced William I and Maurice of Nassau now provided yet another savior. The young leader defiantly opened the dikes in Louis' face, successfully stopping the French offensive. William, destined to become King of England in 1688, was thenceforth to devote his entire life to the defeat of Louis XIV. For the moment, however, he was hard pressed to defend his dank, diked lands at the mouth of the Rhine. Alone he could never overcome France; desperately he sought allies.

England did not join the Dutch at this time. As a matter of fact, English troops aided Louis in his invasion.* Soon, however, William succeeded in ending the final naval war between his beleaguered nation and his future subjects. England withdrew from Louis' expedition in 1674, a year after the Holy Roman Empire had declared war on France. Shortly, Brandenburg, Sweden, Denmark, and smaller states became embroiled, as well as Spain and Holland.

When the Dutch War began, Marshal Turenne was over 60 years old. He had started his martial career as a 14-year-old at the side of his illustrious uncle, Maurice of Nassau. Ever since he had been a soldier, waging war over nearly every

*Two young officers who would one day clash swords as leaders of their respective armies first met on this campaign. John Churchill (later the Duke of Marlborough) and Claude Hector (later the Duke of Villars) went along to fight and to learn what they could by observing the master, Turenne.

Vicomte Turenne

part of Europe from Italy to the North Sea. In the twilight of his life he was better than ever; Napoleon said he was the only one of the great captains whose genius grew bolder as he grew older.

Turenne's name is unalterably linked with the "strategy of evasion." Under him, wars of maneuver—combat without battle—reached the height of perfection. As discussed earlier, battle had become such a costly affair that it was to be avoided whenever possible. Even if one general wanted to fight, he first had to gain the consent of his opponent, for all one usually had to do to avoid a fight was march away. Battle was absolutely a last resort, to be accepted only when conditions were highly favorable, and then only reluctantly. A much more admired method of gaining a "victory" was to cut your foe's line of communication, forcing him to retreat, or to maneuver him into an area in which he would be unable to sustain his force, thereby obliging him to withdraw. Another method employed feints to deceive the enemy into leaving a key position lightly guarded, at which time one swiftly doubled back to seize it. Skillful maneuvers, close attention to logistics, and proper security measures could bring successful results without the discharge of a single musket. It was held that a general could spend an entire career and never participate in a battle—and be the better for it. Indeed, though wars were frequent, battles were few. Time and again, entire campaigns passed with a greater expenditure of shoe leather than gunpowder. This was the type of warfare at which Turenne excelled and in which European generals were schooled and experienced. One point should be noted, however, with regard to Turenne. As a veteran of the Thirty Years' War, he was far less averse to battle than most of his younger contemporaries. Although he was essentially a practitioner of maneuver, he recognized that a battle was not *always* bad. In fact, it might have been that very trait—the ability to envision a careful maneuver culminating in clash of arms—which set him apart from other generals of the period.

Turenne launched a winter offensive in January 1673, striking sharply into Germany. In haste, Brandenburg agreed to peace. Turenne then posted his army to prevent the Imperial army from linking up with the Dutch. Opposing him was another master of maneuver, Montecuccoli. That general, an Italian two years older than Turenne, was a close friend of the French leader. Both had been lifelong professional soldiers.

At first, Montecuccoli was unmatchable. He shrewdly outmaneuvered Turenne, sidestepped him, and moved down the Rhine to join William. Their combined forces then regained some of the overrun Dutch lands. The next year, 1674, was one of mixed success and failure on both sides, with Turenne generally gaining the better position. The stage was then set for his most brilliant campaign. A daring mid-winter march from one end of the Vosges Mountains to the other completely surprised his enemy. Driving his own forces vigorously, Turenne won a decisive battle at Turkheim in January 1675, giving France the entire west bank of the Rhine. That summer the marshal again outfoxed Montecuccoli, forcing him to accept battle in a most disadvantageous position at Salzbach. Never had the old soldier been sharper. Then, in the opening skirmishes, a cannonball smashed through his torso, killing him outright.

Raymond Montecuccoli

Shocked, Louis XIV had Turenne's remains interred in ground reserved for France's kings. To compensate for his loss, the Sun King promoted eight generals to the rank of marshal. "Small-change for Turenne," courtiers whispered. Condé took command, but it had been a long time since the day of Rocroi. His old fire had burned out, and it was not long before he retired from the service.

Military stalemate marked the rest of the war. Louis' troops made some gains in the Netherlands; and then the King, satisfied that he had gained all he could reasonably expect from the war, set in motion steps leading to peace. Meanwhile, in a forecast of things to come, William married Mary of England.

The Dutch War over, France was at the peak of her power. An aggressive foreign policy and an efficient army had seemingly provided a winning combination. But a deeper look would have revealed some leaks in Louis' ship of state. On the outside, hostile nations seethed with bitterness and fear; on the inside, old familiar faces were disappearing. The greatest generals were already gone; Colbert died in 1684, Louvois a few years later. Their successors were by no means as able. Although aging, Louis assumed more and more of the load himself, increasing the centralizing process so long in progress. Vauban remained, old and bent, riding constantly from one end of France to the other, furiously erecting chains of fortresses to stem the approaching flood.

Louis did not see the flaws as he continued to scheme to absorb lands along his borders. Helpless provinces were gobbled up one by one. William of Orange, preying on Europe's fear of France, organized the League of Augsburg in 1686. The formation of the league, which was composed of Holland, Spain, Sweden, the Empire, Bavaria, Saxony, Savoy, and the Palatinate, precipitated the War of the League of Augsburg.

For 11 years (1688–1697) the fracas wore on, mostly in the Netherlands. William proved himself to be a mediocre but stubborn combat leader. France's last outstanding general, Luxembourg, failed to survive the war. The Earl of Marlborough and Prince Eugene were the best allied commanders; the Duke of Villars led the French. In America, French and English colonists bitterly if ineptly fought one another in the first of four colonial wars. Their bushwhacking battles in the thick forests of the New World were entirely indecisive. Similarly, in Europe, France could not defeat the coalition, nor could the coalition defeat France. Mutual exhaustion and war weariness ground the conflict to a sputtering end. Neither side looked upon the war as over, but both wanted a breathing spell.

A delicate balance of power existed. As long as the Allies hung together, France would be stymied. Louis, searching for a means to break the deadlock, discovered hope in the woebegone person of Charles the Sufferer.

The Spanish Succession

Charles had inherited the throne of Spain in 1665, while still a child. Since then he had demonstrated only one outstanding characteristic: he had appeared to be dying for over three decades. Sickly, crippled, and at least partially insane, he had no heirs. Although Spain was no longer a major power, the Spanish crown remained a great prize. Claimants from France and the Empire had equal rights; and whichever one succeeded to the inheritance would be able to tilt the precarious balance of power. Worriedly, diplomats agreed before Charles' death to divide the spoils evenly in order to retain equilibrium and to avoid war. But Charles had the last laugh. Preferring to be followed by a Bourbon rather than to see his empire partitioned, the pitiable ruler changed his will at the last moment, leaving the Madrid crown to Philip of Anjou, grandson of Louis XIV. Charles died on November 1, 1700, and Louis accepted the throne on behalf of Philip. That left other nations no recourse; war was all but inevitable. France and Spain united would soon have been too strong for any other combination to resist.

What slim chance for peace that might have remained was shattered by Louis' next moves. His armies seized possession of Dutch-occupied fortresses along his northern border, and he recognized an exile as king of England, breaking his previous acceptance of William. *(See Map 1.)* England exploded in fury. The entire thrust of her foreign policy had been to preclude France from obtaining control of the Belgian Channel ports, while, domestically, the most critical issue was to exclude from the throne the Catholic branch of the royal family. Louis had most painfully pricked the Island Kingdom on both counts.

Meanwhile, the Holy Roman Empire had not hesitated to debate the Spanish succession with arms. Emperor Leopold sent an army under Prince Eugene of Savoy crashing through the Brenner Pass into Italy. Eugene, one of the greatest battle leaders of the age, promptly outmaneuvered the French, thrashed them at the Battle of Chiari, and drove them in confusion over the Po River. Those were the opening blows of the War of the Spanish Succession. By the end of 1701, England had joined several continental powers in the Grand Alliance, a coalition against France. Fear, of course, was what drew those disparate nations together. English and Dutch money was the glue that kept them united. Each state had its own interests, jealousies, and desires, and each expected to gain from the coalition. (The price for joining set by the Elector of Brandenburg, for instance, was Imperial recognition of him as King of Prussia, an event full of meaning for the future.) Nonetheless, their joint aim was to reverse Louis' blatant aggression and to oblige him to remove Philip from Madrid.

In this war, however, Louis XIV had allies, notably Spain and, soon, Bavaria. He was confident, then, of avoiding stalemate and achieving victory. On paper, the Grand Alliance seemed weaker than in the last war, but it was blessed with a resource of incalculable value, one that cannot be entered on a tally sheet. When all is said and done, the prime factor in warfare is man—and the coalition claimed two of the most splendid soldiers the world has known, Marlborough and Eugene.

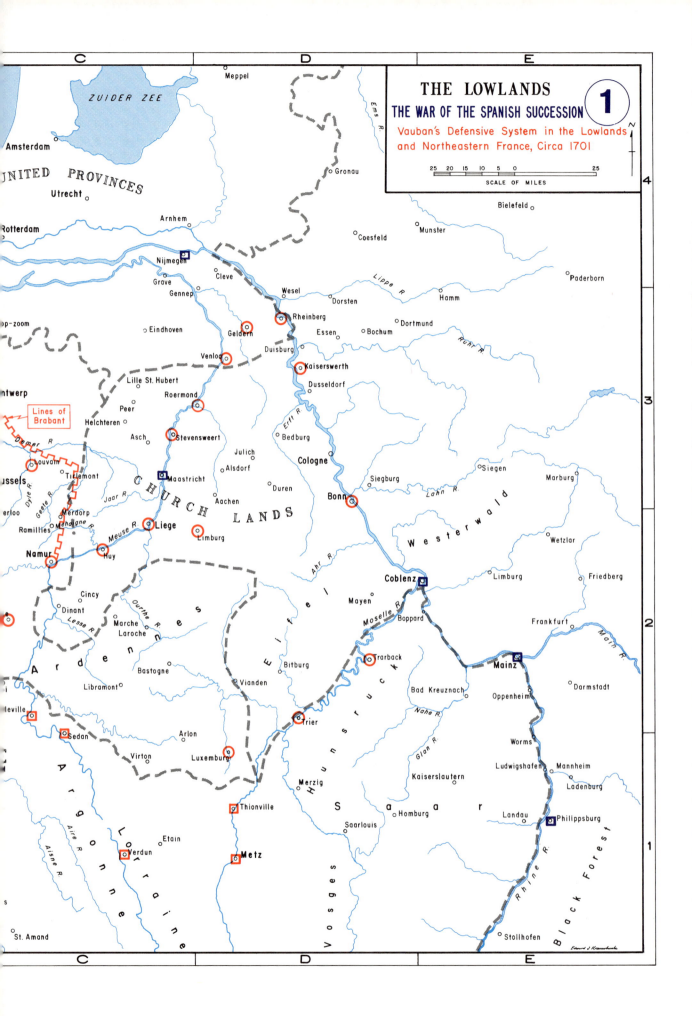

THE LOWLANDS

THE WAR OF THE SPANISH SUCCESSION **1**

Vauban's Defensive System in the Lowlands
and Northeastern France, Circa 1701

SCALE OF MILES
25 20 15 10 5 0   25

LEGEND

□ – Rear line of fortresses in France.

○ – French occupied fortresses in the Spanish Netherlands or in neutral territory.

□ – Allied fortresses

NORTH SEA

ENGLAND

The Hague

Walcheren

Ber

Hulst

Deal

Dover

Ostend

Bruges

Niewport

Dunkirk

Ghent

Dendermonde

Calais

SPANISH NETHERLANDS

Dender R.

Senne R.

Strait of Dover

Ypres

Courtrai

Oudenarde

Menin

Scheldt R.

Boulogne

St. Omer

Hazebrouck

Lys R.

Lille

Ath

Aire

Tournai

Nivelles

Canche R.

Lens

Scarpe R.

Mons

Charle

Crecy

Authie R.

Arras

Douai

Malplaquet

Valenciennes

Maubeuge

Sambr

Abbeville

Bouchain

Philip

Somme R.

Cambrai

Albert

Fournies

Oise R.

Amiens

Peronne

St. Quentin

Cantigny

Montdidier

Noyon

FRANC

Rouen

Laon

Beauvais

R

Compiegne

Oise R.

Aisne R.

Chaumont

Soissons

Vesle R.

Seine R.

Reims

Marne R.

Chateau Thierry

Epernay

Versailles

Dreux

Paris

Ch

Esternay

A   B

Marlborough and Eugene

5

The most renowned commander in Europe at the opening of the eighteenth century was walking proof of Louis XIV's fallibility. Prince Francois Eugene of Savoy had been born in Paris in 1663, and from childhood had wanted to become a soldier. Louis, though, thought him too fragile for war, and wished him to join the priesthood. Stubborn and revengeful, the young man fled to Austria, where he entered the Emperor's service. For over half a century he fought Vienna's wars against all opponents, but most gleefully against France. Daring, resourceful, inspiring, active, dedicated, and intelligent, he climbed quickly. A general at 26, he became commander-in-chief of Imperial forces at 33. His victory over the Turks at Zenta in 1697 temporarily freed the Empire from pressure on that flank, and made Eugene's name known throughout Europe. Twenty years after Marlborough retired, Eugene continued to command—and always from the van. He was never to marry; at his death, innumerable scars on his slight frame offered eloquent evidence of his only passion—warfare.

Marlborough, 13 years older than Eugene, possessed a personality and a past altogether different. When he assumed command of all English, Dutch, and hired German troops in July 1702, Dutch generals fairly rankled with resentment. Deeming their own credentials impeccable, those officers looked down on a commander who was not in their eyes a truly professional officer, and owed his position to court favor and diplomatic intrigue. There was jealousy behind their accusations, but an element of truth as well.

John Churchill obtained his commission through a sponsor's influence, and money from a woman he himself had influenced. Later, gaining combat experience in France, he caught the eye of Turenne and saved the life of a duke. Marital sagacity brought martial success, for his biggest boost up the military ladder came when he wed Sarah Jennings, attendant and best friend of Princess Anne of England. He quickly thereafter became a general, showing some soldiery ability and much diplomatic skill. When William III came to England in 1688, Churchill joined him and linked his prestige to the cause of the Dutchman. That move made him Earl of Marlborough. Under William he conducted solid campaigns, but never displayed the verve with which he was later to startle Europe. One reason was that William, an average general at best, was almost always in the field to exercise top command. As both Churchill and his wife had been old and close friends of Princess Anne, it was not surprising that even more honors came his way after Anne became queen early in 1702. Indeed, one could have excused the Dutch generals their pique.

Prince Francois Eugene of Savoy

John Churchill, the Duke of Marlborough

But they were wrong about his abilities. Beneath his stately demeanor and elegant manners, behind that imperturbable personality, pounded the solid heart of a warrior. That fact would soon become evident. Anne, naturally, would not intrude upon the battlefield; Marlborough, enjoying her complete trust, would for the first time be free to fight as he wanted—to employ his genius without higher restraint.

During the War of the Spanish Succession, France—Spain was more an appendage than an ally—seemed to hold most of the aces: a central position, a single command post in Paris, the larger and stronger military establishment, virtually impregnable defensive systems, and control of the approaches to the Mediterranean. Opposing her was a coalition, with all the weaknesses implied in that word. The contest, however, was not entirely one-sided. The Allies sailed supreme at sea, a not inconsiderable advantage, and they possessed in the tiny body of British troops, the finest fighting force in Europe—the legacy of Oliver Cromwell's New Model Army. Nonetheless, in the ultimate weighing, the generalship of Marlborough and Eugene counted for more than anything else—perhaps more than everything else. In a time when the ordinary officer preferred anything to fighting, Marlborough and Eugene preferred fighting to anything.

War at the Turn of the Century

The marvelous achievements of Marlborough and Eugene can be properly appreciated only if the prevailing mode of battle in the early 1700s is comprehended. By the turn of the century, every musketeer had a bayonet. That technological advance eliminated pikemen in most armies, thus increasing the number of shot in a formation. In Churchill's words, " . . . infantry was not a thing that stood, but a thing that fired." Firing was generally by platoon volley rather than line by line, while infantrymen formed squares to defend against cavalry. The better cavalry charged home with saber, even though vestiges of the caracole survived. Artillery had shown little improvement since the time of Gustavus Adolphus, although armies had more of it. Linear tactics had been adopted by all; but in their efforts to maintain a solid front of fire, generals began losing sight of the importance of battlefield flexibility and tactical mobility. When armies grappled, it was more likely with the muscular embrace of wrestlers than with the slashing grace of fencers.

A famous descendant of Marlborough vividly described battle in the day of the Duke:

> Marlborough's men and their brave, well-trained opponents marched up to each other shoulder to shoulder, three, four, or six ranks deep, and then slowly and

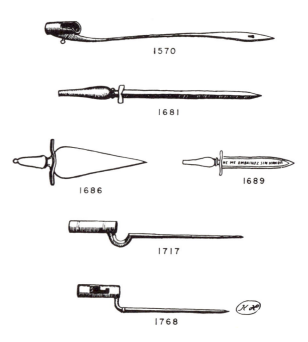

Development of the Bayonet

mechanically fired volley after volley into each other at duelling distance until the weaker wavered and broke. This was the moment when the falcon cavalry darted in and hacked and slashed the flying men without mercy. Keeping an exact, rigid formation under the utmost trial, filling promptly all the gaps which at every discharge opened in the ranks, repeating at command, platoon by platoon, or rank by rank, the numerous unhurried motions of loading and firing—these were the tests to which our forebearers were not unequal. In prolonged severe fighting the survivors of a regiment often stood for hours knee-deep amid the bodies of comrades writhing or forever still. In their ears rang the hideous chorus of the screams and groans of a pain which no anaesthetic would ever soothe.*

No wonder generals and statesmen alike tended to eschew full-scale battles.

It was an era dominated by the negativeness of the defensive—conduct a siege, make a march, threaten a flank, but avoid the enemy army. On such a stage strode Marlborough and Eugene, both having formed unusual opinions: that wars were to be won, that armies were to fight, that the initiative was to be seized and maintained, and that the enemy army was the supreme objective. These were strange ideas, bold ideas, thoughts too revolutionary for warfare in the Age of Reason; but they engendered concepts that bore the seeds of victory and barred the indecision of stalemate. "To crush the French armies in the field, and to pursue their demoralized remnants to the French capital itself," was their conception of how to humble Louis XIV.

The Campaigns of 1702 and 1703

From the outset, Marlborough and his Dutch compatriots clashed, disagreeing strongly on strategy. As a result of French advances, mortal danger faced the United Provinces; Marlborough wanted to assault the invaders, while the Dutch, fearing to commit their army to an offensive, preferred to await the French attack.

The French position was indeed imposing. They garrisoned most of the fortified towns in the Spanish Netherlands that the Dutch had so carefully and at such great expense erected as a barrier. A strong French army under Marshal Boufflers had advanced between the Meuse and Rhine Rivers, penetrating almost to Nijmegen, deep in Dutch territory. *(See Map 2.)* To the south, stretching 70 miles from Antwerp to Namur,

were the famous Lines of Brabant, a defensive system erected under Vauban's personal supervision the year before. That superb system of field works and water obstacles barred a direct Allied approach into France.

Unable to obtain agreement for a direct counteroffensive, Marlborough demonstrated traits that were to serve him well time and again in the years to come—diplomatic finesse and mental flexibility. He quietly bowed to Dutch wishes and sought another solution. A march towards the lines of Brabant, he surmised, would oblige Boufflers to vacate his advance position and hurry back. He was right. Crossing his army over the Meuse at Grave, the Duke struck out for France. Surprised, Boufflers reacted just as Marlborough had anticipated: he raced back in an effort to reinforce the Lines of Brabant before the Anglo-Dutch army could attempt breaching them. The Dutch were ecstatic; without firing a shot they had repulsed the French invasion. That was how they liked war. But Marlborough still wanted a test of arms.

When Boufflers crossed the Meuse at Roermond and angled west, Marlborough saw another chance. The French would have to cross his front. He could take them in flank. For his part, Boufflers recognized the danger, but relied for protection upon darkness and Allied reluctance to fight. Marlborough deployed his army, ordered the men to sleep on their arms, and prepared to pounce at dawn. An easy and decisive victory appeared to be within his grasp—in effect, he would be springing a flank ambush on an enemy in column. It promised to be another Lake Trasimene. But at the last moment Dutch deputies—civilian representatives of the Dutch Government assigned to Marlborough's staff to ensure that he avoided a battle—grew timid. They implored him not to attack. He acquiesced, but made them ride forward with him to see the rare opportunity that had been missed. There, beneath the guns of the arrayed Allied army, strung out helplessly over the level heath, straggled the sorely fatigued French army, wallowing "in the greatest confusion and disorder imaginable."

Shamefacedly, the deputies admitted their error, although the galling lesson in no way made them more aggressive. The very next day, when Boufflers encamped in a most unfavorable position in order to close up his weary units, Marlborough proposed again to attack him. "No," was the predictably timorous Dutch reply. Marlborough the diplomat did not remonstrate; Marlborough the soldier was furious. His professional pride was sorely bruised. It is a curious reflection of the times that he promptly penned a letter of apology to his enemy for having twice failed to attack him. It was not his fault, he candidly informed the foe, that a battle had not occurred.

About that time, Louis XIV unexpectedly came to Marlborough's aid. Enraged at having so swiftly lost the entire lower Meuse, the monarch railed at Boufflers,

---

*Winston S. Churchill, *Marlborough, His Life and Times* (6 vols.; New York, 1935), III, 112-113.

brusquely ordering him to seek battle. Smarting under Louis' sharp reprimand, Boufflers advanced northward on August 9 to threaten the Allied line of communication near Eindhoven. After attempting a trap, which went awry, Marlborough calmly continued south toward the Lines of Brabant. Stymied, Boufflers turned in pursuit. Near Helchteren, as his advance units began to debouch from a defile, the startled French marshal encountered Marlborough's entire army positioned for battle on an open plain. For a third time, Marlborough had maneuvered Boufflers into a position of extreme disadvantage. This time even the ultra-cautious deputies could see advantage in battle.

Watching the French frantically struggle out of the defile while artillery duelled, Marlborough noted the virtually complete disorganization of their left. Quickly deciding to launch his main attack against that vulnerable point, he ordered General Opdam, a Dutch officer commanding the Allied right wing, to advance. Opdam, like nearly every other general in Europe, was trained to do anything but attack. He delayed for hours, finally flatly refusing to go forward, claiming the footing was not firm. Marlborough boiled. The French completed their deployment and awaited assault. Even with Louis' orders to engage in battle still ringing in his ears, Boufflers could not bring himself to attack. Nor would the deputies permit Marlborough to start the fight once the two sides appeared more equal. Boufflers slipped away that night, to Marlborough's supreme chagrin.

Giving up hope of a battle, the exasperated Earl turned his talents to siege work. As the campaigning season ticked away, he methodically cleared most of the Meuse to include the capture of Liége. In November, he put his forces in winter quarters and headed for England. Without a single engagement, Marlborough had pushed the French back to Vauban's defenses in Brabant. Louis was angry, Marlborough depressed, the Dutch delirious, and England buoyant. Queen Anne made Marlborough a duke. However, only in the Lowlands had things gone well for the Allies; elsewhere, French arms had triumphed. Despite the fetters imposed by his cohorts, Marlborough alone had managed to check Louis' aspirations that year.

Crushing frustration was the new Duke's lot in 1703. He advocated a vigorous offensive in Flanders, but the Dutch were stubbornly satisfied to defend. He pressed for battle, but the Dutch permitted only sieges. He planned and initiated a "great design" to capture Antwerp, but Dutch generals failed to cooperate. Discouraged because the Dutch preferred a war with minimum casualties, Marlborough resolved to resign at year's end. When winter arrived, Allied achievements were neatly summed up in the words on a medal struck by the Dutch to honor the English commander: "Victorious without slaughter, by the taking of Bonn, Huy, and Limburg."

Elsewhere, French arms scored real successes. Marshal Villars, a French general who believed in waging offensive warfare, crossed the Rhine, traversed the Black Forest, and linked up with Bavarian allies to defeat an Imperial army on the Danube in September. The path to Vienna lay open— Austria was in peril.

Marlborough was persuaded to continue in command, but he resolved to rid himself of Dutch interference. That decision and the threat on the Danube led him to contemplate shifting his forces southward in 1704.

The March to the Danube

Corresponding during the winter of 1703–1704, Marlborough and Eugene concluded that they must unite their forces somewhere to strike a telling blow at the French. Dutch stubbornness eliminated the Lowlands, distance the Mediterranean. Bavaria, however, appeared to be within reach. Knocking that German state out of its alliance with France would weaken Louis and relieve Vienna. Best of all, Marlborough could leave behind his bothersome Dutch deputies. Bavaria became the objective.

Three major problems immediately faced the Duke. First, of course, he had to organize and equip his army for the long march—no simple task, but one that he and his staff could manage. Second, he had to fool the French, for he would in effect be making a flank march along their entire front—a most dangerous maneuver should they even remotely suspect his intentions. Third, he must mislead his own allies—never would the Dutch knowingly permit him to march off into Germany, leaving them to fend for themselves. Secrecy was the key. Marlborough accepted total responsibility without consulting a council of war. Only a handful of trusted individuals knew of his intentions.

Openly, the English commander espoused an invasion of France from Coblenz up the Moselle Valley toward Metz and Paris. *(See Map 3.)* This was an obvious invasion route, quite believable to the French. Moreover, moving to Coblenz, ostensibly for such an advance, would constitute the first stage on the road to the Danube. Finally, the myopic Dutch leaders could probably be persuaded to allow operations on the Moselle. Through the winter, Marlborough gathered his forces and debated convincingly in favor of his cover plan. By early May 1704 he was ready, having obtained all the necessary authority, supplies, and men. Leaving most of the Dutch Army to defend the Lowlands, he happily headed south on May 19.

Promptly, French forces postured as if to attack the United Provinces—an obvious maneuver designed to cause the English to withdraw. Predictably, the nervous Dutch set up a squeal of protest, clamoring for Marlborough's immediate return. Imperturbably, the Duke ignored the uproar behind him. Seeing their feint fail, the French quickly decided to race for the Moselle in order to block what they believed to be an impending invasion. Immensely relieved, and just a little embarrassed over their premature fright, the Dutch even agreed to forward another contingent of troops to aid Marlborough.

At Coblenz, Marlborough calmly continued southward, surprising his troops, startling allies, and perplexing enemies. Puzzling over maps in an attempt to divine English intentions, Louis XIV and his advisers worriedly concluded that Alsace must be Marlborough's objective. But they remained highly concerned, for the hostile army could always board boats and rush back down the Rhine to debouch in the vacuum left by French forces, which were now hastily converging on Strasbourg.

Marlborough's march was unhurried, but steady. Troops were on the road at dawn and in camp by noon, avoiding the heat of the day. Heavy equipment and supplies were transported by river as far as possible. Extreme care was given to preserve the health of man and horse—the Duke wanted to arrive with a fresh and ready force. Staff planning had been meticulous: a new pair of shoes, for instance, awaited every man at Frankfurt. Everywhere the long, red columns were greeted with buoyant enthusiasm and bubbling curiosity. Never before had an English army shown its face in central Germany, and seldom had any soldiery looked so sharp—and this much-fought-over land had seen enough of wars and fighting men to judge. Disciplined, healthy, and happy, the English and their allies were an impressive bunch as they progressed inexorably southward.

Just beyond Mannheim, on June 7, Marlborough suddenly shifted his advance away from the Rhine toward Ulm. He was then between the Bavarians and the French, and could no longer be prevented from linking up with the Imperial army. On June 10, Prince Eugene rode in, beginning one of the greatest partnerships in military history. Once again, without firing a shot, the Duke had gained a magnificent strategic victory. The threat to Vienna had been countered. The entire panorama of warfare provides few such splendid examples of the strategy of indirect approach.

The Assault of the Schellenberg

The next step was to drive Bavaria out of the war. That meant forcing a passage of the Danube. Marlborough and Eugene decided upon Donauwörth, the site chosen for the same purpose by the great Gustavus Adolphus. Once again, though, coalition difficulties intervened. The two generals were joined by Prince Louis, the Margrave of Baden. A competent commander in the terms of the time, he was plainly pedestrian in the company of Marlborough and Eugene. The Duke hoped to convince Prince Louis to block French forces in the west while he and Eugene cornered and conquered the Bavarian army. Baden, however, would have no part of that plan. He insisted on accompanying Marlborough. Moreover, he demanded equal command status. Reluctantly, Marlborough sent Eugene to hold the French, agreed to share command with Baden on alternate days, and set his army in motion for Donauwörth.

After leaving the last waterway connecting him with the Rhine, Marlborough switched to previously arranged lines of communication stretching through Nuremburg to the Main River. That step shortened and secured his logistical tail, evidence again of the Duke's careful planning and keen foresight.

The Elector of Bavaria, Max Emmanuel, chose to defend on the left bank of the Danube in an impregnable position some 30 miles west of Donauwörth. Marlborough merely bypassed him to the north and pushed rapidly on. Sensing the Englishman's plan, Max Emmanuel rushed 14,000 French and Bavarian troops along the south bank of the Danube into Donauwörth. In heavy rain on July 1, the Bavarians under Count d'Arco began frantically entrenching the Schellenberg, a high, flat-topped hill overlooking the town. Marlborough's forces reached a bivouac 15 miles to the west. Count d'Arco calculated that the Allies would not be able to attack until July 3, at the earliest. His calculations were wrong—Marlborough was no ordinary opponent.

Granted another day, d'Arco would have had time to complete his entrenchments and possibly receive reinforcements. If the Schellenberg were to be taken, Marlborough reasoned, it must be on the morrow. Moreover, the Duke commanded on July 2; he could not depend on Prince Louis to attack a day later, nor could he afford to wait until the fourth when his own turn would come up again. However, an assault on the second could only be launched late in the day, after an exhausting march over boggy roads; and it would have to be an attack from column, for there simply would not be enough time to let the entire Allied army close up. A piecemeal attack with tired troops late in the day against an entrenched enemy meant that the odds were long indeed. Yet, to delay would endanger the campaign. Two final factors were in Marlborough's favor. D'Arco would never expect such an audacious lunge, and the fighting quality of these English soldiers would assure bold and violent execution at the point of contact. The Duke would be taking a risk—but a carefully calculated one. Late on July 1 he began preparations for an attack.

A handpicked assault force of 10,000 men was slogging along the mucky way at 3:00 a.m. the next morning. Marlborough personally led them. Behind hurried the main army under the Margrave of Baden. Nine hours and twelve miles later, the tiring column of assault troops crossed the Wernitz River unopposed. Eight hours of daylight remained. As his troops pressed anxiously on, the Duke rode ahead to reconnoiter, approaching so close to Bavarian positions that he drew cannon fire. Marlborough saw thousands of soldiers atop steep slopes, laboring vigorously to complete earthworks. An old fort, abandoned long ago by Swedes, anchored their center. On the Imperialist left stood the town of Donauwörth, holding very little defensive strength in its obsolescent walls,

but nonetheless creating a serious obstacle in view of the fast dwindling daylight. A thickly wooded area similarly precluded maneuver against d'Arco's right. The assault would have to go straight in. Determinedly, the Duke deployed his mud-splattered storm troops in three broad lines. Close behind he packed three more lines of mixed infantry and cavalry. On a narrow front of about 300 yards he massed, all told, perhaps 10,000 men. Bugles and drums sounded the advance. It was 6:00 p.m.

Waves of scarlet-coated soldiers surged upward. Grapeshot and musket fire mauled them terribly, cutting ragged gaps in the crimson ranks. But screaming, "God save the Queen," the troops advanced unfalteringly. To drown out their unnerving yells, d'Arco ordered his drummers to beat loudly and continuously. The British assault reached the Bavarian line

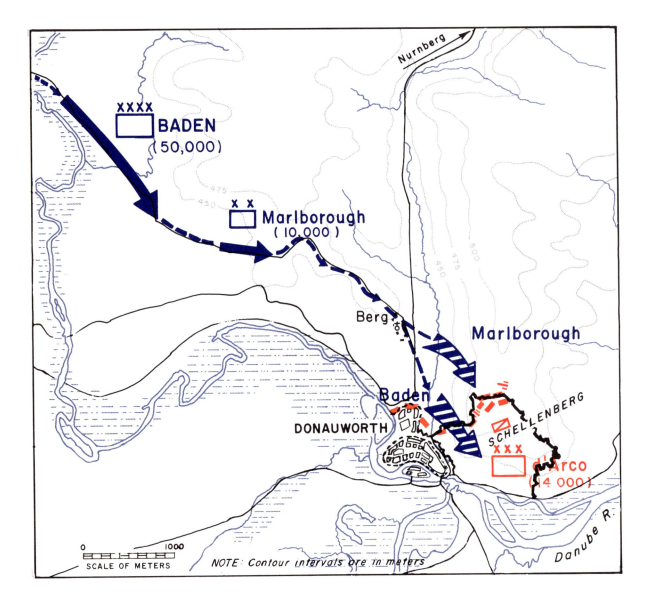

Marlborough's Assault of the Schellenberg, July 2, 1704

of defense before falling back over a corpse-littered field. Undeterred, the redcoats reformed for another attack while d'Arco hurriedly reinforced the bloody angle, which the English were quite obviously going to strike again.

In the smoke and confusion of that cacophonous charge, Prince Louis had hustled troops into position on Marlborough's right. Bavarian lines in front of Louis were being denuded in order to strengthen the area in which Marlborough was even then conducting a second valiant attack. Once more the red wave rolled up the Schellenberg, once more leading elements were wiped out, once more survivors reeled back after reaching the very ramparts, and once more Marlborough grimly rallied his forces for another attack. But this time Prince Louis' troops advanced and easily splintered the thinned defenses, spilling into the center of the Bavarian position. The third English attack, launched at that moment, caught d'Arco's troops between two lines of fire. They broke. In a matter of minutes, while fleeing frantically across the Allied front for the river, the panic-stricken defenders were almost annihilated. Of 14,000 men, perhaps 5,000 survived the slaughter. English cavalry, sabers dripping red, granted no quarter. When the sun set, blanketing bloody Schellenberg in darkness, the Allies had executed a Danube crossing and won a clear tactical victory as well. The cost had been high—6,000 casualties, including 1,500 dead—but the rewards were also great. The cream of Max Emmanuel's army had been decimated; Bavaria lay open before Marlborough. Storming the Schellenberg had been a fitting end, a bold exclamation point, to the march to the Danube.

Maneuvering Toward a Battle

As soon as Allied units had secured a bridgehead over the Danube, Marlborough issued orders to raze Bavaria. Taking first what they needed or wanted, his soldiers mercilessly put Max Emmanuel's domain to the torch, leveling entire towns and villages, and destroying crops, herds, and orchards. A few old-timers remembered the last time their country had been so brutally and so efficiently ravaged—over seventy years before, by Gustavus Adolphus.* But when the terrible Swede had come, warfare had been savage and total, a fact somehow explaining if not excusing his devastation. It was supposed to be different now. War had rules; it was reasonable and limited. It was not intended to be a burden on civilians. Not so in Marlborough's eyes; wars were to be fought and won and ended as quickly as possible, in any manner possible. The swift sword of decision was preferable in every way to

*Turenne, too, had sacked Bavaria toward the end of the Thirty Years' War.

the stalemate of indecision. The English duke would have agreed wholeheartedly with a future American warrior, William Tecumseh Sherman, who described his destructive march through Georgia with the curt phrase, "War is hell!" Marlborough's course was deliberate, if not humane. The Elector had barricaded the remainder of his army in strongholds to await French succor. Marlborough hoped he would capitulate to save his bleeding state, or else would be obliged to gamble on a battle. The rape of Bavaria, then, was simply a military move to achieve a military victory.

Louis XIV loyally supported his beleaguered ally, sending Marshal Tallard with 35,000 troops through the Black Forest to relieve the Bavarians. Max Emmanuel, learning that help was on the way, grimly clung to his fortresses and ignored the havoc being wrought in his country. Marlborough's first attempt to bring about a battle had failed.

Far from being discouraged by the news of Tallard's approach, Marlborough was pleased. Eugene, maneuvering brilliantly, had so frightened the French over the safety of Strasbourg that they had entrenched most of their army there to repulse an imagined Imperial attack. While they huddled in their defenses, too far removed to affect events on the Danube, Eugene was actually on his way to join Marlborough, moving rapidly to arrive at the same time that Tallard would link up with the Bavarians. Thus, the Allies would still possess a superiority of 71,000 to 60,000. Perhaps Tallard could be tricked into a battle.

Beforehand, however, it would be necessary to ease Prince Louis of Baden out of the picture. Although he had supported bravely and well at the Schellenberg, he was cantankerous, stubborn, uncooperative, and worried more about his rights than about ultimate victory. For the coming battle there must be unity of command. With Baden present, that would be impossible to attain. When the three commanders met on August 7, they decided to lay siege to Ingolstadt. Intimation by Marlborough that Eugene should have the privilege of conducting the siege was enough to compel Baden to demand that honor for himself. Closely disguising his glee, Marlborough packed the Margrave off with 15,000 men. Perhaps no other event in history so clearly illustrates the value that wise generals have attached to unity of command— 15,000 troops dismissed on the very eve of battle! Eugene could have been a problem, for he technically was not under Marlborough's command. But he fully appreciated the importance of having a single head in combat. Moreover, there existed between the two men a unique empathy, a total trust, that would assure unfettered cooperation.

Now, the enemy must be enticed into battle. *(See Map 4.)* Prince Eugene's 18,000 men would be bait. They bivouacked west of Blenheim and north of the Danube. Marlborough's 38,000 remained near Rain, south of the river. Baden's departure with 15,000 further added to the impression of Allied dispersion. If Marlborough and Eugene were believable in preparing their ruse, Tallard and Max Emmanuel, with 60,000 massed troops, might consider overpowering Eugene's detached force before Marlborough, who was stationed across a river and miles away, could react. That is precisely what happened. The Franco-Bavarian army crossed the Danube and marched east toward Eugene's position. The bait had been taken.

Obviously, Marlborough and Eugene were not out of supporting distance. The roads and bridges between them had been put in excellent repair, march times had been figured exactly, and units stood ready to move on a moment's notice. Moreover, Eugene had selected a tentative battlefield. North of the small Danube village of Blenheim stretched a grassy, open plain providing limited room for maneuver. Farther east, wooded hills restricted movement almost to the Danube. The battle should take place west of that bottleneck, Eugene declared, because "it is above all important not to be shut in between these mountains and the Danube."

Eugene fell back to a position approximately four miles from Donauwörth and halted. On August 10, Marlborough began moving over the Danube; 20 miles upriver, the enemy crossed. Learning of Eugene's withdrawal and Marlborough's northward movement, Tallard deduced that the Allies were retreating to Nuremburg because of his threat to their line of communication. Immensely satisfied with himself, in spite of missing the chance to attack Eugene's vulnerable force, the French marshal conceived his new mission to be one of simply following the enemy retreat. He had not the least offensive intent, nor the vaguest thought that Marlborough might. On August 11, he selected a camp just west of a swampy stream, the Nebel. It appeared to be a good defensive position. The Danube covered his right, wooded hills his left, the Nebel and three villages his front. Blenheim was the southernmost of the three villages. There he stayed to await reinforcements and to enjoy his foe's retirement.

Tallard had taken the habitual precaution of selecting a defensible bivouac site. However, as a soldier of his era, he had not the slightest suspicion that he would be attacked there. Such a thing would be contrary to all the rules of war as he knew them. Of such complacency is surprise born.

On the twelfth, Marlborough and Eugene rested their forces, while the two leaders themselves went forward to reconnoiter. From a church tower they watched enemy troops occupy positions, Bavarians on the left and French on the right. Surprisingly, most of the cavalry took the center, while infantry units camped on the flanks. From the leisurely manner prevailing in the Franco-Bavarian camp, the two generals realized that they would probably enjoy the benefit of surprise. That meant Tallard would have to fight the battle as he was deployed in bivouac. Cavalry would hold the center—a fatal flaw that the two men in the church tower quickly discerned.

Tallard's troops slept peacefully as Marlborough and Eugene put their men on the road at 3:00 a.m. on the morning of August 13, 1704. In multiple columns they advanced, Marlborough near the river, Eugene by the hills. At 6:00 a.m. they halted to rest, just two miles from the enemy. Marlborough and Eugene rode ahead for a final reconnaissance. Through the mists they perceived Tallard's troops just rousing, unsuspecting, and careless. The two were ecstatic. Finally their foe had been brought to bay; he would have to give battle, and total surprise seemed to be in the offing.

The Battle of Blenheim

Ever since assuming command in 1702, Marlborough had been striving to pit his redcoats in open battle against Louis XIV's regulars. At long last he had such an opportunity, although no other soldier save Eugene would have seen the situation at Blenheim as anything remotely resembling an opportunity. Defeat would likely be absolute disaster, and chances for success seemed slim. Tallard had the larger army, as well as a heavy preponderance of artillery, a strong defensive position, and the not insignificant aura of invincibility attached in those days to French armies. To counter those advantages, the Allies relied upon surprise, the fighting quality of their soldiers, and the leadership of Marlborough and Eugene. Supremely confident, those two thought the risk well worth taking.

The battle was to be a setpiece affair—no headlong charge like the Schellenberg. Time would be consumed in deployment, but that could not be avoided. Marlborough, with 34,000 men, would launch the main attack against the French between Blenheim and Oberglau; Eugene, with the remaining 22,000, would conduct a secondary attack to hold Max Emmanuel's Bavarians north of Oberglau. Peering through the morning mists, Marlborough saw with satisfaction that Tallard's line ran along a crest well behind the Nebel, leaving room for the British squadrons of cavalry to form on the far side of the stream when the right moment came. After confirming their plans, the two Allied commanders rode back to their respective troops to order the advance.

Marching briskly up to the Nebel and fanning out into position while engineers rushed forward to prepare crossing sites, the Allied army at last made known its presence and its aggressive intent. In openmouthed disbelief, Tallard and his army stared across the Nebel as the rise of ground was suddenly transformed from pastoral calm to a swarming anthill of hostile soldiers. The psychological shock could hardly have been greater. Frantically, half-clad officers rushed to ready troops. Signal guns and drummers sounded urgent messages, aides dashed about feverishly with orders, regimental colors were unfurled, and gunners hastily loaded cannon. Hours were to pass before the actual assault, providing Tallard with adequate time to prepare, so that the surprise was more spiritual than tactical, more psychological than physical. But it was nonetheless all-important: Franco-Bavarian units stood to arms where they had slept, failing in their haste, as Marlborough had hoped, to correct their faulty dispositions. The weakest spot was between Blenheim and Oberglau—precisely where the Duke intended to strike his major blow. Moreover, the entirely unexpected apparition of an Allied army preparing to attack unsettled the nerves of officers and soldiers alike, a setback from which they were unable to recover. Thus, in a trice, the Allies snatched the moral ascendancy and retained it.

Rough terrain and greater distance delayed Eugene's preparations. Waiting for his friend to get into position, Marlborough engaged the French in a heavy and prolonged artillery duel. Both sides suffered severely, but stoically accepted the casualties. Tallard, with 90 guns to the Allies' 66, probably had the better of that exchange. While under fire, Eugene's men ate lunch, conducted religious services, and waited. On his left, the Duke sent a strong column across the Nebel toward Blenheim. It halted as ordered about 150 yards before the town, where it, too, waited. *(See Map 5a.)* As the sun climbed toward its midday post, Eugene's sweating men neared their assault position. Marlborough, his only sign of impatience a constant questioning to learn of Eugene's progress, calmly rode along his front, ignoring cannonballs, and inciting his men to fever pitch.

The Duke's plan was simple. He would first assail Blenheim and Oberglau, forcing Tallard to reinforce them from his center. Then, with French infantry tied down near the villages, and the weak middle even weaker, English cavalry in overwhelming strength would smash through that vulnerable point. A penetration having been made, the cavalry would turn right and left to take Tallard's infantry in the rear. Success would depend upon totally unselfish sacrifice on the part of Eugene on the right and the same from Marlborough's own shock troops, which were to be sent against the defended towns.

At half past 12, word came that Eugene was ready. Immediately, Marlborough signaled for the attack to begin. The men in the column near Blenheim rose and marched straight toward the village walls. At pointblank range, massed musket volleys from 16 infantry battalions and great belches of artillery cannister mowed down a third of the attackers, sending the rest recoiling to the rear. Retreat they did, but only to promptly advance again. Shaken, the French commander in Blenheim called in 11 reserve battalions from behind the village and 12 squadrons of dismounted dragoons that had

been guarding his river flank. The English assault reached the very edge of the smoke-shrouded town before devastating fire shredded it once more. Lord Cutts, the commander, casually reorganized, reinforced, and, in full view of the unbelieving defenders, prepared for a third attack. Though beaten back bloodily during the first two attempts, Cutts had done precisely what had been expected of him. Crammed so tightly into Blenheim's tiny streets that they could hardly move, much less fight, were 39 of the best battalions in the French infantry. Marlborough directed Cutts to delay making a third assault, but told him to keep pressure on the village. Meanwhile, there had been intense fighting elsewhere along the line.

Eugene's infantry valiantly stormed Lutzingen, chopping out a toehold. *(See Map 5b.)* A cavalry clash followed, with Bavarian troopers gaining the upper hand and pushing the Prince back over the Nebel. Fierce hand-to-hand fighting marked the seesawing struggle, as each side mounted charge after countercharge. Casualties climbed. In the thick of the fighting, wielding a saber, raging, and leading his men on, was Eugene himself. Profusely cursing every retreat, eagerly encouraging every advance, seeming to be everywhere at once, the fiery leader tightly pinned Max Emmanuel's larger force in place.

Only in the center near Oberglau did Marlborough's plan go awry. Ten of his German battalions had forded the Nebel to attack that village, but a vicious counterattack stopped them in their tracks. The German commander fell, along with most of his lead battalion. Leaderless and in disorder, the Germans flocked back over the Nebel, leaving Marlborough's right flank perilously open. Marshal Marsin, an able French officer working with the Elector of Bavaria, recognized the opportunity and hastily began organizing a cavalry force to crash through the gap—a maneuver that would have ruptured the Allied line, most likely forcing a retirement. Marlborough, too, spotted the danger. Personally taking command at the threatened point, the Duke sent an urgent appeal for assistance to Eugene. That officer, sorely pressed himself, clearly comprehended Marlborough's greater need. Without the slightest hesitation, he sent a strong body of cavalry galloping southward. They arrived in the nick of time, striking the charging French cavalry in flank and scattering them. Granted a respite by his friend's generous act, Marlborough restored the line. Wheeling artillery forward, he smothered Oberglau with heavy fire and ordered another infantry attack. That worked. The French in Oberglau, like their comrades to the north and in Blenheim, were trapped.

Throughout the fighting, those units of Marlborough that were destined to make the main attack had been steadily crossing the Nebel. Infantry led the way, followed closely by cavalrymen. Seeing the redcoats debouching from the

The Battle of Blenheim, 1704

swampy crossings, French cavalry cantered down from the ridge to engage. English infantrymen quickly formed stout squares to resist the attack. Because the French employed the obsolete caracole, Marlborough's men were able to hold their ground until friendly cavalry squadrons emerged to chase away survivors of the French effort. By 4:00 p.m., the entire Allied army had crossed the Nebel.

Marlborough's plan had succeeded admirably. At the decisive point he had massed, fresh squadrons of cavalry and infantry battalions. Opposing them were 60 French squadrons, most of which were already bloodied and tired, and 9 infantry battalions, comprised almost entirely of untrained recruits. But the Englishman waited. He wanted to assure that every unit along the line assaulted simultaneously. Having achieved this much, he was determined not to launch the main attack prematurely. For an hour, aides raced back and forth over the battlefield from Lutzingen to Blenheim, coordinating the final blow. Then, a few minutes before 5:00 p.m., Marlborough rode imposingly to the front and pointed his sword toward the enemy. Thus, the final act of the Battle of Blenheim began.

Moving at a walk so the infantry could keep pace, the 80 Allied squadrons swung majestically up the slope. *(See Map 5c.)* From one end of the battlefield to the other, tired Allied units surged forward with renewed vigor. Smoke, thick and acrid, blanketed the battle as tens of thousands of muskets spoke. But Tallard had eyes only for his center where, much too late, he now realized Marlborough was about to deliver the main blow. Unable to extricate units previously committed to Blenheim and Oberglau, and without a reserve, the French commander apprehensively ordered his cavalry forward. Better trained to begin with, and now fresher and more numerous as well, Marlborough's cavalry quickly repulsed that counterattack. Desperately, Tallard dispatched the 9 battalions of young recruits to cover his cavalry's reorganization. Eager to get into the fight, those green troops, standing in hollow squares, momentarily halted the English advance. Marlborough wheeled forward artillery pieces, which accompanied his lead elements, and methodically blasted the recruits to bits. Holding their ground like veterans, but standing alone, the recruits died in place, their corpses clearly outlining the block-like shape of their formations.

At that point, Marlborough ordered trumpeters to sound the charge. Starting with a brisk trot and riding boot to boot, with sabers waving overhead, Allied troopers gradually gathered speed until they crashed full-tilt into and through the demoralized French cavalry. The French line was severed cleanly; survivors became fugitives. Immediately, Allied squadrons turned right, while Marlborough led the rest to the left. French cavalrymen were destroyed, and infantry in Blenheim doomed. *(See Map 5d.)* On higher ground to the north, Marsin and Max Emmanuel, having perceived the decisive maneuver developing on their right, had hastily organized a fighting withdrawal. An orderly retreat plus the coming of night allowed many of the Bavarians to escape. But the French were not as fortunate. Tallard himself was captured, and at about 9:00 p.m. that night, survivors in Blenheim capitulated.

Victory had cost Marlborough and Eugene nearly a quarter · of the Allied army, including 6,000 killed. Enemy losses in dead and wounded were only slightly greater, but 15,000 prisoners had been taken and another 10,000 or so were unaccounted for, having deserted or drowned trying to swim across the Danube. Furthermore, virtually every item of equipment in the Franco-Bavarian camp fell into Allied hands.

The importance of Blenheim reached far beyond the brilliance of the tactical victory itself. Losing an entire army was an irredeemable blow to the prestige of Louis XIV. Thereafter, French fortunes declined, not to be revived until the advent of Napoleon nearly a century later. Concurrently, Allied morale and confidence increased markedly. One could hardly claim that any single factor forestalled French hegemony over Europe in the eighteenth century, but if pressed to select a single event that made the most significant contribution toward reversing Louis' drive to dominate Europe, the historian would have to point to the battle at Blenheim on the Danube.

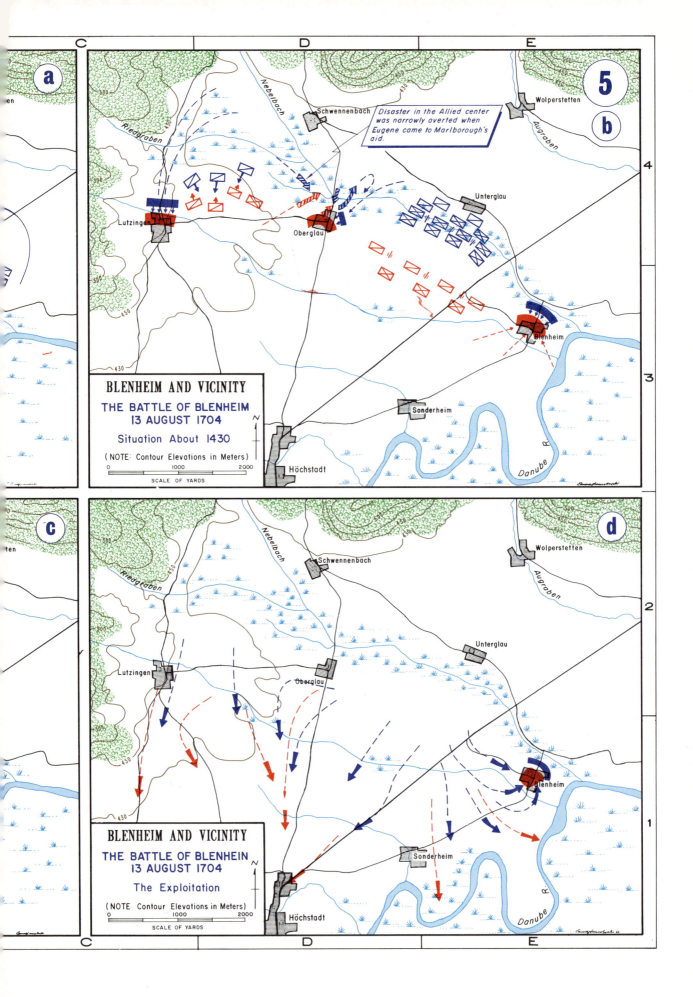

a

b

5

Schwennenbach

Wolperstetten

Disaster in the Allied center
was narrowly averted when
Eugene came to Marlborough's
aid.

4

Unterglau

Lutzingen

Oberglau

Blenheim

3

BLENHEIM AND VICINITY

**THE BATTLE OF BLENHEIM
13 AUGUST 1704**

Situation About 1430

(NOTE: Contour Elevations in Meters)

| | | |
| 0 | 1000 | 2000 |

SCALE OF YARDS

Sonderheim

Höchstadt

Danube R.

c

d

Schwennenbach

Wolperstetten

2

Lutzingen

Unterglau

Oberglau

Blenheim

1

BLENHEIM AND VICINITY

**THE BATTLE OF BLENHEIN
13 AUGUST 1704**

The Exploitation

(NOTE Contour Elevations in Meters)

| | | |
| 0 | 1000 | 2000 |

SCALE OF YARDS

Sonderheim

Höchstadt

Danube R.

C

D

E

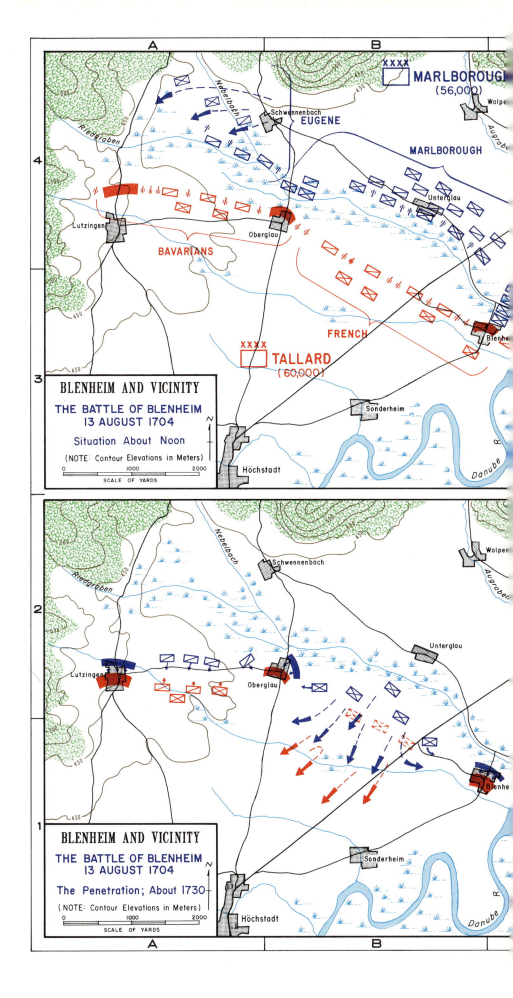

BLENHEIM AND VICINITY

**THE BATTLE OF BLENHEIM
13 AUGUST 1704**

Situation About Noon

(NOTE: Contour Elevations in Meters)

0   1000   2000
SCALE OF YARDS

BLENHEIM AND VICINITY

**THE BATTLE OF BLENHEIM
13 AUGUST 1704**

The Penetration; About 1730

(NOTE: Contour Elevations in Meters)

0   1000   2000
SCALE OF YARDS

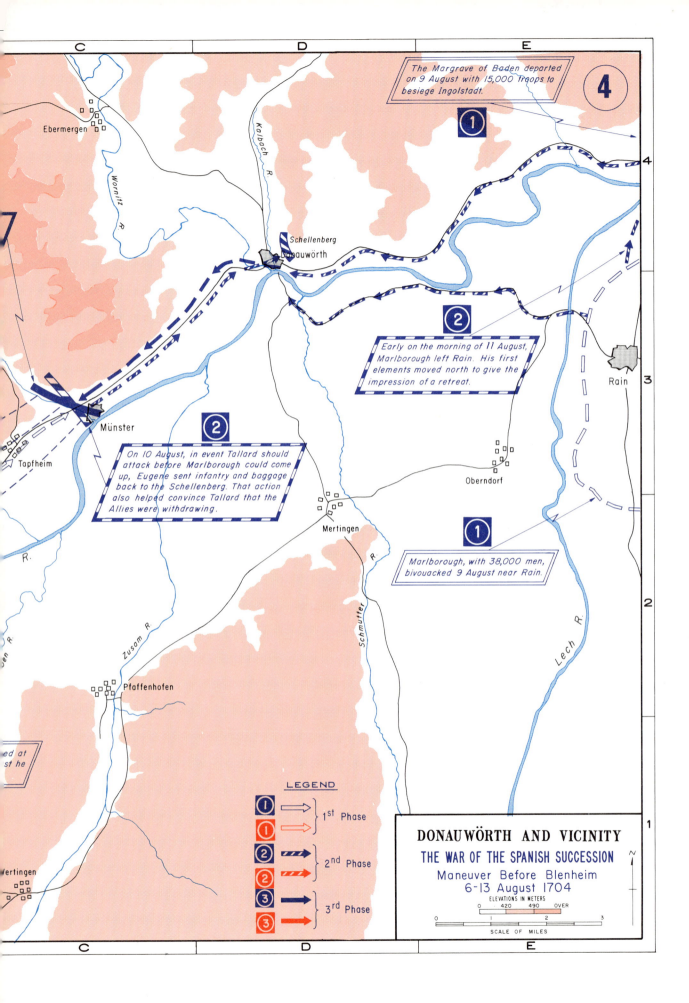

The Margrave of Baden departed on 9 August with 15,000 troops to besiege Ingolstadt.

④

①

Schellenberg
Donauwörth

②

Early on the morning of 11 August, Marlborough left Rain. His first elements moved north to give the impression of a retreat.

Rain

Münster

②

On 10 August, in event Tallard should attack before Marlborough could come up, Eugene sent infantry and baggage back to the Schellenberg. That action also helped convince Tallard that the Allies were withdrawing.

Tapfheim

Oberndorf

①

Mertingen

Marlborough, with 38,000 men, bivouacked 9 August near Rain.

Ebermergen

Wornitz R.

Kalbach R.

Schmutter R.

Lech R.

Zusam R.

Pfaffenhofen

Wertingen

LEGEND

① ⇨ ⟩ 1st Phase
①

② ⇢ ⟩ 2nd Phase
②

③ ➡ ⟩ 3rd Phase
③

DONAUWÖRTH AND VICINITY
THE WAR OF THE SPANISH SUCCESSION
Maneuver Before Blenheim
6-13 August 1704

ELEVATIONS IN METERS
0   420   490   OVER

0   1   2   3
SCALE OF MILES

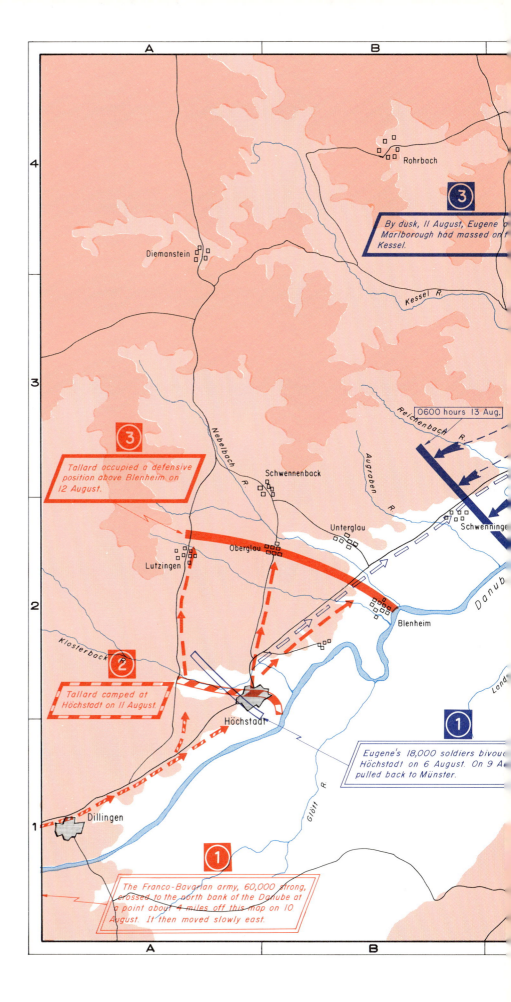

Diemanstein

Rohrbach

3

By dusk, 11 August, Eugene a
Marlborough had massed on f
Kessel.

Kessel R.

Reichenbach R.

0600 hours 13 Aug.

Nebelbach R.

Schwennenback

Augraben R.

3

Tallard occupied a defensive
position above Blenheim on
12 August.

Unterglau

Schwenninge

Oberglau

Lutzingen

Danub

Klosterback R.

2

Tallard camped at
Höchstadt on 11 August.

Blenheim

Höchstadt

1

Eugene's 18,000 soldiers bivoua
Höchstadt on 6 August. On 9 A
pulled back to Münster.

Glöit R.

Land

Dillingen

1

The Franco-Bavarian army, 60,000 strong,
crossed to the north bank of the Danube at
a point about 4 miles off this map on 10
August. It then moved slowly east.

3
C
D
E
1
2
3
4
SWEDEN
DENMARK
BALTIC SEA
Copenhagen
Malmo
Memel
Niemen R.
Tilsit
Konigsberg
PRUSSIA
Danzig
Elbing
Dirschau
Mewe
Marienwerder
Stralsund
Peenemünde
POMERANIA
Lubeck
MECKLENBURG
Hamburg
Stettin
Elbe R.
Weser R.
Bremen
BRANDENBURG
Oder R.
Thorn
Narew R.
Vistula R.
BRUNSWICK
Hanover
Brunswick
Havel R.
Berlin
Zorndorf
Kustrin
Frankfurt
Potsdam
Posen
Warta R.
Warsaw
Magdeburg
Dessau
Jankau
POLAND
Paderborn
SAXONY
Torgau
Glogau
Halle
Breitenfeld
Elbe R.
Cassel
HESSE-CASSEL
Rossbach
Leipzig
Lützen
SILESIA
Neisse R.
Leuthen
Breslau
MARLBOROUGH
(50,000)
Erfurt
Bautzen
Dresden
Oder R.
Jena
Vistula R.
Coburg
Eger
Cracow
Tarnow
Frankfurt
May
heim
WÜRZBURG
BAMBERG
Prague
Elbe R.
Wurzburg
Bamberg
Pilsen
BOHEMIA
UPPER PALATINATE
MORAVIA
7 June
Nuremberg
Zilina
Van R.
Brunn
BADEN
Nordlingen
Regensberg
2 July
Donauworth
TRANSYLVANIA
WURTTEMBURG
Blenheim
Ingolstadt
Isar R.
Passau
22 June
Rain
Landshut
Ulm
XXXX
Augsburg
ELECTOR OF BAVARIA
(45,000)
Danube R.
Vienna
Miskolc
Iller R.
Lech R.
Munich
Landsberg
AUSTRIA
BAVARIA
Salzburg
Marlborough was joined here by Eugene and Baden, bringing Allied strength to nearly 100,000. Eugene then took 30,000 to block Tallard.
Budapest
Tisza R.
Innsbruck
HUNGARY
TYROL
Graz
Brenner Pass
XXX
OTTOMAN EMPIRE
STYRIA
Trent
Ljubliana
REPUBLIC of VENICE
Trieste
Zagreb
XXXX
VENDOME
(50,000)
Milan
Verona
Padua
Venice
Fiume
Pavia
Cremona
Po R.
Ferrara
N
50
0
50
100
SCALE OF MILES

CENTRAL EUROPE

THE WAR OF THE SPANISH SUCCESSION

The March to the Danube, 1704

N O R T H   S E A

Due to severe dynastic and religious strife
during the 17th Century, boundaries were often
subjected to sudden, major displacement. The
extremely fragmented nature of Germany was
another factor accounting for confusion over
political borders. For clarity, boundaries depicted
are very general and simplified; there has been
no attempt to trace them precisely.

ENGLAND

○ Birmingham

Norwich ○

Ipswich ○

Thames R. London

Southampton ○
○ Portsmouth   Dover ○

THE NETHERLANDS

Amsterdam

Rhine R.
Nijmegen

CHURCH LANDS

Ems R.

Ostend ○   Eindhoven ○

19 May

Antwerp
XXXX
OVERKIRK
(40,000)

Cologne

SPANISH NETHERLANDS

Calais ○
○ Dunkirk

Lys R.
Lille ○   Oudenarde ○   Brussels   Maastricht ○

Ramillies ○   Meuse R.   Liege   Aachen ○

Bonn ○

Arras ○   Malplaquet ○   Namur ○
Sambre R.

Coblenz

26 May

Le Havre ○

Caen ○   ○ Rouen

○ St Quentin

Seine R.

Oise R.   Laon ○   Rocroi ○   Sedan ○
XXXX
VILLEROI
(30,000)

Luxembourg ○

Mainz

Moselle R.

LOWER PALATINE

XXX

Worms ○

Soisson ○   Reims ○

Aisne R.

Evreux ○

Marne R.

○ Dreux   **Paris**

Chalons ○

Verdun ○

Mannheim ○

LORRAINE

Metz ○
XXXX
TALLARD
(40,000)

Chartres ○

Toul ○

Nancy ○

Strasbourg ○   Sossba

VOSGES

○ Sens   Troyes ○

ALSACE

Rhine R.

○ Orleans

Loire R.

F R A N C E

NOTE: The French shifted
forces as Marlborough marched
southward.

Turkheim ○

○ Freiburg

Mulhouse ○

Belfort ○

○ Basel

Angers ○

○ Tours

FRANCHE COMTE

Poitiers ○

Nevers ○

Vienne R.

○ Bern

SWITZERLAND

Limoges ○

Loire R.

Geneva ○

MILA

Lyon ○

Rhone R.

SAVOY

Turin ○

○ Valence

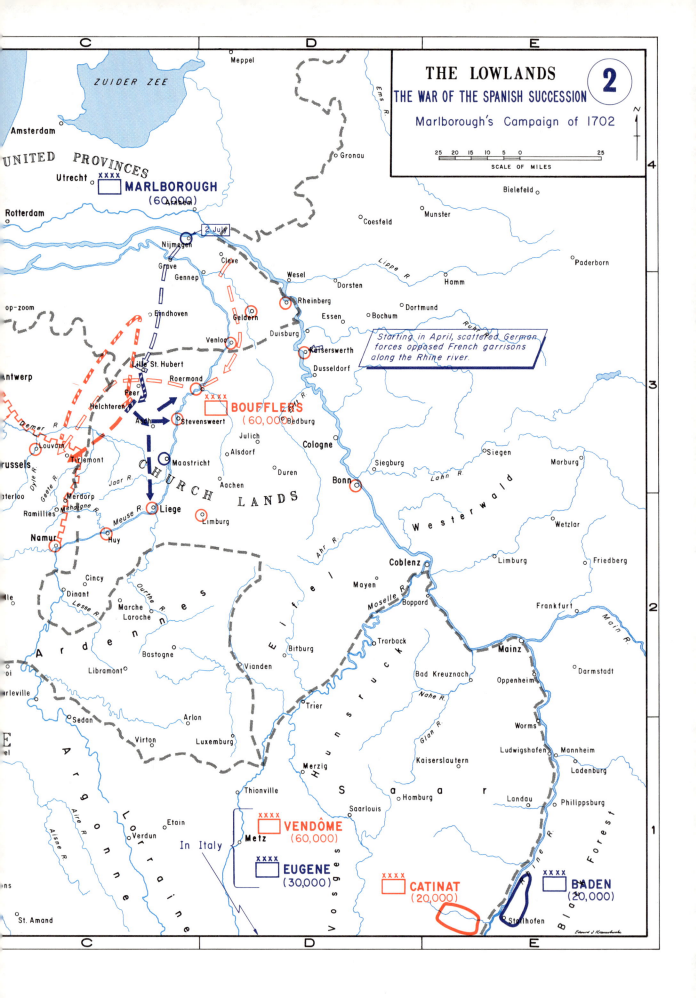

SCALE OF MILES

25 20 15 10 5 0   25

ZUIDER ZEE

Amsterdam

UNITED PROVINCES

Utrecht   XXXX **MARLBOROUGH**
(60,000)

Rotterdam

Arnhem

Nijmegen   2 July

Grave

Gennep

op-zoom

Eindhoven

Venloo

Lille St. Hubert

Peer

Helchteren

Roermond

Stevensweert

XXXX **BOUFFLERS**
(60,000)

antwerp

Demer R.

Louvain

russels

Tirlemont

Merdorp

Ramillies

Meheigne R.

terloo

Namur

Huy

Meuse R.

Liege

Limburg

Geete R.

Jaar R.

Maastricht

CHURCH LANDS

Aachen

Duren

Alsdorf

Julich

Aschen

Bedburg

Cologne

Bonn

Meppel

Gronau

Cleve

Wesel

Rheinberg

Geldern

Duisburg

Kaiserswerth

Dusseldorf

Lippe R.

Dorsten

Essen

Bochum

Coesfeld

Munster

Bielefeld

Paderborn

Hamm

Dortmund

Starting in April, scattered German forces opposed French garrisons along the Rhine river.

Siegburg

Siegen

Marburg

Westerwald

Lahn R.

Wetzlar

Coblenz

Mayen

Ahr R.

Limburg

Friedberg

Frankfurt

Main R.

Dyle R.

Dinant

Cincy

Marche

Laroche

Lesse R.

Ourthe R.

Ardennes

Bastogne

Libramont

Eifel

Bitburg

Vianden

Trarback

Moselle R.

Boppard

Bad Kreuznach

Nahe R.

Mainz

Oppenheim

Darmstadt

Worms

oi

rleville

Sedan

Arlon

Luxemburg

Trier

Hunsruck

S   a   a   r

Glan R.

Kaiserslautern

Homburg

Ludwigshafen

Mannheim

Ladenburg

Landau

Philippsburg

Black Forest

Virton

Merzig

Thionville

Saarlouis

A   r   g   o   n   n   e

Aire R.

Etain

Verdun

Metz

In Italy

XXXX **VENDÔME**
(60,000)

XXXX **EUGENE**
(30,000)

XXXX **CATINAT**
(20,000)

XXXX **BADEN**
(20,000)

Stollhofen

Rhine R.

Vosges

Aisne R.

ns

St. Amand

L   o   r   r   a   i   n   e

Edward J. Krasnoborski

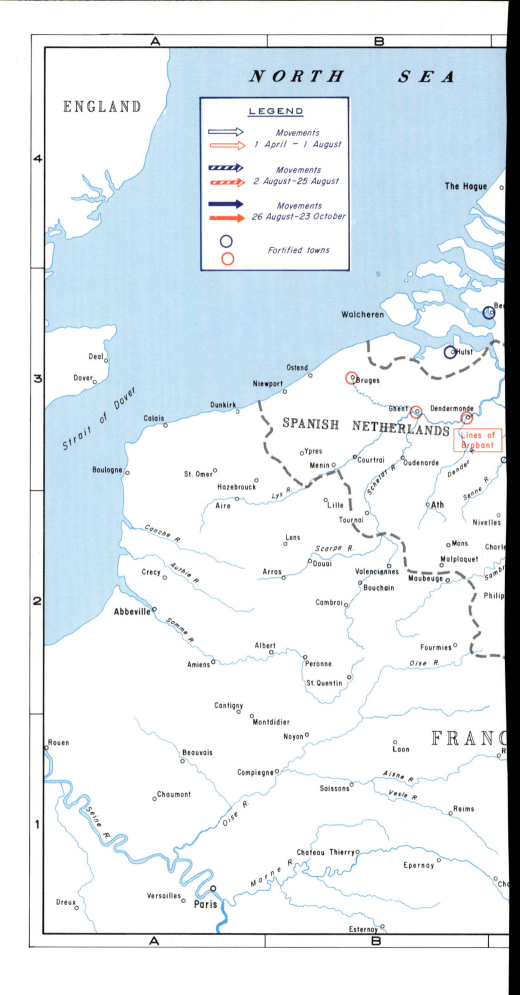

The Decline of France

6

After the Battle of Blenheim, the strategic initiative in the war clearly belonged to the Allies. The blow to French arms had mental as well as physical repercussions. Worried over the drastic turn of events, Louis XIV consolidated his forces and anxiously waited to see where the Allies would next strike. For their part, Marlborough and Eugene had every intention of exploiting the advantage they had gained.

Joined by Prince Louis of Baden, who never quite forgave the Duke for keeping him out of the Battle of Blenheim, Marlborough and Eugene pushed westward, straight for the Rhine. Crossing near Philippsburg, they promptly laid siege to French citadels there. Marlborough, never losing sight of plans to invade France in order to defeat Louis once and for all, began to lay the groundwork for such an invasion in the next year. Leaving his allies on the Rhine that autumn (1704), he made a rapid march directly across the mountains to descend on and capture an astounded enemy garrison at Trier, on the Moselle River. Thanks to Marlborough's rapid movement and the sluggishness of the French, by year's end, Allied armies occupied the entire lower Moselle Valley from Coblenz to Trier. The stage was set for a climactic campaign in 1705.

The Campaign of 1705

Following a busy winter, during which he made preparations for his great invasion, the Duke returned eagerly to the United Provinces in April 1705. He was in the best of spirits; a determined drive, he felt sure, would bring the war to a triumphant close. But his high hopes were rudely shaken by coalition differences. The Dutch leaders did not support his offensive tactics, and the various German princes, no longer fearful of a French invasion, were not overly enthusiastic about meeting Alliance obligations. Marlborough, by dint of sheer persuasion and personality, finally obtained reluctant

Dutch approval; Eugene, by threatening to resign, gained Imperial support for the invasion. But their efforts were in vain. When the Allied army finally assembled, the season was late, supplies were not at hand, units were woefully understrength, and the French blocked the way with a superior force under Marshal Villars, Louis' most able commander. Sadly acknowledging the wreckage of his grand design, the Duke decided to wage a campaign in Flanders, hoping to salvage something tangible from the year.

Using interior lines* made possible by Allied control of the major rivers, Marlborough surprised the French by quickly moving his army to the north. He then outmaneuvered them and succeeded in breaking through the formidable Lines of Brabant near Tirlemont. Saber in hand, the Duke led the cavalry charge which assured that the breach remained open.

A chance to cut off the disorganized enemy force grew dim when Dutch generals refused to support their English comrades. As had so often happened before, frustration stalked the Duke. Time and again, timorous Dutch deputies or generals thwarted his schemes; time and again, French armies walked serenely out of traps. When he could endure the interference no longer, Marlborough petitioned the United Provinces to grant him uncontested control of the Allied forces. In response, the provinces allowed him to make two or three marches without prior approval of a council of war—but Dutch deputies, in any case, had to sanction any contemplated battle.

Resolving to make the most of the limited concession, Marlborough used his three free marches to turn the entire French army. In August, striking first south and then turning sharply west and ultimately north, he passed the village of

---

*A force has interior lines when it can move its units from one part of a battlefield or theater of operations to another part more rapidly than can the enemy force opposing it. The favorable condition (interior lines) is created by the force either occupying a central position relative to the enemy or having superior lateral communications relative to the enemy.

Waterloo and stationed his massed army astride the French route of retreat. Outnumbering his foe by 4 to 3 and occupying a superior position, the Duke was sure that even the Dutch would agree to attack. Still they refused. Bitterly watching the French army file by, Marlborough lamented, "I am at this moment ten years older than I was four days ago."

The year ended on that sour note, although Allied efforts had not been entirely wasted. Two results of the campaign of 1705 combined to make possible a battle in 1706. Louis XIV, wanting to end the struggle, had secretly approached Queen Anne. That move fightened the Dutch, who immediately decided to grant Marlborough freedom of action in the forthcoming year. Also, analyzing events in 1705 with surprising logic, Louis concluded that Marlborough was after all a mediocre commander who owed success at Blenheim to Eugene and luck. The Sun King decided to permit his generals to fight the Englishman—under favorable circumstances, of course. With both friend and foe in agreement on the point, chances appeared good for a battle in 1706. Marlborough, who always sought battle, did not disappoint them.

The Campaign of 1706

Wanting to join Eugene for another campaign far removed from political centers, Marlborough at first contemplated operations in Italy. However, a drive by Villars carried the French back across the Rhine near Phillipsburg and attracted Imperial attention. At the same time, aggressive moves by Marshal Villeroi at the head of a powerful French army in Flanders demanded counteraction. Battle in Italy was no longer possible. Marlborough would have to fight in the Lowlands—and make do without Eugene's invaluable assistance.

Early May found Marlborough at Maastricht, gathering forces for what he assumed would be another interminable season of futile maneuvering. He was never more wrong. For once the Dutch had their dander up, while Villeroi, urged on by Louis, was even then on the march. Puzzled by his opponent's aggressive advance, the Duke nonetheless welcomed it. Quickly moving to meet Villeroi before he could change his mind, Marlborough happily accepted the challenge. Each general, underestimating the other's eagerness to engage, misjudged the rate of closing. As a result, advance guards clashed in the morning fog on May 23, 1706, near the village of Ramillies. Neither commander had intended to fight there, but both knew the ground well from previous occupation. The two armies promptly deployed for battle. Villeroi planned to defend, while Marlborough considered only offensive actions. *(See Map 6a.)*

Villeroi anchored his right on the Mehaigne River and

drew up the bulk of his best infantry and cavalry along the level, open ground south of Ramillies. He also entrenched that town, and stretched lesser forces from Ramillies through Offus to Autre-Eglise. Slopes, orchards, and swamps provided a good measure of protection for his weaker left. A successful attack, he thought, could only strike south of Ramillies—and so many units stood there that any assault would be doomed. Actually, Villeroi's deployment was good, with the exception that he retained no reserve and occupied a concave line. To reinforce either end, French troops would have to march the arc of a curve, while the Allies could reinforce faster using the chord. Moreover, Villeroi's position suffered that liability inherent in any defensive deployment: it forfeited the initiative to the enemy.

Reconnoitering while his army closed on the site, Marlborough immediately perceived the advantage of his tactical interior lines, but also noted a terrain depression leading all the way from behind his right to the open area south of Ramillies. Possessing that intuitive feel for terrain which marks all great battle captains, the Duke immediately devised his plan. He would initially strengthen his right wing and attack the French left, obliging Villeroi to weaken his right-center; then, shifting troops secretly and swiftly from right to left, he would mass sufficient forces to make a penetration south of Ramillies.

Directing his arriving units into position according to his scheme, the Duke confided in no one. Blandly but firmly, he refused to be dissuaded by arguments from subordinates who objected to such a heavy concentration of combat power on the right, where it would be wasted in the rough terrain. At about 1:00 p.m., artillerists commenced that duel of guns which usually preceded eighteenth century battles. An hour later, Marlborough ordered the attack to begin.

Forthwith, Dutch infantry stormed Taviers. *(See Map 6b.)* Their furious onslaught gained a quick lodgment, causing Villeroi to dispatch an infantry brigade from his strong center to support the harried defenders. Those reinforcements, along with 14 squadrons of dragoons, were pulled into the savage struggle and pinned down. Survivors of Blenheim might have had an eerie feeling that they had somehow been through all this before. Just then, Villeroi's attention was drawn toward his left, where English troops were clawing their way doggedly up the rough slopes. Those bright British coats waved a red flag in the Marshal's mind, blinding him to the realities around him.

Louis XIV had precisely and emphatically instructed Villeroi on the tactics to use in a battle with Marlborough. "Pay particular attention to that part of the line which will endure the first shock of the English troops," the monarch had ordered. Under Louis' centralized system of warfare, such guidance was taken as a direct order to be disobeyed at the field commander's peril—no matter that shifting situations on a battlefield demand immediate, on-the-spot assessments and decisions. Accordingly, Villeroi obediently rushed battalions and squadrons from his right and center to reinforce his left, which was indeed enduring "the first shock of the English troops." With that fatal move, he fell in perfectly with Marlborough's scheme.

At about that time, Dutch General Overkirk, at the head of 69 Dutch and Danish cavalry squadrons, clashed with the 68 French squadrons of cavalry and several infantry units that were still in position south of Ramillies. Neither side could gain an advantage, but both continued the fight. Meanwhile, Marlborough began to shift troops from right to left. First came 18 cavalry squadrons pounding up the covered way to raise Allied strength at the point of decision to 87 squadrons. Then, much to the disgust of his countrymen on the right, who had believed all along that they were conducting the main assault, Marlborough withdrew those attacking redcoats and transferred them to the left. On their arrival, the Duke had massed 108 squadrons against his opponents' 68—and the French had not been aware of any lateral movement at all.

Marlborough personally led the grand charge and twice narrowly escaped death. His troops swept through Villeroi's line, shattering and scattering the demoralized defenders. *(See Map 6c.)* While Marlborough then paused briefly to reorganize his troops and to wipe out fanatic resistance in the village of Ramillies, Villeroi frantically gathered battered remnants of his army for a stand along a hastily devised line extending westward of Autre-Eglise *(see Map 6d.).* Marlborough then rolled up the new French left flank with his disgruntled English infantry, and broke Villeroi's front with a headlong cavalry charge. The French stampeded.

Safety for the French, however, did not exist in flight. Brutally and relentlessly, Allied riders, flushed with victory, pursued the fugitives through the night, flashing sabers and doing their macabre work until weary arms were drained of all strength. It was Marlborough's one real pursuit, a most unusual event in that age of overcautious warfare; and it succeeded in destroying the French army. Villeroi brought in to the Fortress of Louvain only some 15,000 dazed and bedraggled survivors—45,000 had been lost. Allied casualties totalled approximately 4,000. Ramillies had been a direct confrontation between Marlborough's unhampered genius and the centralized system erected by Louis XIV. Whether due to flexibility, genius, or both, the Englishman had won decisively.

Marlborough did not pause after the initial pursuit. Following up his victory, he drove his troops almost viciously to take advantage of the temporary French weakness in the Lowlands. *(See Map 7.)* By the time snow ended the campaigning season, he had cleared Louis' troops from the area east of a line running roughly from Ostend to Namur. It had been a disastrous season for the French. Conversely, 1706 may have been Marlborough's greatest year, vying only with 1704, the year of Blenheim.

During 1706, Marlborough's partner in providing outstanding leadership for the Grand Alliance had also been extremely successful. Eugene, in a campaign that can only be described as spectacular, reconquered the Po valley, crushed a French army at Turin, killed Marshal Marsin, and ended the war in Italy.

The high point of 1706 provides a good place to break away from Marlborough's activities to explore other contemporary events. The War of the Spanish Succession was, of course, being waged in many theaters, while another monumental clash, the Great Northern War, transpired simultaneously. Then, too, a trend surfacing in Prussia at this time deserves at least a glance.

The War Overall and Other Developments

The Mediterranean

From the outset, Imperial and French troops had fought over northern Italy, while England's naval superiority had enabled Queen Anne's power to be exerted in the Mediterranean. Trade with Turkey and the Middle East was the magnet irresistibly drawing English interest to that theater. Portugal and England entered into an alliance in 1703, which has endured to the twentieth century. Gibraltar fell under English attack just a week before Blenheim. Several poorly planned and even more poorly executed operations in Spain brought few laurels to English arms, but Spain's very weakness often offset British blunders to give the redcoats victory. Gradually, as the years wore on, English garrisons occupied most of Spain's major coastal cities, although as far as Her Majesty's Government was concerned, peninsular adventures proved singularly unprofitable and indecisive.

The Colonial Scene

American colonists supported their monarch in the War of the Spanish Succession, but they insisted upon naming it Queen Anne's War.

When French settlements sprang up at the turn of the century along the Gulf Coast and near the Great Lakes, English colonists openly feared foreign encirclement. Security, they felt, lay in total ejection of French and Spanish influence from the New World. Thus, when war came, colonial leaders willfully grabbed the opportunity to smite their unwanted and unloved neighbors.

Carolinians noisily if somewhat ineffectively invaded Florida, and New Englanders raised a force to besiege Port Royal. The latter expedition disintegrated from lack of discipline and want of leaders who knew how to conduct a siege. Border raids were launched when one side or the other could entice local Indians into joining the fray. Some colonies, however, remained haughtily aloof from it all, much to the anger of their more aggressive neighbors. Finally, after five years of futility, the colonists sent an agent to England to petition the Queen for a contingent of regular soldiers. Three years later—no one seems to have done things hastily in those days—London agreed to send over a force to cooperate with a colonial army in ousting the French from Canada.

Gleefully expecting assistance, the colonies evinced a greater degree of cooperation than they had previously exhibited by sending 1,500 men to Albany in May 1709. There they prepared for the march north, and waited. Summer passed. Infuriated, the Americans disbanded in September. A month later, word arrived that the British expedition had been cancelled. Colonial military cooperation had been somewhat enhanced, but respect for the mother country was very much diminished.

There was, however, to be another try. A new Tory government in England, looking for a way to counter past Whig victories won by Marlborough, seized upon North America. Colonists gazed in awe as 60 ships transporting 5,000 soldiers anchored in Boston Harbor in June 1711. Remembering how they had been left in the lurch just two years before, Americans reluctantly agreed again to field a body of troops to advance up the Hudson Valley, while the British expeditionary force sailed up the St. Lawrence River. Over some opposition, the colonial force was formed, and tramped off toward Lake Champlain. The fleet headed for Canada and disaster. Rain storms, thick fog, contrary winds, and a negligent pilot contrived to drive eight ships onto rocks, drowning 700 regulars, 35 women, and 200 sailors. Discouraged, the British commander returned to England, leaving incensed Americans staring once more over Lake Champlain's placid waters.

With that, Queen Anne's War ended. Nothing had been resolved. France and Spain still possessed posts all around the English colonies. Compared to the scale of fighting in Europe, the war had been ludicrously small. In 11 years, French and Spanish deaths combined were no more than 60; New England lost some 200 and the Carolinas maybe 150. Indians and drowned Englishmen accounted for the bulk of casualties. Colonial officials had failed to forge any sort of effective military organization, nor had the frustrating attempts to cooperate with troops from England improved

colonial regard for regular forces. One legacy emerged—the indecisive ending assured that the New World would continue to be a battleground in the long contest between France and England.

The Great Northern War, 1700–1721

While much of Europe watched the spectacle of Louis XIV's struggle with England and her allies, a warring Vasa lost the Swedish Empire built by Gustavus Adolphus. Although he first gave them all a terrible fright, Charles XII eventually saw Russia, Prussia, Saxony, Poland, Denmark, and Hanover begin the dismemberment of his domains.

Hegemony over the Baltic region was the source of the quarrel. Since Gustavus had first made Sweden supreme, the balance of power had been upset by the emergence of a new factor: a giant of a Russian leader, Peter the Great. Peter, standing close to seven feet tall, with appetites and aspirations to match his physique, came to the Russian throne in 1689 when he was just 17 years old. Practically by virtue of his own brute strength, Peter dragged Russia out of the backwardness that had for so long shackled that country. An army, a navy, economic and educational systems, a court life—all these and more he determined to have, all patterned after western European models. Although his reforms were far from complete in 1700, Russia's rising strength made a clash with Sweden inevitable.

The time seemed propitious for a trial when a 15-year-old lad ascended the throne of Sweden in 1697. Within two years, Russia, Poland, and Denmark had formed a secret alliance against their northern neighbor. The next year, war began. To everyone's astonishment, however, the young king, Charles XII, was anything but a pushover. Inheriting the Vasa genius—and, unfortunately, the Vasa madness as well—Charles soon blazed for himself a niche in the pantheon of great warriors. Imbued with the offensive spirit of his famous forebearer, young Charles immediately lashed out. An unexpected invasion knocked Denmark out of the war at its very beginning. Then, shifting rapidly across the Baltic, Charles located Peter and 40,000 Russians outside Narva. Unhesitatingly striking in the midst of a swirling snow storm, the young king led his 8,000 Swedes straight for the heart of the Russian horde. Unable to withstand the savage assault, Peter and numbed survivors fled in disorder, leaving 10,000 dead. In a single season, Charles had brought one enemy to heel and had snatched a resounding victory from another. Henceforth, no one took the swaggering teenager lightly.

That winter, Charles made a basic strategic error which eventually cost him the war. Russia, under the driving leadership of Peter, was potentially Sweden's major enemy. Charles should have followed up his victory by destroying Peter,

Statue of Charles XII of Sweden

while the tsar still reeled from the rout of Narva. Instead, the King turned against his third enemy, Augustus of Saxony and Poland.* Marching from one end of their flat country to the other, Charles repeatedly inflicted defeat on the Poles. But, having no natural obstacle against which to pin his opponent, he never managed a battle of annihilation. After each loss, remnants of the Polish forces would assemble in a sanctuary beyond some neutral border, receive new injections of money from Peter—who was greatly benefitting from this war-by-proxy—and appear again. For six years, Charles' Swedes sought final victory—a most elusive will-o'-the-wisp. Augustus, safe in Saxony, was content to have Poles bear the brunt of Swedish rage. Finally, in 1706, Charles invaded Saxony to force Augustus out of the war once and for all. That worked. (Marlborough, worried lest the combative Swede should join the French, hurriedly arranged a meeting. Through a combination of flattery and bribery, the Duke removed any such inclination Charles might have had.) At long last, Charles fastened his attention once more on Russia. But the Russian Army of 1707 was not the whipped shadow that had retreated in disgrace from Narva in 1700.

Peter had used the breathing space to recruit, equip, and train a modern army. His men and officers had learned the art and science of war from imported foreign professional

soldiers, and Peter had staged elaborate war games to perfect their techniques. By 1707, he was prepared to face the Swedes. The Russian Army was in no way a great one, but it was solid, and it was big. Vast Russia herself was an ally. Charles, having erred in delaying his invasion of Russia, erred a second time when he decided to carry out the invasion after Russia had readied itself.

Early in 1708, Charles, hoping for a fight, advanced toward Moscow with over 40,000 men. Peter declined to meet the Swedish army, preferring to trade miles for time. Abruptly, banking on help from a Cossack leader, Charles turned southward and marched toward the Ukraine. However, the expected reinforcements never materialized, while a harsh winter in 1708–1709 reduced Swedish effectives to fewer than 20,000. Russians then blocked all efforts to resupply the invaders, leaving Charles isolated deep in hostile country. Peter finally offered battle at Poltava, near the Dnieper river, and Charles, in desperation, accepted the wild gamble. Outnumbered by more than 3 to 1, he nonetheless chose to attack the entrenched Russians. Just before the battle, Charles received a wound that partially incapacitated him, thus removing him from his accustomed place at the head of his army. He participated in the fight, but from a litter. There are some who argue that had Charles been able to lead in person as was his wont, the Swedes would have won. Perhaps. As it was, they did well in the face of such odds, and once even succeeded in pushing Peter to the point of retreat. However, Charles' strategic blunder was so great that no tactical victory could have redeemed

SHOCK TACTICS OF CHARLES XII

---

*The sire of 354 illegitimate children, Augustus became known as "Augustus the Strong." The eldest of those offspring was Maurice de Saxe, later to become France's leading marshal and a military philosopher of considerable repute.

it. As it was, the Battle of Poltava was a smashing Russian success; the entire Swedish army perished except for Charles and perhaps 1,500 who escaped to Turkey.

Poltava ended Sweden's sojourn as a great power, and signaled to the world the rise of Russia.

Interestingly, during a period in which generals made every effort to sustain an unbroken line of fire, and shock tactics were all but ignored, Charles had gained victory after victory by speed and shock, furious onslaught, and violent impact of flesh and steel. Knowingly or intuitively, he had multiplied mass by velocity to obtain such shock at the point of contact that opponents, arrayed linearly and relying on musketry, were almost invariably overwhelmed. His assaults were tornadoes in an age of calm breezes. Despite Charles' repeated triumphs, however, tactics of shock were not adopted by others, perhaps because such vehement and vigorous methods were essentially out of place in the Age of Reason.

The Rise of Prussia

Between the Thirty Years' War and the end of the War of the Spanish Succession, Brandenburg-Prussia emerged as the strongest of the German states. If that period can be called the beginning of the militaristic state later known as Prussia, it is appropriate and not too simplistic to observe that the country was conceived in conflict, born in battle, and suckled in strife. In retrospect, it would have been surprising had the tiny, landlocked state survived *without* developing a disproportionately large military establishment.

Under timid, vacillating leadership during most of the Thirty Years' War, Brandenburg had been a helpless doormat upon which every army had trampled. The state did not escape the levy of death and devastation which marked that war, losing practically all its industry and trade, and perhaps half its population. Toward war's end Brandenburg lay prostrate. However, the Duchy of Prussia, which had been linked to Brandenburg in 1618, was practically untouched. A young, energetic leader became Elector in 1649: Frederick William, later to be known as the "Great Elector." Building on the base of relatively prosperous Prussia, Frederick William briskly began to resettle and revitalize his razed lands. An inescapable lesson of the Thirty Years' War was that any state which could not defend itself was doomed. Frederick William promptly enlarged his small standing army to over 25,000 men. Wielding that force to defend his lands while mobilizing his population to restore them, the Elector gradually built a viable country.

When Frederick William died in 1688, he handed over to his son, Frederick, the reins of one of the two strongest states in Germany; Prussia's only competitor was Bavaria. As his price for joining the coalition against France, Frederick exacted recognition of Prussia as a kingdom. He was crowned King Frederick I in Prussia in 1701. During the War of the Spanish Succession, Prussia loyally supported Marlborough with soldiers, sending a contingent that ultimately numbered 40,000. Prussians played a part in every one of the Duke's great battles, earning praise and gaining experience. Because Bavaria had chosen the losing side, Prussia emerged from the war unchallenged as the most powerful German state. Frederick I, dying just as the war ended, bequeathed to his son, Frederick William I, a disciplined, industrious people; a reservoir of experienced war veterans; and a militaristic outlook.

Thus Prussia joined Russia in stepping into the vacuum of power left by the demise of Sweden and the derailment of France. Both were destined to become deeply involved in future European wars.

Concluding Years in the War of the Spanish Succession

Following the great victories in 1706, Allied fortunes in the main theater of war took a turn for the worse. Events seemed caught up in a pattern of alternating years of success and debacle. French arms had predominated in 1701, 1703, and 1705; Marlborough in 1702, 1704, and 1706. That cycle was not merely coincidental; it flowed naturally from the Allied concept of limited war. Rather than steadfastly following one clear path through to victory, members of the Grand Alliance were prone to relax once French pressure was eased, reacting only when danger became imminent. Successful endeavors in the field, therefore, tended not to lead to rapid victory, but, ironically, to prolonged warfare.

When nations wage war halfheartedly, they must expect commensurate results. The favorable events of 1706 primed Marlborough to drive in for the kill in 1707; but his allies, complacent and wholly satisfied with limited gains, had neither the Duke's jugular instinct nor his comprehension of what constituted a decisive objective. The Emperor sent Eugene on a useless expedition down the boot of Italy, in Spain Valencia was lost, Dutch deputies refused to consider giving battle in Flanders, and German princes ignored their security. Abruptly ending the Allied repose, Marshal Villars took advantage of his lax enemy to cross the Rhine. Raiding virtually unopposed through central Germany, he sent patrols down the Danube as far as Blenheim. A few marches at the end of the season gained Marlborough some territory in Flanders, but, all in all, 1707 was a wasted year. Marlborough's discussion with Charles XII was nearly the only thing that had turned out well.

Dissension was weakening the Grand Alliance. Fear of Louis XIV had held the coalition together for six years, although Marlborough's diplomatic finesse and military prowess had contributed in no small measure to keeping the disparate nations working together. Now, as the French threat diminished and war weariness increased, latent national rivalries revived. Moreover, unable while campaigning to defend himself from intrigues at court, Marlborough found his political strength constantly eroding. Previously untouchable and once entirely free of political wirepulling from London, the Duke came increasingly under attack and surveillance. For a time he was safe, because the coalition would accept no other commander-in-chief; but unless the war could be ended quickly, a split in the Grand Alliance seemed inevitable.

Events led to battle in 1708. For his part, Louis XIV intended to operate aggressively in Flanders with an army 110,000 strong, putting even more pressure on the quavering coalition and forcing the peace that his bankrupt and fast-weakening state sorely needed. Across the line, Marlborough decided to summon Eugene to Flanders, where the famous pair could act in concert. The Elector of Hanover (one day to become George I of England) commanded 40,000 Germans on the upper Rhine, Eugene had 45,000 Imperialists on the Moselle, and Marlborough led 90,000 Dutch and English in Flanders. According to Marlborough's master plan, Eugene would shift to Flanders in a surprise move, and the combined armies would break through the border fortifications to invade France.

The Battle of Oudenarde

Internal problems in Austria delayed Eugene's concentration, permitting the French to move first in an advance toward Holland. Marlborough countered with a shrewd maneuver, blocking his enemy near Brussels. Both forces waited. When word arrived in early July that Eugene was on his way by forced marches, the French had to act. Marshal Vendôme commanded, but Louis XIV's grandson, the Duke of Burgundy, accompanied the French troops. Burgundy had inherited his grandfather's ineptitude at soldiering, a fact he proved by overruling Vendôme to order a foolish move northward toward Ghent and Bruges. That decision made a battle possible and, for a change, Dutch deputies did not demur.

Eugene arrived three days in advance of his hard-marching army. He and Marlborough agreed to grasp the opportunity then available, rather than waiting for a larger force to be assembled. Accordingly, the Anglo-Dutch army hastened toward Oudenarde to slice across the French line of communication. A race developed. The French attempted to retrace their steps in order to reach Lille and safety, but Marlborough, energetically driving his men through the night of July 10–11,

arrived first. When advance elements made contact near Oudenarde, Vendôme could not believe that he was faced by more than a detachment, for Marlborough's army had been 50 miles away just two days before. Hence, he ordered the "detachment" brushed aside so that his march could continue. As Marlborough's units streamed across the Scheldt River, Vendôme's continued to close on the town. A test of strength there would be, but not the typical setpiece affair. It would be fluid rather than formal, improvised rather than devised. It was to be more a twentieth century melee than a classic eighteenth century clash.

The battle opened in mid-afternoon on July 11, 1708, when English cavalry struck four Swiss battalions in Eyne, capturing three and destroying the fourth. That charge rocked Vendôme's troops back on their heels, a loss of initiative they never regained. Gradually, as more and more units arrived on both sides, the two armies deployed in a ragged line along a muddy stream, the Diepenbeck. *(See Map, page 94.)* Among the first on the scene, Marlborough and Eugene quickly surveyed the situation. The developing line of contact was clearly visible, marked by puffs of smoke and multicolored uniforms. The Allies were fighting with an unfordable river directly to their rear—a defeat would be total, but the two generals seem not to have been greatly worried by that. On the right, the Allied flank hung in the air, dangerously inviting a French envelopment. Marlborough, planning to mass on his other wing, decided to accept the risk, but never for a moment took his eye off that vulnerable point. Only one piece of terrain in the entire area was dominant, the Boser Couter, a large eminence rising beyond and behind the French right. From the first, Marlborough had decided to send his main attack thundering down the slopes of that hill.

Marlborough's major problem was to lock his opponent in struggle along the Diepenbeck, assuring always that his own vulnerable right flank was not rolled up, while rushing enough troops over the Oudenarde bridges to launch the decisive assault from the Boser Couter. To Eugene, the Duke handed the heavy responsibility of commanding the crucial right, thus showing his great concern over that wing. As a matter of fact, Vendôme had seen the flaw in the Allied position, but his attempt to attack there was vetoed by Burgundy, who apparently never managed to comprehend what was happening. Later, when Eugene appeared to be having trouble holding, Marlborough immediately withdrew troops from the center and sent them speeding to the right. Overkirk, the battling old Dutch general who had conducted the decisive attack at Ramillies, finally worked into position atop the Boser Couter, with perhaps an hour's daylight remaining.

The French failed to develop a coordinated plan; troops came into line helter-skelter. At least part of the difficulty was the presence on the field of the heir to the throne, but,

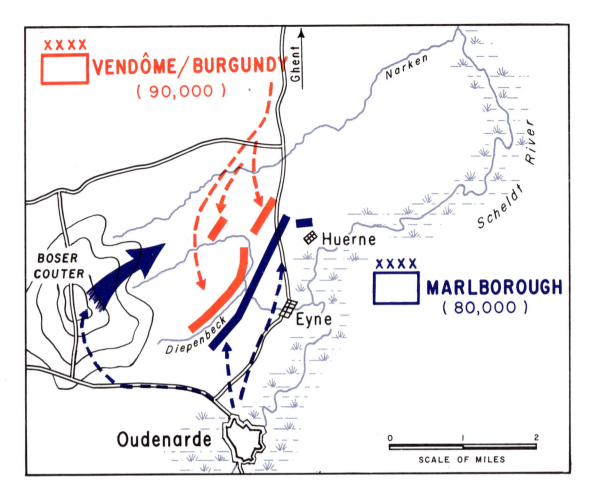

The Battle of Oudenarde, July 11, 1708

in any event, French generals were neither trained nor expected to act flexibly in such a situation. A battle was simply not supposed to unfold on the field. Rules of eighteenth century warfare did not allow it. It was an unreasonable event in the Age of Reason.

But it was happening, and if any doubts remained, Overkirk forcibly removed them when his 25,000 troops cascaded down the Boser Couter to crash with irresistible momentum into the French flank and rear. The rest of the story can be briefly told. Chaos prevailed in the French army; a dark night accounted for the fact that any great number survived. Some 9,000 surrendered, while about 6,000 were killed or wounded. Another 10,000 returned to France as stragglers. Marlborough lost fewer than 1,000 dead, and 20,000 of his troops never even managed to cross the Scheldt in time to participate in the fight. In a fluid battle requiring mental mobility and imaginative flexibility of the highest degree, Marlborough and Eugene had once more far outclassed their commonplace opponents.

With Oudenarde over, Marlborough proposed to invade France by a cross-Channel attack. He envisioned establishing a beachhead around Abbeville—thus turning Vauban's remaining border fortifications—and then marching on Paris. Even Eugene balked at such a rash departure from standard strategy; perhaps, being commander-in-chief of the army of a landlocked power, he was unable to grasp the significant advantage afforded by England's naval might. The Prince contended, conventionally, that Lille must be taken first. His arguments prevailed, and Lille was duly besieged. Defended by a determined garrison, "Vauban's masterpiece" held out until December, thereby dashing Allied hopes of invading France that year.

Futile Peace Negotiations

Sadly, mankind has always demonstrated a marked propensity to sprint into war—and crawl toward peace. In the midst of conflict, people often forget the original cause of struggle and look upon the fighting as an end rather than a means. That phenomenon occurred in the War of the Spanish Succession.

Ever since the disaster at Ramillies, Louis XIV had been seeking a way out of his ruinous war. Now, after the fiasco at Oudenarde, the King made it clear that he would grant almost any terms for peace. France's human losses had been enormous, the economy was a shambles, and peasants teetered on the brink of revolt; widespread wretchedness and despair walked in the domain of the Sun King. Louis' dreams of expansion had been throttled; he strove now only for France's survival. Negotiations began in January 1709. A crushingly bitter winter inflicted appalling agony on Louis' already impoverished people, placing one more bargaining lever in the hands of Allied diplomats. One by one, the French grudgingly conceded every single point for which the Allies had first gone to war: Spain's throne would go to Austria; Louis XIV would recognize Anne as sovereign of England; and the Dutch would gain possession of a barrier line from Ypres to Charleroi. Furthermore, France agreed to demolish Dunkirk's defenses, cede Alsace to the Emperor, and hand Newfoundland over to England. The Grand Alliance had gained its every objective—and more. The war should have been over.

However, flushed with victory, Allied politicians demanded more. Among additional stipulations was one requiring Louis to use French arms to expel his grandson from Spain should he not voluntarily quit that throne within two months. Those extra terms outraged Louis. "If I must fight," he thundered, "it will not be against my own family!" The war continued for four years more.

National Resistance

Allied harshness at the negotiating table sparked a national patriotism across the breadth of France. The enraged population was determined to fight to the end if necessary. Nobles melted personal silver to bolster the treasury; young men flocked to the colors with little or no expectation of pay; peasants quit grumbling over taxes. That patriotic surge, spontaneous enough, was carefully nourished by Louis. The King also appointed capable Marshal Villars commander in chief, despite opposition from courtiers whom the tactless soldier had offended. That assignment markedly raised the Army's morale, for French soldiers, knowing Villars' fighting reputation, had supreme confidence in him. Everywhere, a new spirit surfaced. France, so recently on the ropes, was roused for another effort. There, in letters clear and bold, is a lesson on how *not* to make peace.

The Battle of Malplaquet

Greatly outnumbered, lacking sufficient arms and equipment, and able to distribute full rations only when marching, Villars correctly deduced that he could do no more than act defensively. Accordingly, he erected a barrier to block Marlborough's path, the Lines of La Bassée, a system of field fortifications 40 miles long. *(See Map 7.)*

Marlborough and Eugene, not wanting to attack Villars in a prepared position, decided to draw him out. They knew that of all Louis' generals, Villars was the one most likely to accept combat. First, the Allies laid siege to Tournai. Villars did not budge. When Tournai fell, Marlborough marched toward Mons. The Frenchman could stand idly by no longer; he also moved toward Mons, prepared to give battle if necessary. Choosing a strong position astride a gap between two thick forests near Malplaquet, Villars carefully entrenched his army. After reconnoitering the formidable enemy defenses, Marlborough judiciously waited for reinforcements. When they arrived, nearly 200,000 men were arrayed on the field of battle, the largest number ever assembled in the war. Regardless of the formidable earthworks and the highly restrictive space, the Duke resolved to assail the French. An assault would be expensive, he knew, but if France lost this last army, the strategic gains would be well worth the price.

Attacking on September 11, 1709, Marlborough and Eugene won the furiously fought and brutally costly battle. Allied casualties amounted to 20,000; French, 14,000. Both Eugene and Villars were among the wounded. Villars later reported to Louis XIV, "If God gives us another defeat like this, your Majesty's enemies will be destroyed." It was easily the bloodiest brawl of the entire century; not until Napoleon's day would there be longer casualty lists.

As in all his former battles, at Malplaquet Marlborough had carefully created a situation that enticed his opponent to withdraw troops from a location that would eventually become the point of penetration. Villars' defensive dispositions were one reason, of course, for the sanguinary results, but so too was the aggressive spirit of the defenders. Villars' men met the Allied onslaught with grit, determination, and sacrifice not usually seen in soldiers of that era. Although victorious, the Allies were too exhausted to follow up the success. There was no pursuit.

The Genius of Marlborough

The political clamor in England grew, as Parliamentary enemies fastened onto the terrible cost of Malplaquet to belittle the Duke. Besides that, coalition frictions increased, and Marlborough's health declined. Still, his military reputation remained so great that only he was an acceptable commander to all members of the Grand Alliance. *(See Map 7.)* Hampered and harassed by political restrictions throughout 1710, the

Duke managed nonetheless to pierce the Lines of La Bassée and maneuver the French back even closer to Paris. Before the campaigning season of 1711 arrived, Marshal Villars erected a vast defensive barrier called the Lines of "Ne Plus Ultra," which roughly translates into "No Farther." In a clever and nearly bloodless stroke, Marlborough broke through that final line on August 5, 1711. It was a fine climax to a fabulous career. In 10 campaigns, despite tribulations that would have broken a weaker man, the Duke had halted Louis XIV's aggression and, for the time being, had precluded French hegemony in Europe.

Marlborough occupies a unique place in military history. Stacking his accomplishments beside those of such illustrious predecessors as Alexander, Hannibal, Caesar, and Gustavus, appears at first glance to diminish the Duke's stature. The same is true of a comparison with two future lights, Frederick and Napoleon. But before forming conclusions one must examine Marlborough's deeds in the context of his time. Severely inhibited by as cantankerous a coalition as was ever

devised, serving as a theater commander without a monarch's power to shape overall strategy, opposed by an enemy at least as strong and possibly stronger, and limited by the very nature of eighteenth century warfare, he nonetheless persevered to make those gains summarized on Map 7. Although these are miniscule conquests when contrasted with the results achieved by the warriors mentioned above, they were magnificent almost beyond imagination in Marlborough's era.

Strategically, Marlborough always saw the big picture, kept the grand view. Even when intimately involved in one theater, he retained the rare ability to see the war as a whole. Nor did he ever lose sight of the true objective: to destroy the enemy's will and ability to fight, and to eliminate the French Army, thus forcing Louis XIV to terms. If he was ahead of his age in strategic grasp, he was equally so in appreciation of seapower and the possibilities it provided for amphibious maneuvers. Even though all of his campaigns were on land, he devised numerous plans hinging on the use of naval forces. So, too, did he live in the wrong time with

The Battle of Malplaquet, 1709

regard to his offensive spirit. His constant strategic aim was to bring the enemy to battle, and he repeatedly outmaneuvered the French to achieve just that—only to be thwarted again and again by his allies. Due to the timidity of the Dutch, Marlborough, in 10 years of constantly seeking battle, fought only five times. Nevertheless, though it galled him no end, he was far and away the outstanding general in the game of maneuver preferred by most of his contemporaries. In the realm of strategy, Marlborough walked alone. He had no competition.

Even so, he was a better tactician than strategist. In a day when even good generals were poor tacticians, and the best only mediocre, Marlborough was brilliant. He possessed an unfailing feel for terrain, an uncanny ability to discern the flaw in his foe's disposition, and a practiced gambler's touch in calculating and contesting odds. Simplicity stood as a hallmark of his operations, along with deception and violent execution. The complete coordination of arms—a judicious mixture of firepower and shock action—might have been his supreme contribution to the conduct of his battles. Finally, his record itself speaks eloquently of his tactical ability: he never lost a battle nor failed to take a fortress that he besieged.

The Duke was a superb diplomat, at home whether working with clamorous and panicky foreign governments or dealing in private with heads of state. His diplomatic skills served him equally well when he dealt with subordinates. His men adored "Corporal John." His meticulous care and obvious interest warmed them, while his cool bravery and unerring judgment inspired them. Voltaire placed at the top of Marlborough's traits "that calm courage in the midst of tumult, that serenity of soul in danger, which is the greatest gift of nature for command." More simply, Marlborough was one of the handful of great soldiers, a genius at war.

Nonetheless, his government treated him shabbily. Arriving in England late in the autumn of 1711, the Duke found his last political capital expended. Queen Anne spitefully relieved him of all duties in December. Disgraced, he left his country to live in exile while awaiting the verdict of history.

Without Marlborough to contend with, Villars managed to regain much territory in 1712. A year later the war ended with the signing of the Treaty of Utrecht. Ironically, the war that had been waged to block Louis' grandson from the throne of Spain ended with the Allies agreeing that he could keep it.

Thus, there is an element of bitter truth in the final lines of Robert Southey's poem, "The Battle of Blenheim":

> "And everybody praised the Duke,
>   Who this great fight did win."
> "But what good came of it at last?"
>   Quoth little Peterkin.
> "Why, that I cannot tell," said he,
> "But 'twas a famous victory."

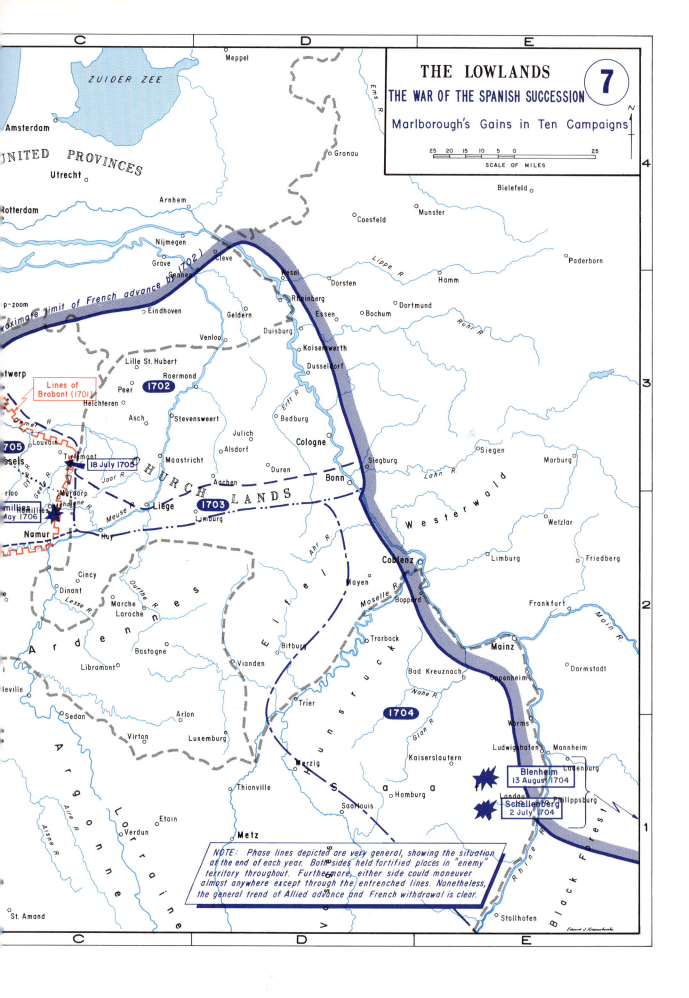

THE LOWLANDS
THE WAR OF THE SPANISH SUCCESSION
Marlborough's Gains in Ten Campaigns

7

25 20 15 10 5 0   25
SCALE OF MILES

ZUIDER ZEE

UNITED PROVINCES

Amsterdam

Utrecht

Rotterdam

Meppel

Arnhem

Gronau

Bielefeld

Munster

Coesfeld

Paderborn

Nijmegen

Grave

Cleve

Gennep

Wesel

Dorsten

Hamm

Lippe R.

p-zoom

Proximate limit of French advance 1702

Eindhoven

Geldern

Rheinberg

Essen

Bochum

Dortmund

Ruhr R.

antwerp

**Lines of
Brabant (1701)**

Venloo

Lille St. Hubert

Duisburg

Kaiserswerth

Dusseldorf

1702

Roermond

Peer

Helchteren

Asch

Stevensweert

Siegen

Marburg

705

Louvain

Demel R.

Tirlemont

18 July 1705

Maastricht

Julich

Alsdorf

Bedburg

Erft R.

Cologne

ssels

Dyle R.

Geete R.

Merdorp

Oudenarde

Aachen

Duren

Siegburg

Lahn R.

Westerwald

Wetzlar

rloo

Liege

1703

Limburg

Bonn

milliles

Meuse R.

Jaar R.

HURCH LANDS

Limburg

Friedberg

May 1706

Namur

Huy

Ahr R.

Coblenz

Moselle R.

Mayen

Frankfurt

Main R.

Cincy

Ourthe R.

Boppard

Dinant

Lesse R.

Marche
Laroche

A r d e n n e s

Bastogne

Libramont

Bitburg

Vianden

E i f e l

H u n s r u c k

Trarback

Bad Kreuznach

Mainz

Oppenheim

Darmstadt

leville

Sedan

Arlon

Trier

Nahe R.

1704

Worms

Ludwigshafen

Mannheim

Virton

Luxemburg

Kaiserslautern

Glan R.

Ladenburg

Aisne R.

Aire R.

L o r r a i n e

Etain

Verdun

Merzig

Thionville

Homburg

**Blenheim
13 August 1704**

Landau

Philippsburg

**Schellenberg
2 July 1704**

St. Amand

Metz

Saarlouis

Rhine R.

Black Forest

Stollhofen

NOTE: Phase lines depicted are very general, showing the situation
at the end of each year. Both sides held fortified places in "enemy"
territory throughout. Furthermore, either side could maneuver
almost anywhere except through the entrenched lines. Nonetheless,
the general trend of Allied advance and French withdrawal is clear.

Edward J. Krasnoborski

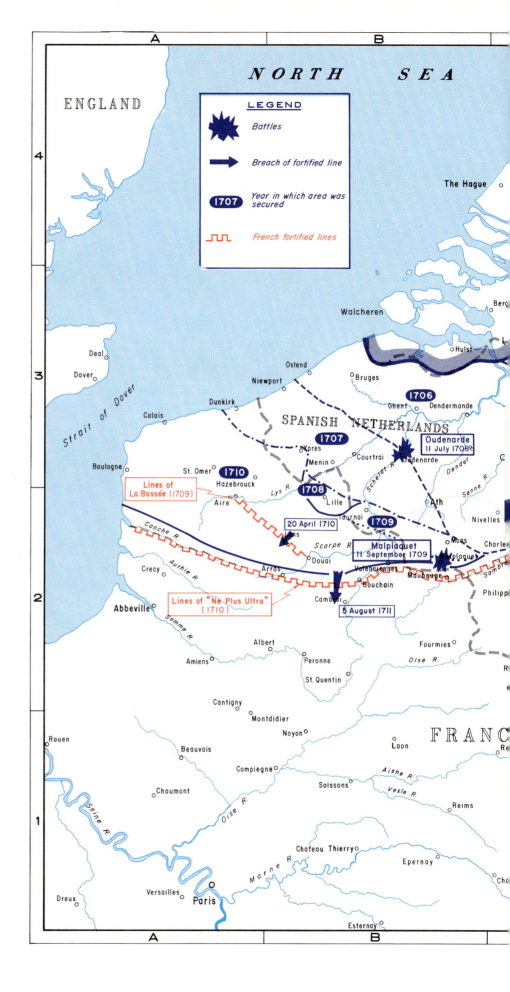

ENGLAND

LEGEND

Battles

Breach of fortified line

1707 Year in which area was
secured

French fortified lines

The Hague

Berg

Walcheren

Hulst

Deal

Ostend

Bruges

1706

Dover

Niewport

Ghent Dendermonde

Strait of Dover

Dunkirk

SPANISH NETHERLANDS

1707

Calais

Ypres

Oudenarde
11 July 1708

Boulogne

St. Omer

1710

Menin

Courtrai

Oudenarde

Dender

Hazebrouck

Lines of
La Bassée (1709)

Lys R.

1708

Lille

Scheldt R.

Senne R.

Aire

Tournai

1709

Ath

Nivelles

Canche R.

20 April 1710

Scarpe R.

Mons

Malplaquet
11 September 1709

Charlei

Crecy

Authie R.

Arras

Douai

Valenciennes

Malplaquet

Abbeville

Lines of "Ne Plus Ultra"
(1710)

Cambrai

Bouchain

Maubeuge

Sambre

Somme R.

5 August 1711

Philipp

Albert

Fourmies

Amiens

Peronne

Oise R.

St. Quentin

Cantigny

Montdidier

FRANC

Noyon

Laon

R.

Rouen

Beauvais

Compiegne

Aisne R.

Soissons

Vesle R.

Chaumont

Oise R.

Reims

Seine R.

Chateau Thierry

Marne R.

Epernay

Cha

Dreux

Versailles

Paris

Esternay

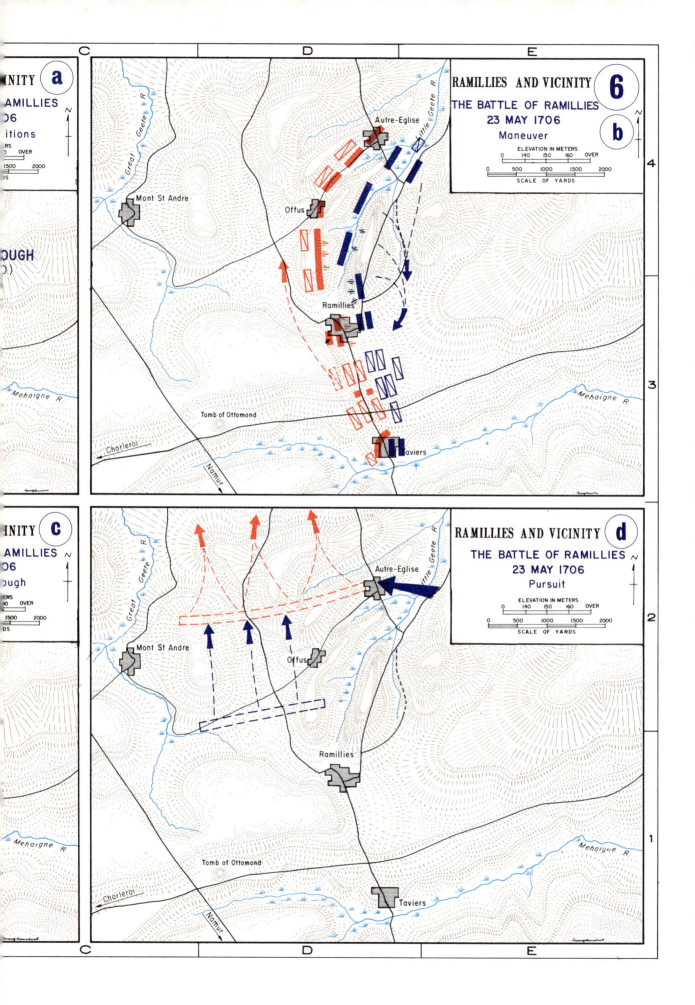

RAMILLIES AND VICINITY

6

THE BATTLE OF RAMILLIES
23 MAY 1706

Maneuver

b

ELEVATION IN METERS
0   140   150   160   OVER

0   500   1000   1500   2000
SCALE OF YARDS

Autre-Eglise

Mont St Andre

Offus

Ramillies

Tomb of Ottomond

Charleroi

Namur

Great Geete R.

Little Geete R.

Mehaigne R.

Taviers

Mehaigne R.

RAMILLIES AND VICINITY

d

THE BATTLE OF RAMILLIES
23 MAY 1706

Pursuit

ELEVATION IN METERS
0   140   150   160   OVER

0   500   1000   1500   2000
SCALE OF YARDS

Autre-Eglise

Mont St Andre

Offus

Ramillies

Tomb of Ottomond

Charleroi

Namur

Great Geete R.

Little Geete R.

Mehaigne R.

Taviers

Mehaigne R.

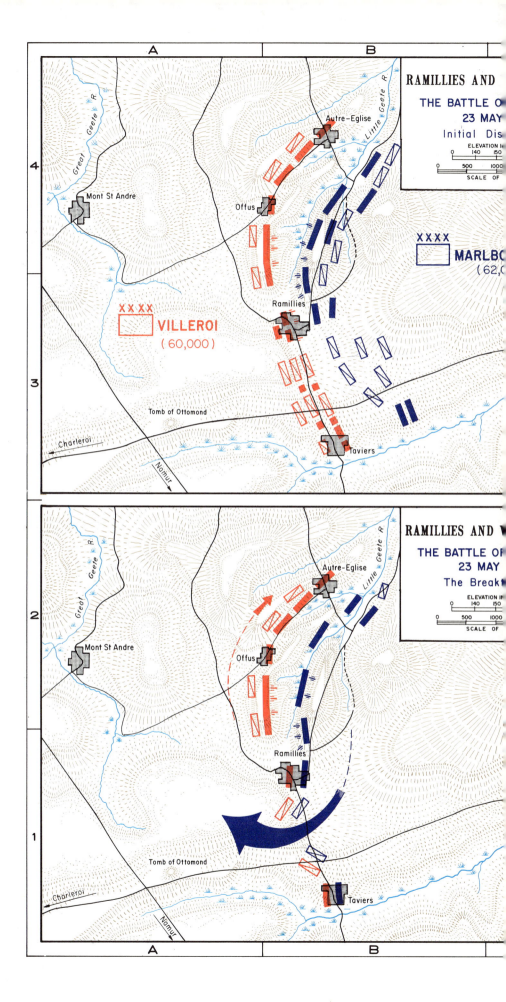

RAMILLIES AND

THE BATTLE O
23 MAY
Initial Dis

ELEVATION I
140   150
0   500   1000
SCALE OF

XXXX
MARLBO
(62,0

XXXX
VILLEROI
(60,000)

RAMILLIES AND

THE BATTLE O
23 MAY
The Break

ELEVATION I
140   150
0   500   1000
SCALE OF

Prussia's Rise to Power

7

Late in the afternoon of April 10, 1741, on a snow-swept field in what is now East Germany, an anxious young man, as yet unhardened by battle, was listening to the advice of Count Curt von Schwerin, a veteran of 20 years. Riderless horses galloped madly about, stung by the crack of artillery and the vengeful pursuit of Austrian hussars. Crisis prevailed.

"Your Majesty, the battle is irretrievable," implored the old warrior. "But what is the loss of a battle to that of Your Majesty's own person? You must save yourself."

Considering the flight of the Prussian cavalry, which was being rushed off the field by its sturdier opponents, Schwerin's advice made sense. After days of forced marches through drifting snow, the movement to contact appeared to have failed, and Frederick's first campaign seemed finished. There was no other alternative. The young king accepted the judgment of his senior general and fled from the battlefield at Mollwitz, not to reappear for 16 hours. It was an ignoble performance in his first test of arms.

Reputation and honor were all the more tarnished when Frederick returned to his troops in the morning. He was greeted with the news that the tide of battle had miraculously turned. The Prussians had rallied, exhorted by the indomitable Schwerin. What the King could not do, his infantry had done for him. That steady line of infantry was to become famous.

In evaluating Frederick's place in history and his right to be called a "Great Captain," a word of caution is in order. It is important not to judge him strictly by modern standards. Like Marlborough, he must be viewed as an individual working within the constraints of his time. To understand his concept of command, one must first know something about Frederick, and then examine the nature of warfare in the eighteenth century. Why were wars undertaken, and with what kinds of armies were they fought? There were also external forces that must be comprehended: Prussia's geographic vulnerability in a competitive Europe, and its inherent strengths and weaknesses in comparison with its rivals. (*See*

Map 1.) One might question if it was indeed true that Prussia was forced to expand or perish.

The Prince

The military heritage of Prussia was rooted in the bitter memory of devastation by foreign invaders. To prevent a repetition of the Thirty Years' War experience, when Swedish, Austrian, and French mercenaries systematically ravaged the north German plain, Frederick William, the Great Elector, established a standing army of 27,000. To maintain this force, he imposed taxes on the northern provinces, especially Brandenburg and

The Grenadiers at Mollwitz

King Frederick William I

Prussia. Thus the financial backing for an army became the cause of the state's formation. After the War of the Spanish Succession, this groundwork was consolidated by his grandson, King Frederick William I, a harsh, autocratic ruler with a thirst for beer that eventually killed him. Althogh he had no appetite for battle, Frederick William steadily increased the size of the Army to over 80,000 men. If one recalls that in 1740 the population of Brandenburg-Prussia numbered less than two and a half million, the predominance of the Army is evident. The twelfth largest state in Europe possessed the fourth largest army. It could truly be said that the Army was the soul of Prussia.

The influence of Frederick William's Army extended beyond the dominance of numbers. If the poor Prussian land was to support a large army, efficiency must be practiced. Frederick William solved this problem by virtually mobilizing his subjects for life. Visitors to Berlin remarked that everyone—nobility, townspeople, and clergy—acted like soldiers in an armed camp. Not only the military, but also the economic and social life of Prussia was channelled into the service of the Army. The iron discipline of the barracks became the model for all of Prussia.

Into this militaristic atmosphere Frederick II was born in 1712. It would be an understatement to say that his upbringing was stormy. Inspired by his mother and encouraged by his sister, Frederick sought the pleasures of music and literature; the sensitive and thoughtful youth turned deliberately away from the Brandenburg-Prussian tradition of martial life. Attempting to impose his own crude pattern of behavior on his heir, Frederick William insisted that the young prince emulate the rough manners of his drinking circle and join in the barbarous hunts that offended the Queen. Misinterpreting his son's taste for art as weakness, he subjected the boy to violent

abuse, often in public. On one occasion, the daughter of a school official attracted Frederick's attention by her beautiful voice. Learning that Frederick had given her gifts, the King ordered her stripped and whipped, even after her innocence had been proven. It is hardly surprising that the talented Frederick sided with his mother against his brutal master.

The climax of Frederick's unhappy boyhood nearly ended his life. Unable to endure the increasing intemperance of his father, Frederick deserted. He and an accomplice were caught, and both were convicted by court-martial. The King considered executing his errant son, but was dissuaded by his court. Instead, he ordered the beheading of Frederick's friend, and directed that Frederick be forced to watch the execution. The prince collapsed, and is reported to have suffered a severe mental breakdown. By some mysterious process, the period of Frederick's recovery brought about a reconciliation with his father. There was continued animosity, which produced stubbornness on both sides; but while the father failed in controlling his temper, Frederick learned that the only way to survive was to conceal his emotions. His unyielding nature was molded in these years; at an early age, he learned the value of self-discipline.

Frederick William interpreted his son's compliant behavior as a change of heart, and restored him to duty. In 1733, Frederick was married to a minor German princess, chosen by the King to revitalize his faltering foreign policy. Although he had no desire to wed the girl, Frederick submitted to his father's orders without complaint. In the bargain, he gained some measure of freedom and established his own household in the palace of Sans Souci. When not required to be with his regiment, he hastened to this retreat, where he could play his flute and talk with men of ideas. It was during these relatively peaceful years that Frederick became acquainted with Voltaire. Correspondence with the French philosopher played a major role in the development of Frederick's way of thinking.

Anticipating the day when he would assume the crown, Frederick pursued a rigorous apprenticeship in the art of the soldier and ruler. He visited the provinces to discover at first hand the problems of government, and accompanied the renowned Eugene on campaign in 1734. He read widely in history to improve his awareness of political and military affairs, and tried to clarify his own approach to problem solving by composing philosophical essays. Truly a product of the Age of Reason, Frederick's precision in writing was matched by a belief in the value of logic. No difficulty, not even his own personal torment, was too serious an obstacle to be surmounted by the intellect.

Frederick's character was the result of tradition, resistance to his father's demands, and a desire for self-improvement. Perhaps his most important accomplishment during these formative years was the standard of discipline he evolved for himself. His most lofty ideal was a strong sense of duty. Thus was the prince trained for command.

The Sword Unsheathed

For over 20 years, Europe had laughed at Frederick William I, the Sergeant-King, whose favorite hobby was drilling his giant grenadiers. Of what use are soldiers if they never fight? The derision seemed all the greater when his son ascended the throne. This unsoldierly young king cared nothing for battle; he was more concerned with feats of art than of arms.

Frederick's sudden thrust into Silesia in 1740 put an abrupt end to the laughter, and propelled him into the center of a tumultuous diplomatic stage. Six months earlier, the death of Charles VI, nominal Holy Roman Emperor and ruler of Austria, had left the Hapsburg domains without an effective sovereign. With no male offspring, Charles had foreseen the emergency 15 years earlier, and pronounced the Pragmatic Sanction. In that announcement, he willed that the rights of succession belonged to his daughter and that the Hapsburg lands, including Silesia, should remain inseparable from Austria. A number of European courts now sought to break away from Hapsburg control by questioning the legitimacy of this dynastic arrangement. The newly crowned Austrian Queen, Maria Theresa, was caught without allies in a moment of financial and political distress. Seeking to profit from her unreadiness, Frederick undertook the rapid seizure of Silesia, thus beginning the War of Austrian Succession. The polyglot Empire, torn by internal and external dissension, was unable to react before he completed his conquest. Henceforth, Prussia would weigh strongly in the European balance of power.

The Widening War

Frederick's first campaign in Silesia was an eruption that brought several long-simmering feuds to a boil. Alliances and mutual interests helped to expand the conflict. France readily joined the Prussian cause, if for no other reason than to continue a tradition of warring with the House of Hapsburg, her major rival on the Continent. England promptly backed Austria with financial and limited military support, but technically remained at peace with France. Contested areas included the peripheral holdings of the Hapsburg Empire (the Netherlands, Alsace, Tyrol, and northern Italy). Also at stake was the entire North American continent and the trade routes between it and Europe.

Prince Frederick

1739–1741: **War of Jenkin's Ear**
Britain vs. Spain

1740–1748: **War of Austrian Succession** (King George's War)
Prussia, France, Spain vs. Austria, Britain

1740–1742: First Silesian War
1744–1745: Second Silesian War

1756–1763: **Seven Years' War** (French and Indian War)
Prussia, Britain vs. France, Austria, Russia, Sweden

Wars in the Mid-Eighteenth Century

In America, war continued in one form or another, even after the Treaty of Utrecht halted active fighting between French and British colonists in 1713 (the War of the Spanish Succession). For 30 years, French activity was limited to the strengthening of defenses along the St. Lawrence and Mississippi rivers. Expanding British settlements now brushed against struggling Spanish outposts in the south. French and Spanish differences over control of the Mississippi were quickly resolved in recognition of the growing strength their common enemy was displaying in the New World. The founding of Savannah in 1733 initiated a virtual guerrilla war with the Spanish and the Indians. Since the buffer colony of Georgia could not be tolerated by Spain, a crescent of forts was built to protect Savannah. Later, a fumbling attempt to take the offensive lapsed into an indecisive siege of St. Augustine. In an unconventional display of backwoods brawling known as the Battle of Bloody Marsh, a small band of Highlanders and Rangers under the command of part-time soldier and statesman James Oglethorpe finally disposed of the worst Spanish threat to Georgia.

Meanwhile, England and Spain contended on the seas. Both sides violated treaty agreements, and a number of British ships were seized. In 1739, an obscure ship captain named Jenkins declared before Parliament that Spaniards had boarded his ship. When he also announced that the Spaniards had cut off his ear, public opinion was outraged, and war with Spain became inevitable. This chain of grievances helped to draw the lines for the next round in the larger contest between England and France, and the parallel, but localized, struggle between Prussia and Austria, known as the Second Silesian War.

Before tracing the events of that war, it is necessary to examine the Prussian art of war. Frederick's Army was the best Europe had yet seen. It is therefore appropriate to consider his era as a landmark in military history and to explore the details of Prussian military practice. The lessons Frederick learned from his first combat action crystallized into a system of organization, tactics, and command; but throughout his life the general continued to learn, realistically altering doctrine in accordance with changing circumstances. An understanding of his concepts will facilitate the analysis of his wars.

The Prussian Way of War

During Frederick's reign, warfare altered only slightly from that practiced by Turenne and Marlborough. Differences were caused by the nature of the society that Frederick tapped for his soldiery, the slow progress of technology that equipped his army, and the singular manner in which he commanded. Therefore, change was not especially rapid, and the direction in which the art of war evolved during this period is somewhat indistinct. Possibly, Frederick succeeded because he saw the dim path these changes were taking; however, he was careful to keep to the main trail. Instead of reforming his army, as Gustavus did, he perfected the one that he had.

The most expensive, and hence the most important, military resource in Prussia was the soldier. The state could afford only so many men. If the Government were to remain solvent, the productive members of society had to be exempted from military service. This left only the nobility to lead the regiments and the indolent to fill the ranks. There were more nobles than regiments, but the underpopulated provinces could not produce sufficient jailbirds and laggards to keep the regiments at more than half strength. To maintain a large standing army, the ruler was forced to recruit outside the country:

He halted sadly at the door of an inn. Two men dressed in blue noticed him. . . . They went up to Candide and very civilly invited him to dinner. "Gentlemen," said Candide with charming modesty, "You do me a great honour, but I have no money to pay my share."

"Ah, Sir," said one of the men in blue, "persons of your figure and merit never pay anything; are you not five feet tall?" "Yes, gentlemen," said he, bowing, "that is my height." "Ah, sir, come to table; we will not only pay your expenses, we will never allow a man like you to be short of money; men are only made to help each other."

"We were asking if you do not tenderly love the King of the Bulgarians." "Not a bit," said he, "for I have never seen him." "What! He is the most charming of kings, and you must drink to his health." "Oh, gladly, gentlemen." And he drank. "That is sufficient," he was told, "you are now the support, the aid, the defender, the hero of the Bulgarians; your fortune is made and your glory assured." They immediately put irons on his legs and took him to a regiment.*

One should not be misled by Voltaire's clever description of eighteenth century recruiting practice, as Candide was deceived by the recruiters; it was the Prussian army, not the Bulgarian, for which the unwary ragamuffin was destined. Once recruited, the soldier had to be fed, clothed, armed, and trained. The first three requirements took money; the fourth took money and time. A soldier who developed proficiency with the musket and learned to carry out the maneuvers of the drill field represented a considerable investment to a government of limited resources. Such a costly commodity must only rarely be risked in battle. On the other hand, he must not be permitted to desert.

The entire first page of Frederick's famous *Instructions for his Generals* is devoted to his greatest problem, desertion. The Prussian regiments consisted half of citizens and half of mercenaries. Most of the former were needed to prevent the latter from disappearing. To impress the soldier with the hopelessness of escape, Frederick ordered extraordinary measures. He avoided camping near woods; required the soldiers to forage and bathe in ranks, and then only when accompanied by an officer; refrained from night marches except when absolutely essential; never informed the troops of projected movements; and established hussar patrols along each route of march. These procedures imposed severe limitations on the commander's freedom of action. Long-range reconnaissance, night attacks, and aggressive pursuit were almost out of the question. But it was better to have an army that resembled a prison than no army at all. Small wonder that Frederick is reported to have said, "If my men ever began to think not one would remain in the ranks."

*Voltaire, F. M. in *The Portable Voltaire*, edited by Redman, B. R. (New York, 1963), pp. 232-233.

To ensure that the soldier did not think, Frederick intensified the disciplinary regimen of his father. Although one of his first acts after accession was to abolish torture and brutality in civil life, the young King realized that only fear could govern the rabble that formed his infantry. He insisted on severe punishment for the slightest deviation from his orders. "If a soldier during an action looks about as if to flee, or so much as sets foot outside the line, the non-commissioned officer standing behind him will run him through with his bayonet and kill him on the spot." From the general to the private, discipline demanded obedience. Except for trusted independent commanders, the freedom to reason had to be surrendered; the individual became a part of an increasingly efficient machine.

Throughout Europe, numerical strength was considered to be the most important index of an army's wartime caliber. Frederick, however, saw that there were additional determinants of combat power. Striving to maximize fighting effectiveness for a given expenditure of capital, he diligently studied the force structure of his Army. After his soldiers, weaponry was the most vital concern.

Advances in weapons development were remarkably rare during the Enlightenment. It is uncertain whether this was due to the soldier's inability to communicate his needs to the scientist, or to the limited development of management, which was incapable of gearing the inventions of science to military requirements. Regardless of cause, technological progress had not substantially improved the capabilities of weapons. Action still progressed at the speed of man and horse; commanders still relied on the charge of infantry with musket and bayonet to decide an encounter. But in spite of this lull in the evolution of arms, there was some improvement in the employment of weapons. To such a careful planner as Frederick, the art of victory consisted in properly fitting contemporary technology to the capabilities of his men.

The basic weapon of the Prussian Army was the infantry musket. The standard caliber .75 model was long, heavy, and poorly balanced. Its flintlock mechanism assured greater reliability than the old matchlock, but its smooth bore and loosely fitting ball ammunition did not improve the firer's chances of hitting the target. At any range over 100 paces, the musket would miss as often as it hit, and some soldiers claimed that it was more inaccurate when they tried to aim. In short, the combination of soldier and smoothbore musket was a system of inaccuracy.

The most important lesson of the Battle of Mollwitz was lost on neither the soldiers nor their king. It was not well-aimed fire that had won the day, but volume of fire. Since it was senseless to concentrate on marksmanship, Frederick prescribed a training program that taught his troops to perform the 19-step load-and-fire drill as rapidly as possible. Aiming

Prussian Musket

was forbidden, since it reduced the rate of fire. Volleys, rather than well-aimed shots, were desired, and these were fired only on command. In practice, the side that was steady enough to wait until its opponenets fired first gained an advantage: its first volley would catch the enemy while reloading, and would be fired at closer range. Hence the expertness of reloading, which was enhanced by a Prussian innovation—the iron ramrod—became a major factor in infantry tactics. The psychological impact of fire, as well as its lethal effect, was the goal of musketry.

The employment of artillery was similarly affected by technological limitation, and also suffered from lack of imagination. Cannon of this period, like muskets, were still smoothbore, because no one could find a way to apply the concept of rifling to hard iron shot. Pieces were still loaded from the muzzle, a function of skill and courage since the cannoneers were often first to face the enemy. The weapons' tubes were fashioned of cast iron or bronze, and the science of smelting had not yet sufficiently advanced to allow any significant improvement in ballistics over the Swedish culverins of the previous century. Also, cannon and munitions were expensive. The main drawback, however, was that the King remained unconvinced of the full value of artillery until the Seven Years' War. He even allowed an 86-year-old officer to serve as General of Artillery, a choice hardly calculated to inspire aggressive and decisive action by his gunners. This failing is hard to reconcile with Frederick's search for perfection and penchant for squeezing every bit of fighting capability out of available technology. Perhaps the slow, clumsy movements of manually operated cannon contrasted too sharply with the crisp, disciplined maneuvers of the infantry. An immobile weapon could have only a limited role in Frederick's military system.

Experiments were later conducted in an attempt to produce lighter artillery pieces that could keep up with the infantry. Heavy artillery was positioned in key fortresses to protect the forts, and when needed, to reinforce infantry and cavalry forces maneuvering nearby. Eventually Frederick organized horse artillery. Using a technique that had fallen into disuse after the time of Gustavus, he made guns, horses, limbers, and drivers organic to the battery. Once again, after a century of neglect, artillery was mobile and could accompany cavalry, or be shifted during battle from one flank of the army to the other. Frederick also introduced howitzers, which, because of their higher trajectory, could reach over terrain masks and hurl a 10-pound ball to a range of 1,300 meters. As the strength of his infantry was reduced by attrition, the number

Royal Guards in the Process of Loading Muskets

of his cannon was increased. Toward the end of his reign, after the Seven Years' War, he was finally to admit, "artillery decides everything, and infantry no longer does battle with naked steel."

Cavalry was as much affected by doctrine and tradition as by the slow growth of technology. Still another century would pass before the deadly use of rifles could empty saddles in quantities sufficient to change the main role of horsemen, decreasing the importance of en masse charges in favor of dispersed reconnaissance and security operations. Frederick's cavalry followed the standard pattern of all European armies. The hussars, or light horsemen, were best suited for close-in patrolling and the policing of stragglers. Dragoons used heavier mounts and were also equipped to fight as infantry. The armored cavalry were called cuirassiers for the heavy breastplate that enhanced their ability to work against opposing horsemen. The main problem, as in all other aspects of the Prussian Army, was economic. Every year, Frederick's ministers had to struggle to obtain the number and type of horses he demanded for his steadily growing arm of decision.

Because of Prussia's limited resources, strategy and tactics were virtually governed by logistics. More than ever, the Army depended on supply depots and magazines, since the troops could not be trusted to forage on their own. The decision to give or refuse battle was not infrequently dictated by the level of stocks remaining in the nearest depot, and the distance a force dared venture from it was determined by the amount of supplies it could transport. It was considered an exceptional risk for an army to overstep the conventional "five-day tether." Nor could technology provide the solution to this problem. Transport relied on wind, water, and muscle. Roads were often no more than rutted mud tracks. Tactics, strategy, and organization were bound by the fixed parameters of supply. It would take generations before political and industrial revolutions released warfare from such constraints.

The proper blend of men and weapons in an effective fighting organization has been a problem confronting commanders since the first clash of tribes. Like Gustavus, Frederick developed the best system in Europe for his time. Unlike Gustavus, Frederick inherited the pattern for his formations when he ascended the throne.

The basic tactical unit of the Prussian Army was the infantry battalion. It was developed by a shrewd regimental commander, Leopold of Anhalt, "the Old Dessauer," who had fought under Eugene at Blenheim and Malplaquet, and against Charles XII at Stralsund. Leopold's creation was a force of 700 men, composed in peacetime and during routine marches of five musketeer companies and one grenadier company. When the army commander reckoned that contact with the enemy was imminent, each battalion performed a sort of metamorphosis in which the company structure dissolved and

Leopold of Anhalt, the Old Dessauer

the fighting battalion emerged in eight musketeer platoons. At the same time, the grenadier company marched off to join a consolidated grenadier battalion, which was placed in a key position, usually on the tactical flank of the army.*

The battalion normally marched in column of platoons, and fought with platoons in line, each platoon of 75 men forming in three ranks. To shift from column of platoons to platoons on line, the battalion executed a right turn and then

left wheel by platoons. Essential to the success of this maneuver was the proper selection of the points at which the column movements and wheels were to be made, and a level and open piece of ground on which to fight.

The line formation placed maximum musket power at the front, especially when the front rank kneeled and the second and third ranks fired over its shoulder. Firing could be accomplished by platoons or battalions, the latter being preferred for maximum effect. Firing was on command of the platoon leader or battalion commander, and the decision as to the mode of fire was made by the commander in chief. Because of the Prussians' ability to fire at least twice as fast as their adversaries (five shots to the Austrians' two at Mollwitz), the Prussian battalion became known as "a walking battery." Its combat power was close to three times that of a corresponding Austrian or French infantry battalion.

Appreciating the need for artillery to be responsive to his infantry, Frederick assigned light artillery pieces in direct support, normally two 6-pounders per front line battalion. Twelve-pounders and howitzers were retained in general support for employment in batteries as directed by the King. The light artillery was positioned 50 paces in front of the forward line of battle, firing shot at long range to soften up the enemy, and grape at close range to open a gap in his lines.† Infantry

---

*Grenadiers initially were infantrymen who were armed with grenades. The term, however, gradually came to mean an elite soldier.

†Shot consisted of a solid projectile, usually an iron ball, that had no exploding charge inside it. Grape was an antipersonnel projectile; the projectile was made up of small iron balls that were joined together by wire or rods and, as a group, encased in burlap or metal. Upon being fired from an artillery piece, the joined balls separated from the casing shortly after leaving the muzzle and spread apart en route to the target.

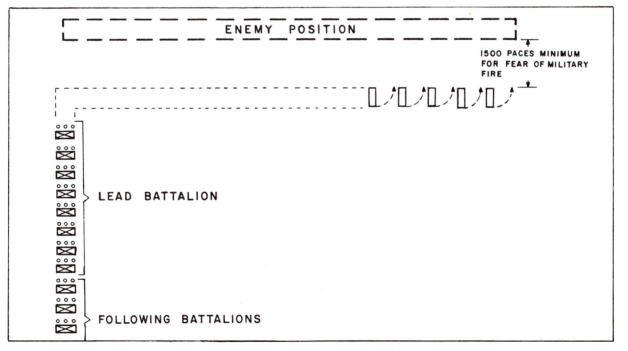

Frederician Battalion Deployment From Column to Line

The Advance of the Prussian Army

was thus assured of artillery fire at the crucial moment when shock met shock, and the victor was often decided in a matter of a few hours. The side that most effectively brought its available combat power to bear in a unified effort usually blasted a less strong-nerved opponent off the field.

Infantry battalions were drilled to advance shoulder-to-shoulder. Small gaps were left on the flanks of each battalion, enabling the light artillery to be pushed forward to cover the opening moves of the infantry. Once his battalion deployed in line, the battalion commander made no decisions. His unit was now a part of a long, thin line which advanced and fired as an integral part of the army. The fact that two battalions formed a regiment and two regiments a brigade made little difference in the assault. The movement of each piece was regulated by the progress of the whole.

No one piece could move ahead of the line, and none was permitted to fall back. Only by pushing the advance forward all along the attacking wing could the Prussian Army win, while minimizing its losses, which were always heavy. Delay only increased the time under fire, while speed diminished this exposure and hastened the moment when the decisive clash of infantry would occur. At that point, it was most probable that the discipline of the Prussian soldier, stiffened by the bayonets behind him, would triumph. It almost always did. Frederick observed that ". . . it is the ground gained and not the number of enemy dead that gives you victory. The most certain way to insure victory is to march boldly and in order against the enemy, always endeavoring to win ground."

The Archetype for Victory

Since many of Frederick's tactical concepts were distilled from a thorough analysis of the Battle of Mollwitz, it is instructive to examine this action in closer detail.

Frederick invaded Silesia in December 1740 during the First Silesian War; in April 1741, an Austrian army, advancing from the southwest, cut his lines of communication near Brieg. The Prussians marched to counter this threat, preceded by an advance guard of dragoons. Not until noon on the day of battle, when the cavalry vanguard brushed aside a patrol of enemy hussars, did either army accurately determine the other's location. The opposing forces were then less than two miles apart.

The Austrian commander, Marshal Wilhelm Neipperg, had ordered a day of rest for his men. The noise of the cavalry skirmish alerted him, but for two hours the Austrians were vulnerable, for the army was widely dispersed in its quarters among three local villages. Instead of seizing the opportunity, the Prussian advance guard commander followed his orders and methodically continued the march, timing his rate of movement by the progress of the main body behind him.

When the Prussian army drew within a mile of its rapidly assembling opponent, deployment into line of battle commenced. At this point only the Austrian cavalry was completely formed. The infantry was still arriving. The opposing forces were nearly equal in strength, each having roughly

22,000. Frederick was superior in artillery, 60 to 18, while the Austrian cavalry outnumbered the Prussian, 8,600 to 4,000.

The Prussians were disposed in standard formation: two lines of battle arranged in the normal three-rank alignment, with cavalry squadrons divided about equally between the two wings. *(See Map 2.)* Frederick initially directed the grenadier battalions into positions between the cavalry squadrons on each wing, to reinforce the outnumbered horsemen and extend the line to natural obstacles on each flank. During the evolution from column to line, inadequate space was left in the right wing. As a makeshift solution, three of the grenadier battalions deployed between the first and second lines of battle, facing to the northeast. It was an expedient that unexpectedly was to prove decisive.

At approximately 2:00 p.m., the Prussians advanced, with music playing and cannon firing. The Austrians were ready on their left, but still gathering on their right. As the distance closed, Frederick's artillery poured shot into the enemy cavalry. This fire, which could not yet be answered, caused the Austrian cavalry to charge, unsupported by infantry, against the Prussian right wing. In the melee that ensued when Frederick and his cavalry were put to flight, it was the

three grenadier battalions holding "like a dam" that barred the way and prevented an Austrian envelopment of the Prussian right wing. For four hours, Neipperg tried to break that small block on the Prussian right. First his cavalry, then his infantry tired of the bloodshed. Sensing that crisis had passed and the moment of decision was at hand, Schwerin tightened his ranks, swung into the offensive, and herded the Austrians off the field. Prussian losses were 4,600, Austrian 200 less, but the ground belonged to Frederick. Neipperg evacuated lower Silesia.

Frederick learned more from this rude introduction to the reality of combat than many generals learn in a lifetime. Cavalry had proven irresistible in the attack, except when it ran upon the hard rock of unflinching infantry. The first step in revitalizing the Prussian cavalry was therefore to ensure that it always retained the initiative. Frederick instructed his cavalry officers never to allow themselves to be attacked, but always to attack first—the cuirassiers against enemy cavalry, the dragoons against the flanks of enemy infantry after the fight for cavalry superiority had been decided on each wing. In Frederick's mind, the measure of the cavalry's worth was its readiness, on short notice, to charge, sword in hand, at the moment when he judged his opponent to be faltering and

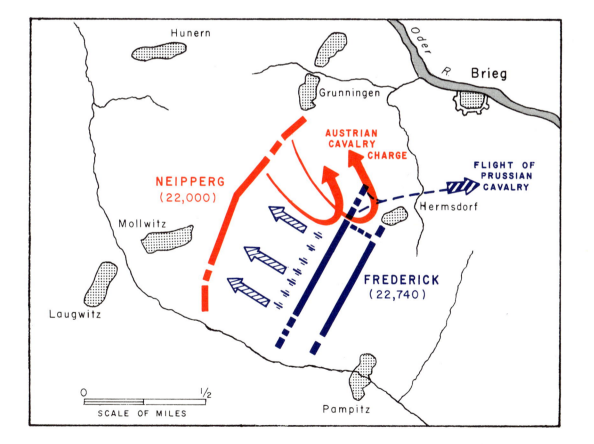

The Battle of Mollwitz, April 10, 1741

ripe for the kill. Although his cavalry squadrons cannot be considered strictly a reserve, the boot-to-boot charge of horsemen was intended to exploit the success of the attack and was almost always launched at Frederick's personal command.

If the cavalry action was not entirely successful, the infantry was expected to strike the deciding blow. Commencing its advance as soon as deployment from march column was completed, its only function was to continue the assault, firing while on the move. This doctrine created a dilemma that Frederick never fully resolved: the relative importance of fire and movement. To allow his troops to fire during the assault would slow the advance and disrupt the integrity of the formation. To order his men to hold their fire was to give up his trump card—the fastest firing infantry in Europe. Frederick's ideas changed as the fortunes of his Army rose and fell, but essentially he favored movement over fire. At the moment of decision, it was the will of the fighter, not his numbers, nor the caliber of his weapon, that settled the outcome. In his instructions of 1746, Frederick emphasized his concept of the moral impulse in infantry action, "During the heat of battle, the infantry must steadily be pushed forward, in order to force the enemy to give ground, at which moment confusion will inevitably set in his ranks."

Another lesson learned at Mollwitz involved the influence of logistics on tactics. Each soldier had been issued 30 rounds, which was believed sufficient for a full day's work. However, the rapidity of the Prussian's fire and the unexpected duration of the engagement caused some soldiers to run out of ammunition. It was this compelling factor that finally caused Schwerin to order the Prussian line of battle forward to bring the fight to a conclusion. Frederick never forgot that infantry charge, but, characteristically, directed that the basic load of the musketeer be increased from 30 to 60 rounds in order to sustain him during a prolonged fight.

Tactics in the Prussian Army was a precise art. The goal was to deploy quickly from column into line, while the enemy was still groping for position. Then, the synchronized advance of those rigid lines of soldiers, following their covering artillery, and flanked by cavalry straining to charge, would overrun anything in their way. The execution of a perfectly coordinated attack is the rarely fulfilled dream of a general. Mollwitz taught Frederick how to realize the dream.

The King's Staff

It is not surprising that the king who reserved all decisions for himself would find little need for a staff. Aside from his four aides and a hard-riding corps of messengers, there were no individuals employed in what can be termed military staff

work. There was a need for specialized skill in the fields of administration, recruiting, procurement, and movement of supplies. These functions were gradually incorporated into the centralized Prussian bureaucracy, which was more of a civilian war department than a military planning staff. Within this agency, only the quartermaster general had a military function. It was he who planned the construction and defense of fortresses.

The vaunted Great General Staff had yet to make its appearance. While the origins of the general staff can be traced to the innovations of Gustavus, its development was definitely retarded by Frederick. The causes of its decline in favor are not entirely clear. In all armies there was a natural tendency to use effective subordinates in both staff and command roles. A trusted assistant might render advice as a sort of chief of staff in the morning and lead a charge in the afternoon, as Schwerin did at Mollwitz. Also, in an age when a commander could view the whole field of battle from the crest of a well-chosen hill, the difficulty of acquiring information and transmitting tactical orders was minimal. These conditions served to reinforce Frederick's method of command, which, based on the precept of obedience, did not admit of the need for staff assistance. In both peace and war, he dealt personally with every subordinate commander, garrison or fortress chief, and provincial official. Prussian tactics were simple, requiring relatively few decisions. These decisions were made by the King, who personally wrote or dictated all campaign plans and battle directives, including the sketches showing routes of movement and lines of deployment.

In the sphere of strategy, operations were more complicated, and as the scope of Frederick's wars enlarged, the disadvantages of his system came home to haunt him. Personal command over great distances was hindered by lack of personal contact. Orders were often sent based on information that was already out of date when it was received. The misunderstandings that inevitably followed cost him in distant theaters. In an effort to minimize these failures, Frederick furnished guidance to independent commanders in massive detail. His secret *Instructions* was written partly to provide a Standing Operating Procedure. Although he recognized the flaws in his method, he preferred to accept them rather than to decentralize authority. In eighteenth century Prussia, the King was not only his own general, but his own chief of staff, and, typically, he did his own staff work.

The Second Silesian War

The Treaty of Breslau ended the fighting between Prussia and Austria in June 1742. Frederick had two costly victories,

Mollwitz and Chotusitz, to his credit, and the province of Silesia in his grasp. Austria might write off the battles, but Silesia would not be forgotten. With silent fury, Maria Theresa accepted peace as an expedient, in order to first deal with France before returning to the battleground in central Europe. The campaigns that followed underline the difficulties of coalition warfare. Frederick abandoned his French ally by breaking off the First Silesian War. As a consequence of this dereliction he was forced to intervene in her behalf two years later in the Second Silesian War. But he impulsively overextended his army, and in turn was abandoned by the French. For Prussia, 1744 was nearly a year of disaster.

The scramble started with Frederick's escape into neutralism in 1742. The French commander in Bohemia awoke to discover his main army surrounded by Austrians at Prague. A desperate breakout was followed by retreat toward the Rhine. In June 1743, a new army challenged the French; it was a slow-moving force, composed of British and Hanoverian units under the command of British King George II, and it appeared in the Main valley on the French northern flank. The Battle of Dettingen ensued, a French trap that snared only France's own unskilled commander. The outpaced George II emerged from this poorly fought battle with the laurels of victory by luck alone. It was the last time a British monarch led troops in battle. It also made Frederick see the danger that a force composed of Austrian and British armies might pose to his Silesian quarry.

A well-thought-out estimate is the best prelude to a decision for action. However, Frederick displayed more of the daring resolve for which he has been acclaimed, and less of the mature strategy that marked his later years. His goal was to secure the expanding Prussian kingdom; his enemies were Austria, England, and perhaps Saxony, depending on where the Saxon king saw the greatest threat to his crossroad kingdom. In the east, Russia could always interpose to take advantage of western strife in order to add to her Polish domains. In Frederick's mind, these various threats were offset by his new alliance with France, which was in turn allied with Spain and now actively at war with England. The permutations and combinations possible in this maze of threat and counterthreat would have given Frederick pause 15 years later. But now, in the summer of 1744, he was possessed by the spirit of opportunism. Having pushed west of the Rhine, the Austrian army, under the command of Charles of Lorraine, was vulnerable to a counterstroke into Bohemia. Such an opportunity could not be allowed to pass. *(See Map 3, Chapter 8.)*

Frederick marched on August 15. Demanding free passage through the gateway of Saxony, his troops, 80,000 strong and supported by 480 supply boats on the Elbe, rapidly converged on Prague, the capital of the ancient kingdom of Bohemia. One month later, after a brief siege, Prague was in Prussian hands.

A careful defensive was now suggested, but with hardly a look to his support from the French, Frederick plunged boldly southwards toward Vienna, leaving behind the magazines on which his army depended for foodstuffs. Still worse, the movement left open the southwestern alleys leading from Bavaria through the Bohemian mountains into his right flank. A hundred years earlier Gustavus had decided against using this difficult route. To further hazard the young commander's daring gamble, swarms of Hungarian light horsemen interdicted his line of communication. The people of southern Bohemia, unlike the easily pacified Saxons, resisted him, hiding their grain and fleeing into the barren countryside. Progress was slow over rough terrain, and with summer fading, one of Frederick's basic calculations was shattered. France saw her main interests threatened not by Austria in Germany, but by England in Holland. The French failed to cooperate with a vigorous offensive, and allowed Charles' army to slip away.

Relying on his ability to maneuver, the Austrian commander avoided decisive engagement, and by positioning his army in northern Bohemia, forced Frederick to withdraw from his grand project. Weakened by lack of supplies, hussar raids, and wholesale desertions, Frederick surrendered Prague and retired into Silesia. His invading army had shrunk to almost half its original size, and predictably, Saxony turned against him.

Frederick grimly prepared for the next campaigning season, well aware that favorable weather would bring with it the advance of Prince Charles' army into Silesia. Since the mountains dividing Silesia and Bohemia were crossed by numerous roads and trails, the problem in 1745 was to determine where the enemy would make the main crossing and to decide if all of Silesia should be held. Frederick decided to concentrate his troops in northern Silesia. As soon as spring weather permitted, he moved into position to await the Austrian attack.

The next move in this whirlpool war came unexpectedly from the Netherlands. Maurice de Saxe, one of the most famous French marshals, stampeded the British lines in a classic battle at Fontenoy. The news of this reverse suffered by his ally galvanized Charles into motion. In May, the Austrians finally advanced, shielded from Prussian reconnaissance by a screen of Tyrolean Pandours, the hard-to-catch irregular light troops.

To the astonishment of his generals, Frederick decided not to seek battle in the mountain defiles, but to defend in the vicinity of Schweidnitz. Hiding his army in haze-cloaked valleys that extended into the foothills, he baited his opponent by allowing an Austrian spy to learn of his supposed concern for the Prussian line of communication to Breslau. On June 1, Charles took the bait. The Austrian army, swelled to 70,000 by the addition of 20,000 Saxons, crowded through the mountain pass near Hohenfriedberg.

The Attack of the Bayreuth Dragoons at Hohenfriedberg, 1745

Frederick prepared his ground well, while his enemies were off balance and surprised. The Saxon contingent, feeling the first blow of Prussian infantry and cannon on the flank, disintegrated in a cauldron of fire. The Austrian infantry were unexpectedly immovable, until the deciding shock of Prussian dragoons melted their resolve. Although it was still early in the morning, this awesome display of combined arms power convinced Charles that he had seen enough. The Austrian troops receded into the mountains.

Even this great triumph at Hohenfriedberg did not compel Maria Theresa to accept her loss of Silesia. Three more times in 1745 the weakening Prussians were forced to fight, and all three times Frederick emerged victorious. Significantly, however, it was a British threat to cut off aid that finally ended the Austrian drive. The Second Silesian War was over, but the cause of war remained, and in its wake, new causes would arise.

The Military Philosopher

The Age of Reason generated extraordinary interest in the art of war. Since its beginnings, there has been a flood of literature dealing with military institutions and policy. Historians, critics, and theorists have related the course of battles, argued why they were won or lost, and suggested reforms to improve old methods. Frederick's writings fit comfortably into none of these categories, but unquestionably they have influenced the practice of war in a profound way. He was a prolific writer; his collected works are in 10 volumes and his memoirs in 30. *Anti Machiavel, The History of the House of Brandenburg*, and a number of military-political essays appear to have been composed in a philosophical vein, as much to exercise his mind as to record anything of immediate significance. Most of his subsequent writings took the form of an authoritative and practical journal.

In 1746, Frederick produced a small treatise entitled *The Principles of War*. It was to this work that his well-known *Instructions for his Generals* was appended. *Instructions* was intended primarily to preserve and disseminate the lessons learned during the two wars for Silesia. Outside Prussia, it was an Aladdin's lamp eagerly sought by soldiers who hoped to duplicate Frederick's battlefield magic. Although it became obsolete half a century later, it details the best of eighteenth century warfare, and reveals a professional's concern with maintaining the finest fighting machine in Europe.

The *Military Testament of 1768* was written after reflecting on the terrible experience of the Seven Years' War. Appalled by the carnage of that long conflict, Frederick now emphasized the limitations of power. Although his views on the discipline of the soldier and the essence of battle had changed but little, on the broader issues of policy and strategy his thought process showed a distinct conservative trend. Such decisive maneuvers as the audacious conquest of 1740 and the march into Bohemia were no longer considered feasible. Frederick's route to maturity can thus be traced through the chronicle of his thoughts.

The evolution of Frederick's character can best be painted against a canvas of his battles. Experience, not idle theory or armchair philosophy, provided material for his thoughts. The sweep of his changing ideas during the convulsions of the Seven Years' War betrays the impact of that unforgettable struggle. It was the supreme test of an army and its general.

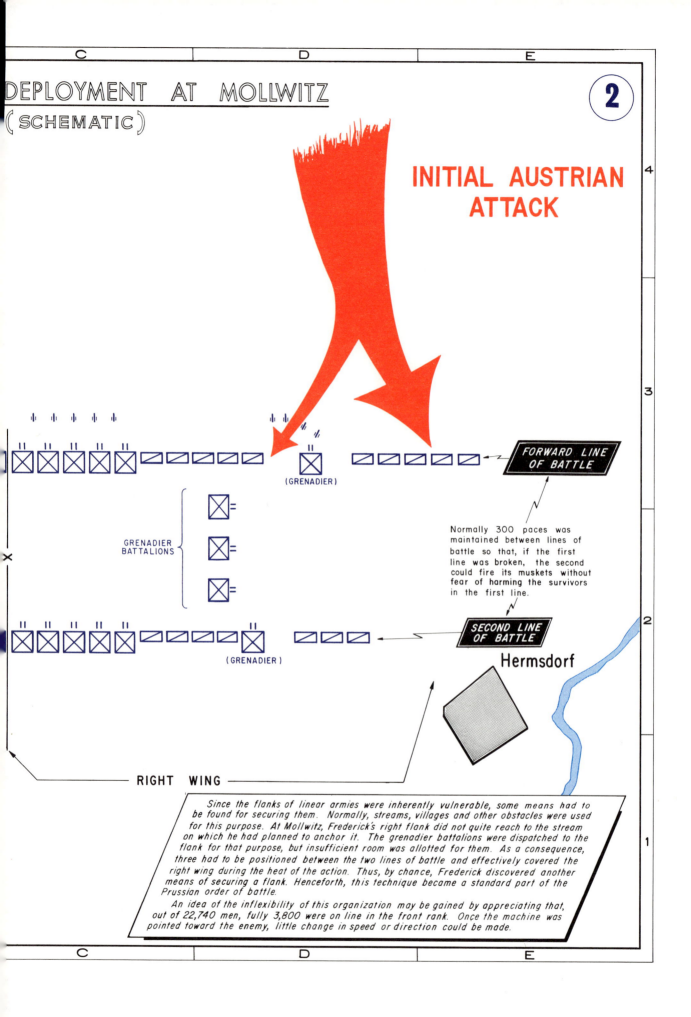

DEPLOYMENT AT MOLLWITZ
(SCHEMATIC)

INITIAL AUSTRIAN ATTACK

(GRENADIER)

FORWARD LINE OF BATTLE

Normally 300 paces was maintained between lines of battle so that, if the first line was broken, the second could fire its muskets without fear of harming the survivors in the first line.

GRENADIER BATTALIONS

SECOND LINE OF BATTLE

(GRENADIER)

Hermsdorf

X

RIGHT WING

Since the flanks of linear armies were inherently vulnerable, some means had to be found for securing them. Normally, streams, villages and other obstacles were used for this purpose. At Mollwitz, Frederick's right flank did not quite reach to the stream on which he had planned to anchor it. The grenadier battalions were dispatched to the flank for that purpose, but insufficient room was allotted for them. As a consequence, three had to be positioned between the two lines of battle and effectively covered the right wing during the heat of the action. Thus, by chance, Frederick discovered another means of securing a flank. Henceforth, this technique became a standard part of the Prussian order of battle.

An idea of the inflexibility of this organization may be gained by appreciating that, out of 22,740 men, fully 3,800 were on line in the front rank. Once the machine was pointed toward the enemy, little change in speed or direction could be made.

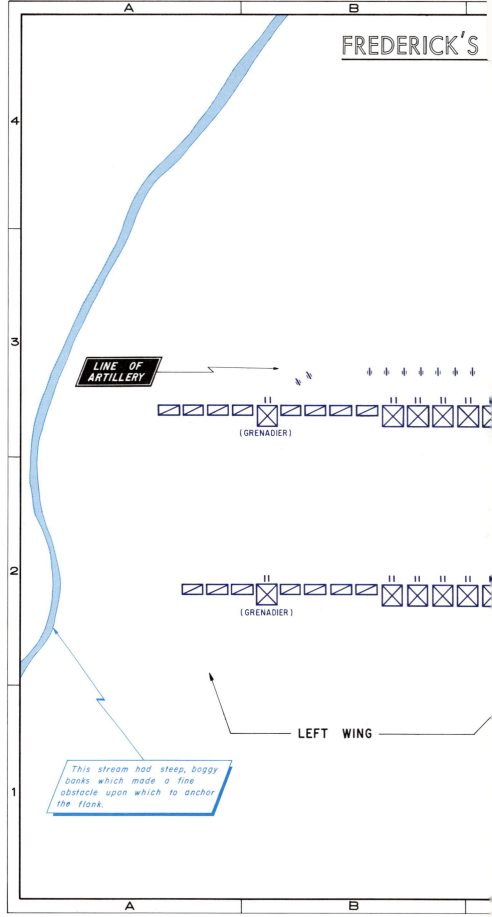

LINE OF
ARTILLERY

(GRENADIER)

(GRENADIER)

LEFT WING

This stream had steep, boggy banks which made a fine obstacle upon which to anchor the flank.

CENTRAL EUROPE

CIRCA 1740

SCALE OF MILES

50   0   50   100

N O R T H   S E A

The territorial fragmentation of Europe increased as the Holy Roman Empire continued to break up in the 18th century. In Germany alone there were roughly 300 principalities, duchies, and imperial cities. For simplicity, only the major political units are depicted. Boundaries are located as confirmed by the Treaty of Utrecht, in 1713.

Birmingham

Norwich

Ipswich

Amsterdam

UNITED   NETHERLANDS

Rhine R.

Ems R.

Thames   R.   London

Nijmegen

Southampton

Dover

Ostend

Eindhoven

Portsmouth

Calais

Dunkirk

Antwerp

IMPERIAL TERRITOR

Cologne

AUSTRIAN

Lys R.

Oudenarde

Brussels

Maastricht

Aachen

Lille

Ramillies

Meuse R.

Bonn

NETHER   LANDS

Arras

Malplaquet

Namur

Liege

Coblenz

Sambre R.

Le Havre

St Quentin

Sedan

Moselle R.

Mainz

Caen

Rouen

Laon

Rocroi

Luxembourg

C

Seine R.

Worms

Oise R.

Aisne R.

Soisson

Verdun

DUCHY OF

PALAT

Evreux

Marne R.

Reims

LORRAINE

Mannheim

Dreux

Paris

Chalons

Metz

Chartres

Nancy

MTS

Toul

Strasbourg

VOSGES

Orleans

Sens

Troyes

ALSAC

Rhine R.

Sossba

Angers

Loire R.

BADEN

Tours

Turkheim

WÜR

F R A N C E

Mulhouse

Freiburg

Belfort

Poitiers

Nevers

Basel

Vienne R.

Bern

SWITZERLAND

Loire R.

Limoges

Geneva

Lyon

Rhone R.

SAVOY

MIL

Turin

Valence

The Soldier-King 8

It is natural for men to consider peace as normal and war as the exception, even during periods of prolonged conflict. In Prussia this attitude was reversed, and it is no accident that the roots of German belligerence are often traced to 1740. From then on, Prussia's wars were energetically waged, and, under masters like Frederick, the Army was usually ready to fight them. Preparedness does not come easily, however, even to an absolute regime, which has the entire material and human resources of the state at its command. Prussian readiness was energized by two extraordinary forces: the hostility of surrounding neighbors, and the driving will of her Soldier-King.

The two Silesian wars were tests of strength that substantially improved Prussia's strategic posture and shattered the prestige of the Hapsburg Empire. Frederick had no illusions that what had been won by the sword could be defended in any other way; therefore, prosperity depended on keeping the sword sharp and resolving to use it when necessary. Since the Peace of Dresden did not end the war with Austria, but only interrupted it, the King decided to put the intermission to good use. Fortunately for Prussia, he was granted nearly 11 years.

Readiness in Peacetime

Domestic affairs now came under the monarch's close scrutiny. In his characteristic style, he worked hard to improve his Government and to expedite the absorption of Silesia into the Prussian economy. Impatiently prodding his ministers, just as he urged his generals in battle, Frederick personally saw that laws were reformed, marshes reclaimed, finances put in order, and industry expanded. This intense pace of progress increased the Government's annual income from 6 million thalers in 1740 to over 12 million in 1752, while the annexation of Silesia increased the population from 2.2 to 3.9 million. Enlargement of the state obviously favored the Army, which continued to have first claim on Prussia's growing resources.

In view of Hapsburg intentions, there was no relaxation in the ranks. In times of peace, regiments were dispersed among their home provinces. However, discipline and training were still closely checked by the King, who spent almost half of each year on field visits, ensuring that his directives were being carried out to the letter. He continued to demand parade ground precision, and, when personally checking regimental reviews with his stopwatch, Frederick more than once expressed dissatisfaction by dismissing a commander. Even Henry, his capable brother, was restricted to his quarters for slipshod work with his regiment, and the famous Bayreuth Dragoons were summarily penalized with three months extra drill for failing to meet the King's standards on the drill field. In a comprehensive test of overall readiness, Frederick assembled the Army once a year for maneuvers. The generals, as well as the troops, demonstrated their proficiency. Marches, tactics, logistics, and new equipment were subjected to the King's scrutiny. Every detail passed or failed his exacting inspection. "Unless every man is trained beforehand in peacetime for that which he will have to accomplish in war," wrote Frederick, "one has nothing but people who bear the name of a business without knowing how to practice it."

This obsessive pursuit of excellence was accompanied by a steady increase in the size of the Army. In 1740, Frederick had inherited an Army of 80,000 men; by 1756, it numbered 150,000. The artillery had doubled and the cavalry had increased from 114 to 211 squadrons. Like all other armies of that time, it depended on magazines and depots for supply. Frederick hastened to stock quantities of gunpowder, grain, boots, sabres, and muskets in key Silesian depots. At the same time he labored to build forts to protect them. Schweidnitz, Glatz, Neisse, and Glogau were the most important of

Frederick, Returning From Maneuvers

seven bastions that were built or improved in Silesia. *(See Map 3.)*

What spurred the Prussian ruler to these consuming peacetime exertions? A close reading of recent events, no doubt, and the knowledge that his antagonist, Maria Theresa, was using the interlude for the same sort of preparation. Seeking to understand the cause of Austrian defeats, she learned of slack discipline, mismanaged logistics, and ineffective training. These deficiencies called not for improvement, but fundamental reform of the Army and the Government. A committee directed by the experienced General Leopold Daun revamped Austrian tactical doctrine along Prussian lines. Summer training camps were arranged for infantry and cavalry, and new regulations were written. But an army is no better than the society from which it is derived. If the country is backward and its people divided, volumes of new regulations will not modernize its military instrument overnight.

If Austria's halting reforms only began a needed revitalization, in France there was no reform at all in an Army that suffered from deep and diverse ills. Standardization was not practiced in training, organization, or supply, and high commanders rotated frequently because of court intrigues. To aggravate these problems, military commanders and civil intendants did not work together, a condition that promised serious troubles during mobilization and deployment. Lack of interest on the part of the indolent Louis XV was undoubtedly the direct cause of the once proud Army's decline, but it would have taken a general of great originality and influence to arouse the French Army from its slumber. Who dared to change the methods that had won victories for Enghien, Turenne, Villars, and Saxe?

Other European armies similarly displayed the strengths and weaknesses of the countries they represented and the regimes they served. The Russian Army was the most national in composition, except in the highest ranks, where foreigners had long dominated the positions of responsibility. The strength of the Russian field army lay in its size, which was generally around 130,000. Neither the Swedish nation nor its small Army had recovered from the exhausting Great Northern War and the vigorous campaigning of Charles XII. Rather than allow a regular army to develop, the British imported mercenaries to protect the home isles. Since the time of Cromwell, military professionals had been suspect. Regular land forces were employed for the most part in far-off places like India and, more recently, America.

It may appear strange that the contest between England and France over possessions in distant lands should govern the destiny of Frederick's continental kingdom. The diplomatic revolution, which determined the lineup for the Seven Years' War, however, was a by-product of this continuing rivalry. A brief survey of the colonial scene, therefore, is essential if one is to understand how the imaginative and dynamic statesman, William Pitt, resurrected British strategy and built an empire.

The French and Indian War

The French and British clashed in nearly every corner of the globe. India, the West Indies, and North America all became battlegrounds in a common war. The Seven Years' War in Europe and the French and Indian War in America, however, were the principal localized clashes in this worldwide contest for supremacy. The basic issue in the colonies was commercial, as mercantilistic states hungrily sought raw materials to feed their factories and bullion to pay their armies. In North America, colonial expansion aggravated the struggle for trade. As settlers from Virginia and traders from Canada pushed into the hinterlands, inevitable skirmishes occurred. Far-off European cabinets were powerless to control these encounters, satisfying only themselves by proclaiming vague boundaries, which often conflicted on the map and were, in practice, meaningless. In this way, the Ohio Valley suddenly became a major focus of conflict.

The French might not have gained that key waterway had the British colonies learned to work together. Virginia took the lead in 1753 by sending a 21-year-old militia officer named George Washington to reconnoiter the basin west of the Appalachian Mountains. Washington returned with unsettling reports that French agents were staking out vast claims in the untouched wilderness. He recommended that a fort be built to command the junction of the Allegheny and Monongehela Rivers. However, the other colonial governors were unconvinced of the urgent need to divert men and money from business activities to defend a remote frontier against French explorers and a few Indian tribes. Virginia undertook the project alone, and in the summer of 1754, the small militia band covering the construction site was ejected by a French contingent of over 1,000 men. George Washington had suffered his first defeat.

French commanders quickly appreciated the significance of the key position astride the forks of the Ohio, and promptly constructed Fort Duquesne at that location. British efforts to dislodge them failed; General Edward Braddock's attempt in 1755 ended in disaster. Like Oglethorpe's unsuccessful siege of St. Augustine, Braddock's failure was due to his use of conventional methods of warfare. Imported from the drill fields of the Continent, these methods were of little use in a war whose topographic, political, and economic conditions differed so greatly from those in Europe.

At this low ebb in British colonial influence, William Pitt, "the Great Commoner," rose to pre-eminence in the conduct of foreign affairs. His first ministry lacked the support of King and Parliament, and was unsuccessful. But England caught the fire of his personality. In June 1757, a government was finally formed in which ministerial powers were shared, but the dominant post in the cabinet was reserved for the popular and eloquent Pitt. As one of two coequal secretaries of state, Pitt quickly established his prominence in the cabinet, and set to work inaugurating his system of colonial policy. Under his direction, British fortunes overseas rapidly improved. Incompetent commanders were replaced with aggressive young men like Major General Jeffrey Amherst and

William Pitt

Brigadier General James Wolfe. The colonies were encouraged to participate in their own defense, and were informed of projects contemplated against the French.

Pitt not only animated the Government but also activated strategy. Canada became the objective, a three-pronged offensive the strategy. In 1758, Wolfe recaptured Louisbourg,* opening access to the St. Lawrence River. Shortly thereafter, Brigadier General John Forbes, in command of a combined British and American force, occupied Fort Duquesne, and renamed it Fort Pitt. In the following year, Wolfe scaled the heights of Quebec with 3,000 regulars. He died valiantly, winning fame for himself, and most of Canada for England.

Pitt's greatest achievement was the shaping of strategy that conformed to global policy and fully utilized available means. Broadly stated, his aim was "to conquer America in Germany." British troops were sent to the colonies, but British money went to the Continent, creating a diversion and absorbing the attention—and Army—of France. To ensure the effectiveness of his secondary effort in Europe, Pitt was willing to plunge the Government into debt. Presumably, London merchants supported his financial ventures in anticipation of

---

*The colonists had taken possession of it 10 years earlier, only to lose it to France at the peace table.

special trading rights with America. Meanwhile, the Navy blockaded French ports, raided enemy bases, and interdicted reinforcements intended for the New World. It was an unconventional scheme, but it relied on common sense. Pitt allocated his resources with an eye to the commercial and maritime strength of his nation. He also saw the importance of the role to be played by Great Britain's chief ally, and he cultivated Frederick with masterful care.

The Diplomatic Revolution

Is it true that war begins only when diplomacy fails? Consider Europe in 1756. England, France, Austria, and Russia were the weights in the power balance, while Prussia stood at the fulcrum. If peace depended on maintaining equilibrium, it was necessary that the weights be evenly distributed and Prussia remain at the pivot. But statesmen were intent on disturbing the balance, and to Frederick, the safety of Prussia was more important than the stability of Europe. King George II, also, was little concerned with the larger continental issues, but he was concerned for the security of his native Hanover. It had become obvious that England's Hanoverian-based dynasty required a more reliable guarantor than the erratic Hapsburg Empire, which increasingly shrank from commitments that were far removed from Austria and Hungary. An agreement signed with Russia in 1755 proved less than satisfactory for England's purpose, but it did prod the vigilant Frederick away from his fitful ties with France. To him, the thought of Russian troops marching across Silesia was almost as menacing as the Austrian threat. Thus, the diplomatic about-face that was now to sweep Europe was triggered by the British. In January 1756, Prussia and Great Britain signed the Convention of Westminister, with Frederick promising to defend Hanover against France, and England serving as a brake on Russia. Ironically, the man who ultimately profited most from this alliance—William Pitt—objected the loudest, claiming that it tied England too tightly to continental affairs.

No one foresaw the effect of this defensive alliance on the agitated Hapsburg court. The "Ten Years' Peace" had only served to inflame Maria Theresa's desire for vengeance. Her chief minister, Prince Wenzel Kaunitz, adroitly managed Austrian affairs, and aimed at directing these shifts of interest toward Prussia's destruction. Having served as ambassador in Paris, he had little difficulty reminding the Bourbon court of Frederick's betrayals. He could point to the new treaty with England as further proof. Skillfully turning France against her genuine interests, he escalated bad feelings to enmity. On May 1, 1756, France and Austria ended their century-long vendetta, and became allies. Russia had not yet formalized her entry into the anti-Prussian league, but the Tsarina was sufficiently outraged by Great Britain's sudden alliance with the impertinent Frederick to respond eagerly to Kaunitz's grand design. In this manner, using distrust and intrigue, a formidable coalition was engineered.

By its very nature, a coalition tends to be an unreliable machine. Hampered by the necessity for constant agreement among its various parties, it rarely demonstrates decisive action, and normally the threat of aggression by a strong common foe is required to cement its combined resolve. For the moment, Kaunitz had conjured up a credible menace, with the help of European ignorance, arrogance, and fear. Typical of the prevailing climate of mistrust was Frederick's lifelong judgment of his chief antagonist: "an ambitious and vindictive enemy, who was the more dangerous because she was a woman, headlong in her opinions, and implacable."

Frederick was kept well-informed of the forces operating against him. It was impossible for Austria to conceal either the flow of supplies to depots in Bohemia or the bristling camps in Moravia. A particularly ominous piece of intelligence brought the news that a train of pontoons was assembling in Vienna. Not only were enemy capabilities disclosed, but intentions were also telegraphed. Prussian spies in Saxony had no trouble uncovering reliable evidence of Kaunitz' offensive plan, while reports from East Prussia confirmed that 70,000 Russian troops were in motion toward that province. Even a report that the attack would be delayed until the following spring did not dispel the danger, but only forecast a larger one in 1757. Frederick's dilemma was the opening of an act that Prussia was fated to rehearse for a century and a half: how to prevent a war on multiple fronts.

Under the pressure of that summer's tension, the Prussian court suffered its hawks and doves. The fiery Hans von Winterfeld, one of the few generals enjoying Frederick's complete trust, argued for attack, "since they only wait to attack us." The King's brother, Prince Henry, was less restive and counselled moderation, rather than plunging the overmatched Prussian state into a futile *Götterdämmerung*. Frederick watched and waited.

Pre-Emptive War

Without warning, three Prussian columns invaded Saxony on August 29, 1756. An unsatisfying exchange of notes with Austria had ended four days earlier, when Frederick's latest demand that Vienna explain its warlike moves met with a contemptuous and evasive reply. Perhaps associating the first-strike style with the *blitzkrieg* pattern of the twentieth century, critics have accused the King of commencing a Germanic age of conquest. Pro-Germans contend that Frederick launched his offensive to prevent a larger war. There is an element of truth in both claims, but neither offers more than a partial solution to a chronic strategic problem. A mere Silesian-type surgery could not cure his encircling enemies of the war disease. In any event, the days following the invasion soon disclosed that a far larger operation was intended; one that would only deepen the wound. *(See Map 4.)*

The first moves were designed to speedily overrun Saxony and secure the Elbe for transport of supplies. These preliminaries completed, Frederick planned to carry the war into Bohemia. One week after the invasion began, the three separate columns of the Prussian main army met near Dresden. But the Saxons chose not to fight, and retired with their king into the formidable fortified camp at Pirna. Frederick had not anticipated this Fabian move, and now encountered a familiar problem. To press into Bohemia without securing his line of communication was to risk certain defeat, as the memory of 1744 reminded him. On the other hand, the campaigning season was already far advanced. A drawn-out siege in Saxony would limit, and perhaps prevent, the decisive thrust into Bohemia.

Determined to prevent the Austrian Army from relieving its Saxon allies, Frederick chose to retain the initiative, using as many battalions as he could afford from the indecisive affair at Pirna. Winterfeld was left to keep a hammerlock on the inactive Saxons, while the rest of the Army pushed south to secure the passes into Bohemia. In a change of the mission, Schwerin was given discretionary orders. He was to draw the enemy in Bohemia away from Saxony, and, if the situation favored it, advance into Bohemia. The old gladiator, now 72, dutifully advanced, but was halted by Prince Piccolomini's strong positions near Königgrätz, and had to be content with foraging the country clean all around his immovable opponent. Meanwhile, Maximilian Browne, an Irish emigré in Hapsburg uniform, proceeded majestically to the rescue of Saxony, but halted shortly at the Eger River until the arrival of bridging from Vienna.

For a week, both sides remained in a sort of suspended animation. Neither was willing to risk a costly assault on the other's strong position, and neither was able to bypass strongpoints that could interdict logistic lifelines. Operations subsided into the classic pattern: the clash of hussar patrols and foraging parties. Saxon biscuits dwindled, but so did Prussia's summer. Frederick broke the spell.

On learning of Browne's delay at the Eger, the King decided to push forward to seize the high ground west of Lowositz. Characteristically, he rode to join the vanguard, and on October 1 personally evaluated his foe from the vineyard-covered hill overlooking the town. Early morning fog shrouded the valley, but could not conceal the signs of an army—wisps of smoke, the restless movement of patrols, and Pandours crouched behind low walls. Burning to end the suspense as well as the stalemate, he flung the Prussian cavalry, cannon, and foot soldiers down the terraced vineyards onto Browne's unready army. Anchored on high ground to the south and the Elbe to the north, Prussian infantry repeated the Mollwitz maneuver, repulsing Austrian cavalry and then rolling through vineyards, Austrians, and town. Using artillery to keep the Prussians at bay, Browne managed to stabilize his position just east of Lowositz. Only Frederick's strong threat to turn the Austrian south flank forced the Austrian commander to yield his position late in the day.

Shocked by this repulse of their deliverer, the weakening garrison of Pirna broke out two weeks later in a desperate attempt to join Browne east of the Elbe River. Hard rains, low temperatures, and inept generalship doomed the venture to failure and the Saxon army to captivity. The next morning Frederick dismayed ally and enemy alike by inducting the vanquished Saxons wholesale into the Prussian Army. The much trampled electorate bitterly yielded the ultimate in defeat; Prussia coldly added 20 battalions and 80 cannon to her trophies.

Voltaire satirically compared the abduction of the Saxon Army to the subjugations of Alexander. The rest of Europe howled piracy! Frederick did not allow these noises to deaden his political and military sensibilities. If the fact of a hostile coalition had ever been uncertain, the sack of Saxony removed any further doubt. During the all too brief winter of 1756, Frederick withdrew from Bohemia and marshalled his energies for the battles that he knew would follow. In this expectation he was not disappointed. The second year of this rancorous war produced a kaleidoscopic turmoil of renewed aggression, vindictive retaliation, and the most breathtaking trek in history from one battlefield to another to preserve the kingdom threatened with annihilation. It was raw drama, and the underdog played the leading role.

Examining his resources in preparation for the next round, Frederick conceded the superiority of the forces arrayed against him. *(See Map 5.)* Opposed to his field armies of 160,000 men and his 48,000-man army of observation in Hanover, the armies of Austria, Russia, France, Sweden, and the petty German states numbered well over 300,000. Reserves could swell the odds. Inaction was no remedy for this mathematical nightmare. Movement had to multiply his numbers. Frederick's offensive instinct needed no further actuation. In April 1757, he entered Bohemia again. *(See Map 6.)*

Prussian formations advanced dispersed, in a rare preview of nineteenth and twentieth century warfare. From Silesia, Schwerin debouched through Landshut, where snow still lay deep in the pass. A smaller force, commanded by the Duke of Bevern, marched from Lusatia. Two armies also filed out of Saxony; the larger, commanded personally by Frederick, moved slowly, while Maurice, the "Young Dessauer," threw a fake at his opponent and slipped through the Commotau gap, thereby driving the Austrian covering force out of its position in front of Frederick. Schwerin bypassed General Johann Serbelloni and narrowly missed cutting off the retreating Konigseck, who had just experienced a sound thrashing in a sharp encounter with Bevern.

The Austrian reaction to these four relentlessly merging forces was hampered by an unready system of command. Prince Charles was the nominal commander in Bohemia, but he waited for more than a month after his appointment to leave Vienna and assume control of operations. In the interim, responsibility for the defense fell to Browne, who was now stricken by disease. Bewildered by the Prussian concentric advance, and unable to direct widely separated border fights,

he ordered a delay, hoping to offer resistance somewhere between the frontiers and Prague. But initiative once lost is not easily regained. As the badly coordinated Austrians withdrew, Browne called councils of war to try to persuade his generals to fight. When Charles arrived in Prague on April 30, he was shocked by the confusion that gripped both city and army. Meanwhile, Marshal Daun lethargically gathered his forces and prepared to move toward Prague. Frederick made certain that he would arrive too late.

Prague: The Indecisive Victory

As the Prussian advance guard thundered at the heels of Austrian troops retreating down the west bank of the Elbe,

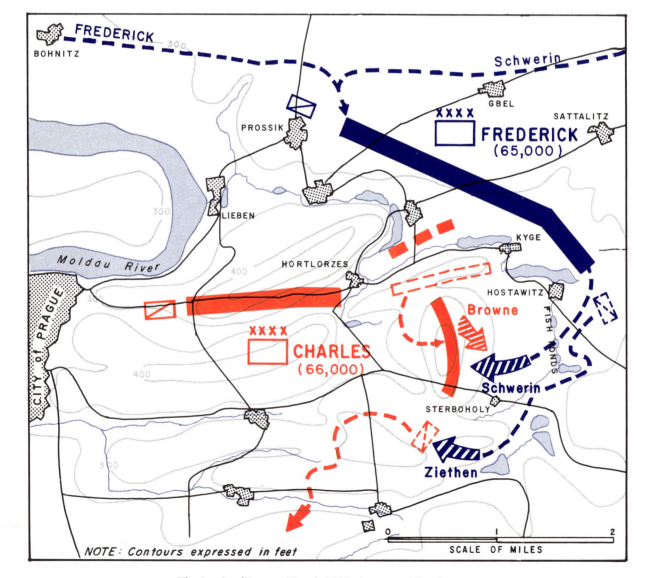

The Battle of Prague, May 6, 1757: Attempted Envelopment

it was evident that a major engagement could not long be avoided. The only question was whether it would be a battle or a siege. The choice was up to Charles, who convened another council of war. Reinforced with cautious advice, he promptly overrode Browne's plea to attack before Frederick and Schwerin joined. It was safer to take position on the high ground east of Prague within sight of the city gates.

The terrain around Prague is steep and rocky, and is dominated by an irregular ridge running several miles to the east. The western spurs of this terrain block were protected by the battlements of the city and the serpentine twist of the Moldau River. The north and east were covered by a curving chain of lakes joined by a deceptively small stream and some empty fishponds overlaid with green mud.

Charles recognized this gift of nature, but wavered between the unhappy options of defending it, retreating into the city fortress, and abandoning Prague altogether. Frederick's priority was the consolidation of his armies, a chore fraught with danger in the face of a more determined opponent than Charles. While a detachment advanced down the west bank of the Moldau, Frederick crossed the main body to the east in a rush, and then signaled the waiting Schwerin to move. Early on May 6, the junction was completed and the united army deployed into standard lines of battle. Frederick's next action was to reconnoiter.

Swirls of dust, the gleam of bayonets, and rows of tents marked the trace of Charles' unassailable front. A tired Marshal Schwerin was dispatched to find a way around the flank; the eager Winterfeld echoed the King's resolve to attack that day, while Daun was still away. None of the three was alert

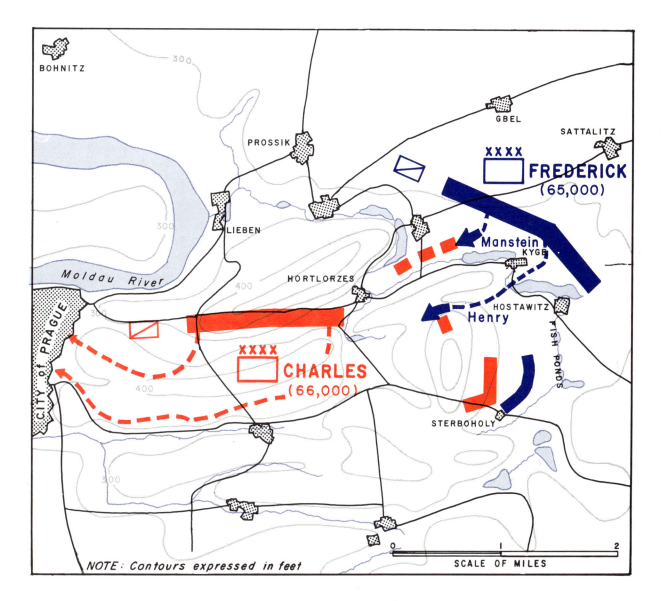

The Battle of Prague, May 6, 1757: The Penetration

to the subtle flaws in terrain south of Hostawitz. They saw only "green meadows," where cavalry and infantry might deploy to climb the slopes. *(See Map, page 116.)*

Ziethen's cavalry splashed around the camouflaged fishponds, but Schwerin's infantry went in over their knees, and his artillery sank to the trunnions, choking the narrow causeways leading through the villages. The Prussian ranks were thus frozen like toy soldiers in a panorama, and the Austrians were shifting guns and grenadiers to bear on the struggling, cursing men below. Shot and grape tore at the desperate Prussians as Browne at last found his chance to strike. The Austrians swarmed from their cannon-covered hill and met the dripping Prussians rising from the muck. In these straits, only valor could retrieve what error had all but thrown away.

There was valor aplenty, and not all of it anonymous. Commanders and troops alike lunged to close the distance; many went down before they could level their bayonets. Winterfeld was hit in the neck, and had to be dragged from the mire by his men. Prussian blue littered the slopes less than a hundred paces from the enemy lines. It was the high-water mark of the infantry advance in the south, although Ziethen's hussars and dragoons eventually succeeded in putting their opponents to flight. Trying to rally his disintegrating regiments, Schwerin dismounted and grasped a flag—"Come on my children, follow me!" Tired men responded to his impulsive cry, but not before a shower of grape struck him down. *(See Map, page 117.)*

Bravery had not won the slope, but Schwerin's heroic death inspired his followers to launch another attack. Responding to this new attempt, more of the Austrian right wing infantry crowded southwards toward Sterboholy. Shortly afterwards, Browne was hit. From then on, control of the Austrian right was lost, especially at the moment when control was most important to their cause. A mile to the north of the Sterboholy action, a gap opened in the Austrian lines. Caused by the stretch of the right wing toward Sterboholy, it could not be soon filled by the inactive portion of Charles' army, which was still oriented to the north. It was a big enough hole to drive a brigade through, and a quick thinking Prussian brigadier named Manstein decided to try, even though his orders called for march column to the south. It was a classic abandonment of mission, and would probably have failed if Prince Henry had not seconded the move with a similar effort through the passageway between Kyge and Hostawitz.

Quick to perceive the opportunity, Frederick reinforced success, feeding the remainder of the Prussian right wing into the point of decision. Too late, the leaderless Austrian troops near Sterboholy discovered Prussians above and behind them. Browne lay mortally wounded, and Charles was called to save the crumbling right wing. At the moment of decision,

the hapless commander in chief was struck with a seizure, and, unable to utter a word, was carried from the field of Prague. His army acknowledged defeat by following him into the city.

Frederick could not take the credit for having ordered the famous penetration of opportunity that to this day is called "the Prague Maneuver." However, the King was quick to exploit the occasion, and thus make use of an advantage that was offered to him. Like Alexander at Gaugamela, the general made the key decision, although, as usual, it was the discipline of the infantry that carried it out. It was also the infantry that suffered, losing over 3,000 killed, including 5 generals and 6 regimental commanders. The old soldier who had taught his captain could never be replaced. Frederick was right when he said, "The pillars of our infantry have fallen." What was worse, the bulk of Charles' men now lay secure behind the walls of Prague, and there were indications that Daun and 40,000 more were loitering within five miles of the city. The toughest fight of Frederick's career had confirmed his generalship, but it had been far from a conclusive victory.

The Ring Tightens

To complete the work begun at Prague, Frederick now had to dispose of the army of Daun. *(See Map 7.)* Bevern, with a detachment of 25,000 men, advanced to locate Daun and bring him to battle. The clever Daun, whose army was being steadily strengthened by daily reinforcements, backpedaled, drawing Bevern away from Frederick, away from his supplies, and into rough ground where irregulars harassed his rear and hussars obscured his view. Neither side could long postpone the fight—Daun because of Charles' worsening condition in Prague, Frederick because of alarming rumbles in the rear of his troops. Two French armies, totaling nearly 100,000 men, were flowing across the Rhine and through the Hessian plains toward Saxony, the linchpin of Prussia's strategic bastion.

Marshal Daun

Time was critical for Frederick. A battle must be brought off and quickly consummated if freedom of action were to be preserved. The war of conquest was over; now would begin the fight for space and time.

Hurrying out of Prague with 10,000 men, Frederick marched to reinforce Bevern. The Prussians met Daun's countermarch on June 14 in the hills near Kollin. Frederick's deployment was well conceived; weakening one flank and pulling it back for protection, he massed his strength on the other flank, where he intended to strike his main blow. But the execution of his plan went astray. Maurice misunderstood Frederick's orders and missed the proper angle of attack, while the impetuous Manstein prematurely committed the Prussian right wing. This time the odds were 1 to 2, and there was no one to bail Manstein out. With all of his combat power committed, Frederick had no means to restore the line against the grinding advance of superior numbers and guns. The gamble failed, and 13,000 more men were killed or wounded. Irritated by his brother's aggressive actions, Henry muttered, "Phaeton has tumbled." Frederick realized that he could no longer besiege Prague with his pared-down army.

Although men and territory were lost, time was not. The retreat to the Bohemian frontier allowed the army to concentrate within range of Saxony and Silesia. *(See Map 7.)* The retrograde movement proceeded, marred by accidents and dissension between Winterfeld and Prince William, who commanded the column retreating into Lusatia. On July 20, William allowed himself to be maneuvered out of Zittau. The loss of this important trading town and route of escape from Bohemia was the first puncture of Frederick's inner defenses. The second occurred just one week later, when the Duke of Cumberland was beaten at Hastenbeck and forced to withdraw to Hamburg. Hanover was virtually ceded to the enemy. August brought no better tidings. The leisurely advance of Prince Soubise gathered momentum as Imperial princes and dukes gave their loyalties and regiments to the French cause. The whole western frontier was now aflame. *(See Map 8.)*

To arrest the blaze, a "fire brigade" was formed—a corps of cavalry and infantry about 14,000 strong. Leaving Bevern with 36,000 men and instructions to guard the passes into northern Silesia, Frederick led the small force westward on August 15. As he passed through Dresden, Maurice joined him. Prussian hopes now rode on a force of over 25,000, which arrived in Erfurt on September 12, prompting Soubise to recoil. Five days later, a young cavalry commander named Seydlitz rode through the gates of Gotha at dusk and tumbled the French headquarters out of town. It was an affront the French could not ignore, especially since the addition of Prince Hildburghausen's corps three weeks earlier had swelled the Allied strength to 54,000. Frederick was confident that he could best his French antagonist, but he needed time to over-

take him. Eschewing rash moves, he settled in Leipzig so as not to be pulled too far from Silesia, and there established a loose defense to draw on his opponent.

Once more his intentions were upset by bad news from other theaters. Charles was pressing Bevern, and Winterfeld had been killed guarding the route to Lauban. At the opposite corner of the embattled kingdom, Marshal Lehwaldt had been beaten by the Russians, and at the same time Sweden had begun to move. Fixed by the motionless threat of Soubise, Frederick was powerless to aid his eastern defenders. Waiting with sinking spirits, he wrote Voltaire, "All men are but the sport of destiny."

The break came in mid-October in an unexpected way. Haddick, leader of Austria's Croatian irregulars, set out from an encampment near Dresden with a band of 4,000 men and descended on Berlin. Ill informed of Haddick's strength and fearing that the Austrian was working in concert with the Swedes, Frederick gave chase with a small force from Leipzig, rousing his garrisons in eastern Saxony to intensify the pursuit. By October 20 the raid was over. The capital had been ransomed for 300,000 thalers in true medieval style, and Haddick's Croats had vanished back into the Lusatian forests. Relieved, Frederick wearily turned the "fire brigade" back, to resume the western vigil. Encouraged by the King's hurried departure, Soubise had already set his men in motion toward Leipzig, the commercial center of Saxony and a fine place to winter his ill supplied French troops. A battle could now be gained; the ransom paid to Haddick was more than worth a fight with the French. Destiny was indeed at work, and Frederick meant for it to work toward a decisive victory for Prussia.

Rossbach: Decision in the West

Frederick's swift return from the futile hunt for Haddick threw the Allied camp into consternation. Leaving small covering posts at Halle, Merseburg, and Weissenfels, the main body retired to a central location west of the Saale River, while Soubise coordinated with Richelieu to the north, and Hildburghausen looked to his supplies in Thuringia. Frederick sped through Leipzig on October 30 and rudely chased Hildburghausen's grenadiers out of Weissenfels, but not before the bridge was burned. Determined not to miss his opportunity, the King quickly erected bridges across the Saale, forced a hasty crossing, and sent messages directing Prince Ferdinand to move his forces across the river at Merseburg and Halle. Ferdinand expertly feinted toward Richelieu and swung south; another column followed the retreating Soubise. It looked like the start of another Prague, as relentless columns converged on a bewildered prey. But how to fashion a win with 22,000 opposed by 54,000?

Frederick first had to fix the target, and then devise some way to smash a part of it with a hastily forged hammer. While Prussian columns formed on the flat, open ground west of the Saale, Frederick rode forward to inspect his opponent's dispositions. *(See Map 9.)* The Soubise-Hildburghausen force was distributed over a hill, looking north across a stream. The French command had finally decided to fight, and erroneously assumed that the northern Prussian columns constituted the main approach. Banishing the worry that his opponents might still evade him, Frederick hastened to profit by their first tactical mistake. Moving at daybreak on November 4, the Prussian army deployed into a formation similar to that envisioned at Kollin. The device for overthrowing his stronger enemy was framed in Frederick's mind. He would advance suddenly, throw the bulk of his army against the enemy's open flank, and use the refused left wing to fix the enemy's right or act as covering force in case of defeat. The scheme had to be put aside, however, for Frederick soon discovered that the French had moved during the night.

Their new position was more formidable. It was anchored by obstacles on both north and south, and the high ground was well laced with cannon. While observing this imposing sight, Frederick, who was positioned in front of his chafing horsemen, was saluted from the French side by a vigorous cannonade. Disgusted with this turn of fate, he made the difficult decision not to commit his meager forces. Instead, he withdrew about two miles onto defensible terrain. It was a wise move, although it was interpreted by the French as a loss of nerve.

What occurred on the following day reads like fiction, especially for the eighteenth century. In November, armies usually ended campaigns and looked for places to hibernate. No commander stayed longer in the field unless dire circumstances threatened. Soubise and Hildburghausen were not exempted from the fetter of this prevailing rule, and the ramshackle French supply system made it all the more imperative either to withdraw to Erfurt or advance to Leipzig. There was no possible compromise, and there could be no delay. Although there were clear indications of the proper course, Soubise and Hildburghausen took the wrong one.

Mistaking Frederick's rearward move for rearward thinking, the Allied army sought to catch him in retreat with a bold maneuver. Soubise suggested to his nominal superior that they undertake a wide southward swing to threaten Frederick's bridges over the Saale, and thereby force him to withdraw. Hildburghausen concurred with the direction of attack, since it ensured his southern line of communication, but, trying to be faithful to the overall Austrian strategy, he argued for a more decisive goal. In an early morning meeting

on November 5, the two agreed to aim at the destruction of Frederick's small army.

While commanders assembled for briefing, orders went out recalling foragers from their plundering. *(See Map 10.)* Count St. Germain moved with 6,000 cavalry and infantry to screen the main attack with dust and noise. While this was being reluctantly carried out, the German cavalry led by Soubise headed the main body, which began its move toward noon. French infantry and cavalry followed, interspersed with artillery and German infantry. The movement was ponderous and confused, as the three hurriedly formed columns jammed together. Like the Romans at Trasimene, the French made only a feeble reconnaissance. There was no attempt to push an adequate screen up to the higher ground beyond Rossbach to survey Prussian moves and prevent Frederick from seeing theirs.

Frederick watched this amateur generalship with disbelief. At first, he suspected that the crawling columns were withdrawing toward their supplies in the south. The prancings of St. Germain were readily identified as an ineffective cover for the main body. The King sat down to lunch and the Prussian army remained still, silently observing the clumsy procession that was intermittently, but clearly, visible as it wound across the bare, rolling country south of Branderoda and Gröst.

At length, lunch finished, Frederick took anther sighting. The enemy columns pointed due east. What magnificent luck! Commanders gathered to receive the order. Thirty-eight squadrons of cavalry quickly assembled under the operational control of quick-thinking, fast-moving Friederich von Seydlitz, a pipe-smoking ramrod, born to horse and to command. He was only 33 years old, and older generals grumbled, but Seydlitz quickly silenced the rumblings of dissent: "Gentlemen, I have got to obey the King, and you have got to obey me." At last the King unleashed the coiled storm of that waiting, brooding cloud of men.

Within 30 minutes the entire army, minus seven hussar squadrons left to amuse St. Germain, was on the move. Seydlitz trotted east, concealed by Janus Hill. Prince Henry followed with seven infantry battalions and eighteen 12-pound guns. The King watched from Janus Hill and, for once, let his lieutenants have their day. Riding the crest of the ridge, Seydlitz saw his adversaries toiling up the hill, thinking that the Prussians were fleeing and that they were pursuing. The Prussian cavalry wheeled into line, dragoons in front of cuirassiers. The signal to charge was Seydlitz' pipe thrown high in the air.

No violence done by man can ever surpass the brutality of the Rossbach death ride. Repelled by the shock of Seydlitz' first thunder, Soubise's cavalry was shattered. Part of the enemy cavalry splintered to the east, and many, having rolled

Friedrich von Seydlitz

back upon their comrades, were struck a second, third, and fourth time. Meanwhile, Prince Henry's battalions deployed and swept down from the crest. It was a masterful combined performance. The iron bracelet of guns around the slopes of Janus broke the Allies' spirit while Seydlitz broke their cavalry. The remainder of the Prussian army arrived after the decision; strung between Lundstedt and Reichertswerben, it swept the fugitives from the field, aided by a final vicious burst from the wounded but still fighting Seydlitz. Four thousand cavalrymen, 18 guns, and 7 battalions of infantry had whipped 50,000 men and demolished the myth of French superiority.

Rossbach was an odd encounter. The standard patterns did not hold true. It was a contest between an agile army with brains and a clumsy army without any. The result should never have been in question. Prussia lost 300 men, France lost 800 killed, 6,000 prisoners, 72 cannon, and reputation by the yard. Although the battle does not rank as one of the most decisive in history, French and German attitudes were deeply affected by the explosion at Rossbach that lasted less than an hour and a half.

Crisis in Silesia and the Classic Battle of Leuthen

The echoes of Rossbach immediately and permanently altered the complexion of the war in the west. The other French commander in Germany was warned not to tamper with the brand of dynamite that had just blown the roof in on his hapless colleague to the south. To encourage the French to depart from Prussia's western tongue of territory, Frederick left Henry in charge of 7,000 men in Magdeburg, and sent his best independent thinker, Prince Ferdinand, to revive the Hanoverian force near Hamburg. In less than six months, an applauding England commenced outright subsidies to sustain Frederick's emptying treasury. More important, Rossbach removed one major threat from Frederick's catalogue of worries. He now turned his attention to the east, where his presence was badly needed to cope with a more dangerous opponent.

Probably no separate commander worked under a greater handicap than the Duke of Bevern. When Frederick rode west in August, this brave soldier accepted the command of Prussian forces in Lusatia and Silesia with a dutiful but hesitant heart. *(See Map 8.)* His orders were clear enough; he was to cover the Zittau gap and prevent the Austrian army from gaining access to Breslau or interposing itself between him and Frederick. Even outnumbered by more than 2 to 1, it was a reasonable assignment; 36,000 men could surely block the northern exits from Bohemia. But if Charles' 90,000 should break through, which mission took priority? It was an insoluble dilemma, and the only man who could make the proper choice was 200 miles away when the Austrian juggernaut rolled over Prussian outposts in early September and smashed Winterfeld's counterattack. The loss of Winterfeld removed the one man on Bevern's team who might have suggested what Frederick would have done.

Pressured by reports that Austrians were now in possession of Bautzen, Bevern chose to cover Silesia, but failed to move decisively until after his provisions in Görlitz had been exhausted. He withdrew north toward Glogau, abandoning Liegnitz on September 27, while Charles methodically snapped up the mountain strongpoints protecting Breslau from the west. Wavering between the logistic attractions of Breslau and Glogau, Bevern finally realized that Charles had captured nearly all of the strongpoints in northern Silesia. With a sudden burst of energy, he cut his ties with Glogau and marched round to the east of Breslau, barely reaching that city before his pursuers, who had been shepherding him along.

Having thus far missed the main object of his campaign, Charles now preferred a battle, but the cautious Daun convinced him that the risk of attacking Bevern's positions could be lessened by first taking the fortress of Schweidnitz. The next three weeks were devoted to this furious siege, which ended on November 11 with the Prussians losing 6,000 men and many supplies, and Bevern losing his composure. Then Charles received news of Frederick's Rossbach coup, and from Vienna came an order: take Breslau! Charles and Daun, with 83,000 men, proceeded to do just that. After a poorly coordinated defense, the city fell on November 22, and Bevern was captured the following day. The Prussian general had become a victim of both Frederick's method of command and the improving Austrian Army.

Fragmentary reports of these unfortunate events reached Frederick at various stages of his trans-Prussian odyssey. Each new report altered elements in his basic plan, which was to eventually seek battle in Silesia. Time, the constant factor, pressed friend and foe alike; enemy and weather, the imponderables, affected calculations unequally. To balance an equation with so many unknowns, a commander's mind must be free to reason, to adjust, to decide. Well-drilled troops freed Frederick's, as he departed from Leipzig on November 12 with 16,000 men, his exact thoughts known only to himself. Instructions had already gone out to Bevern: hold Schweidnitz to block Charles' rear, and prepare to join the King for the showdown on the Oder River.

En route, Frederick learned that Schweidnitz had already surrendered. Now he wrote to Bevern to forget about blocking Charles and to attack him instead. Nearing Liegnitz, he received the bad news about the loss of Breslau and the capture of Bevern. Frederick also learned, however, that General Hans von Ziethen, the well-known hussar leader, had escaped with the remaining half of Bevern's force and the heavy guns from the fort at Glogau. The King continued to grapple with the task of regaining the initiative.

Frederick surveyed his reunited forces on December 2. Half of the men were downcast from their defeat in Silesia, while the others were buoyed by their win at Rossbach. The King had beaten fate before, and it could be done again. But first the tired and dispirited must be given rest and a cause for which to fight. Two precious days were set aside to restore morale. Every tool of leadership was needed to fire the will of soldiers who had tramped the hills of Bohemia, the Saxon plains, and the forests of Brandenburg, winning victories and losing comrades, but still not winning the war. The memory of battles fought that year alone was already receding into the dim past; Prague and Kollin could hardly be distinguished from Mollwitz and Hohenfriedberg.

Speaking to his generals, Frederick made it plain that regardless of the odds he intended to attack. "I should consider that I had accomplished nothing if I left the Austrians in possession of Silesia." He then went on to remind them that numbers were of secondary importance; the bravery of Prussian troops and the proper execution of his orders were paramount:

I shall immediately after the battle dismount and convert into a garrison regiment that cavalry regiment that does not immediately, on being ordered, burst impetuously

on the foe. The infantry battalion which, whatever the obstacles, halts for a moment, shall lose its standards and swords . . . *

Somewhere between Liegnitz and Breslau, Charles' army must be found. On December 4, the advance began. That day, Ziethen's hussars encountered and put to flight 4,000 Croats. A hundred bodies and over 500 prisoners were counted, and 80,000 loaves of bread, freshly made by the Austrian field bakery, fell into Prussian hands. This brief encounter gave both commanders their first hard intelligence, and foretold the cataclysm to follow.

Before dawn the next day (December 5), Frederick's relentless columns marched, Ziethen moving through a clinging December fog to scour the route ahead. Surprised by Frederick's pace, Charles relied on 70,000 men in position to defy the outnumbered "Potsdam Parade." Against the advice of Daun, he had already decided to fight, and, prepared for the fifth time to meet the "anti-Christian northern devil." For the fifth time Charles learned that the teaching of Saxe was true—that war *is* a science covered with shadows. The first shadow that darkened his day was the sudden flush of his covering force at Borna by Ziethen's cavalry. When this fracas was over, Frederick was in possession of the high ground at Borna, and with it, the initiative for the rest of the day. *(See Map 11a.)*

Riding close behind Ziethen's galloping pursuit, Frederick mounted a slight rise, and viewed the Hapsburg ranks stretched before him. He knew the terrain well, for it had been a Prussian maneuver ground during the 10 years of peace—gently rolling country, flecked with tiny villages and scrub forest. Charles' right flank nestled in the woods of Nypern, an entangling snare of peat bogs and swamp. His center was stitched along a line of hamlets, each one having been converted into a miniature citadel of masonry, men, and guns. The Austrian left disappeared into the dwindling haze south of Leuthen, after bending sharply toward the river at Sagschutz Hill. Charles' line stretched nearly five miles from flank to flank, a picture of immobility. The maneuver that had failed at Kollin and been rejected at Rossbach could now be resurrected. To make it work, however, the Austrian commander must be deceived.

Already the Austrians were at work deceiving themselves. Shaken by the sight of Ziethen's hard pursuit toward Nypern, Luchesi, the Austrian cavalry commander on the right wing, convinced himself and Charles that the Prussian main attack would be made there. Skeptical at first, Daun was finally persuaded. Cavalry from reserves and the left wing were

*Jay Luvaas, *Frederick the Great on the Art of War* (New York, 1966), pp. 234-235.

hurried to reinforce the threatened right, leaving Württemberg auxiliaries and a few cavalry at Sagschutz. Frederick exulted at this unexpected turn of events, but remained concerned over how long the Austrians would remain immobile.

Now that the fog was lifting, the north-south line of swells to the east of Borna was Frederick's only screen. By carefully positioning Ziethen's horsemen, he meant to preserve it. Behind this natural curtain, the Prussian war machine flowed round Borna, precisely converting four eastbound columns into two southbound columns. A scant two miles away, Daun and cavalry were proceeding in a parallel but opposite direction. *(See Map 11b.)* For two hours, Frederick and hussars presided from the ridge, guiding the grim procession southward on its lethal errand. Past the hills of Borna it secretly moved, but Charles soon began to wonder. The road to Breslau lay east, not south. Daun offered the opinion that Frederick meant to avoid a fight. Instead of taking action, Charles pondered. At 1:00 p.m., it was too late.

From atop the windmill at Lobelintz, Frederick saw his columns approaching Sagschutz, and saw the Austrians stirring. Part of the advance guard, Ziethen's cavalry, slipped to the right and was promptly struck by a ferocious Austrian charge downhill from Gohlau. Prussian flank guard infantry absorbed the shock and fought it off. At the same time, the remainder of the vanguard attacked the Austrian elbow at Sagschutz, and Frederick gave the command for the main body to attack. The two long columns shuddered to a stop as each platoon crisply executed its left wheel and then marked time. Starting from the right, the assault began, each battalion standing still until its right-hand neighbor had covered 50

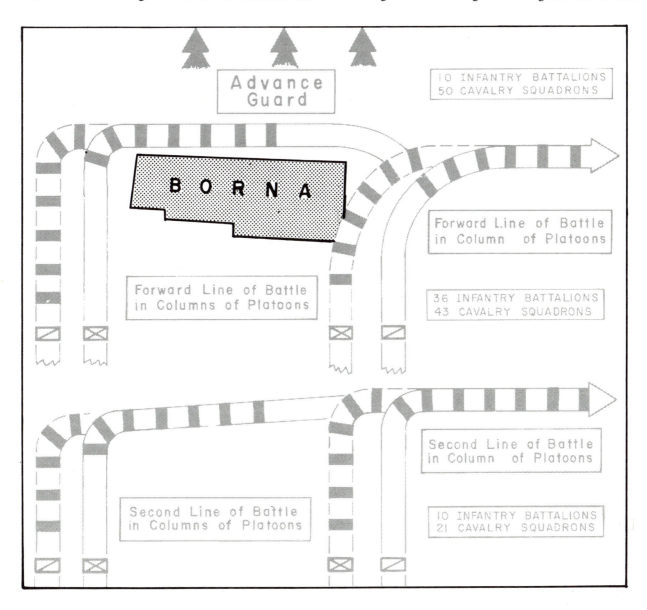

Frederick's Deployment From Column to Line at Leuthen

paces. In this manner, an oblique advance commenced at the moment when the advance guard rammed into the strongpoint at Sagschutz.

For a short time, the issue at that key point was in doubt. But superior fires soon told on the stunned defenders and their shocked commanders. Ten battalions under Maurice overpowered the Württembergers while a battery of 12-pounders enfiladed the Austrian forward line and poured a world of devastation on frightened men. Assaulted in front and flank, Charles' left wing collapsed and rolled back across the hill. *(See Map 11c.)*

Charles and Daun tried to make a fight of it, reinforcing piecemeal from their second line while struggling to realign the unwieldy front from west to south. At Leuthen, an irregular wall of men was pieced together to break the Prussian wave. Bitter fighting whirled around the churchyard, which was not captured for an hour. Thus far, Frederick's left wing remained unengaged, but he shifted Driesen's cavalry north to cover the open flank. Now Luchesi's cavalry made its heroic charge, aiming for the battery of cannon that was now repositioned north of Radaxdorff. At this climactic moment, Driesen's mission became operative. The Bayreuth Dragoons came out of nowhere on Luchesi's flank, shouldered aside the Austrian cavalry, and plunged into unprotected infantry. It was a deluge for which there was no dam. *(See Map 11d.)* Ziethen, now in open country, drove the Austrian left back to Rathen, and the Prussian riptide flowed around and through the broken town of Leuthen. The finest Austrian army since Eugene's day fled across the bridges of Rathen and Lissa, leaving 10,000 dead and wounded to mark its trail.

Frederick never duplicated his feat at Leuthen, and the western world has never forgotten it. The battle is in itself a complete lesson in tactics—deception, maneuver, inspiration, and resolve—gathered together into a volume on generalship, with not one chapter missing. It was also a solid exclamation point to a year that had plumbed the depths of the Soldier-King. More crises were coming, but he would weather them all, doggedly insisting that, "those who cannot survive disaster do not deserve success."

A Strategy for Survival

Two centuries later, it became fashionable to talk of the "discipline of power." No statesman or general ever understood the naked meaning of the phrase better than the bent, prematurely-old cynic in smudged field uniform, who spent seven straight years on campaign. Consider his frame of mind after winning the battle—and immortality—at Leuthen. His victory had shattered the Austrian Army, but it had not ended the war. Nor had it dispelled the ring of danger surrounding the House of Brandenburg, nor guaranteed that next year the peril might not be greater. How then did Frederick reconcile his glowing faith in the Army with his despair of ever gaining safety with it?

Part of the answer can be found in the underlying aim of his strategy. *(See Map 12.)* His most decisive triumphs on the battlefield could not be useful if they did not serve his policy. The general must be subordinated to the King. It is by examining his decisions to accept or to avoid battle—the why rather than the tactical how—that Frederick's strategic schemes can best be understood.

His strategies for 1756 and 1757 were expedient. He fought to retain the initiative with rapid, darting thrusts. In both years, these drives degenerated into desperate, squirming movements designed to preserve his freedom of action, although interior lines and unity of command made his mission easier against an uncoordinated coalition squeeze.

The following year, Frederick resolved to carry the war into Moravia. By capturing Olmutz, Hapsburg strength would be diverted away from Silesia and Saxony. An Austrian alliance with Russia would also be prevented. The campaign started on an auspicious note as Frederick recovered Schweidnitz in April. But Olmutz was too far away and too difficult to capture. Supply trains were ambushed, the enemy could not be made to fight, and Russia threatened from the east. After raising the siege, Frederick withdrew into Bohemia. He then marched to fight the Russians to a bloody draw at Zorndorf, and countermarched to lose at Hochkirch in October. Not one clear victory had been gained in three major actions, "and nothing has come of it on either side but the death of a great many honest people, the misery of a great many poor soldiers maimed for life, the ruin of some provinces, and the ravaging, pillaging, and burning of some flourishing towns."

But, in fact, a great deal had come of it. The events of the next two years demonstrated that Frederick's opponents were gradually losing the stomach for this costly, indecisive war. It was becoming a struggle of moral attrition, with England weakening France while Frederick held off Austria and Russia. In 1759, Frederick stood guard on the Oder, while Prince Henry secured the Elbe and Prince Ferdinand covered Hanover. Daun remained immobile at Landschutz, paralyzed by Frederick's ability to move swiftly in any direction. On August 1, Ferdinand won a major battle over the French at Minden. At the same time, Frederick dashed to meet the Russians and lost a headlong, uncoordinated fight at Kunersdorf. Three generals were lost, and Frederick bitterly said, "it is my misfortune that I am still alive." With half of Prussia's Army felled, the Russian Army paused. The other half was still very much alive, and Russian supply lines were stretching. The Russians withdrew. It was the "Miracle of the House of Brandenburg." In 1760, the indomitable warrior won two more battles that were tactically indecisive. But Frederick more often avoided battle, except to prove that Prussia could not be beaten. Not to be destroyed was to win.

It was Pericles' strategy in the modern age—the strategy of survival. The side with adequate logistics and superior willpower must eventually prevail in this protracted conflict. Great Britain supplied the gold and Frederick the determination. At the same time, British efforts at sea and in the colonies should not be overlooked. French fighting power steadily declined. In 1762, the Russian Empress Elizabeth died. Her successor openly admired Frederick's bravery and resolution, and Russia withdrew from the war. Sweden quickly followed, and the coalition disbanded. Europe's convulsions were over; Frederick's precious army was drained, but his state was preserved.

Frederick the Great

The Legacy

Like Shakespeare's Henry V, Frederick believed that "every subject's duty is to his king, but every subject's soul is his own." This held true for every man in Prussia but one—the man who now labored for 23 years to rebuild his faithful Army and restore his ravaged lands. His duty *and* his soul belonged to Prussia. "I am the first servant of the state," he declared. When his death was announced in 1786, a Swabian peasant is said to have exclaimed, "But who is now to rule the world?"

With the death of Frederick the Great, an epoch passed. Perhaps but for his genius it would have ended sooner. The military revolution wrought by Maurice of Nassau and spread by Gustavus Adolphus ironically reached its pinnacle of achievement at the very moment when it was about to be swept abruptly into history by an even more far-reaching revolution in warfare, one that burst forth with the societal upheaval known as the French Revolution.

From Gustavus to Frederick, warfare had been severely limited in scope. It was an almost private affair between heads of state—a polite, albeit bloody way to debate. Strategic thought and execution, if not wholly atrophied, had been more or less restricted; generals only rarely perceived anything

past the next fortress or supply depot. Victory was defined as not losing. Tactics had evolved from the rather flexible linear formations of Gustavus to Frederick's marvelously inflexible, precisely formed Prussian lines. Shock action, mobility, and flexibility had generally been sacrificed to attain maximum firepower. Limited warfare, formalized and linear, was essentially perfected under Frederick; no one could do better. Yet, there remained obvious deficiencies. A better way had to be devised.

The answer, of course, lay not in the continued improvement of a system that was even then encased in stone, but in an entirely new system. That new system existed already in the imaginations of military philosophers. For its adoption, however, society itself had to change. That change came in the streets of Paris just three years after Frederick the Great died, and only six years after America secured her independence. The French Revolution, and the advent of Napoleon Bonaparte, ushered in a new era in warfare. The art of war as it was practiced in the seventeenth and eighteeenth centuries was no more. It ended as it had begun—with a military revolution.

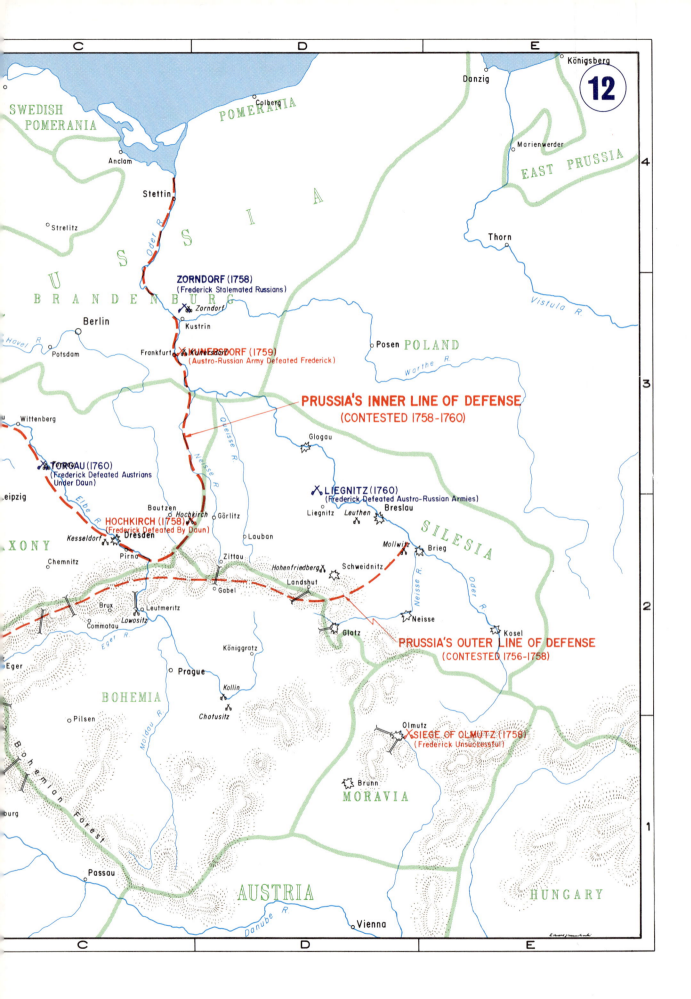

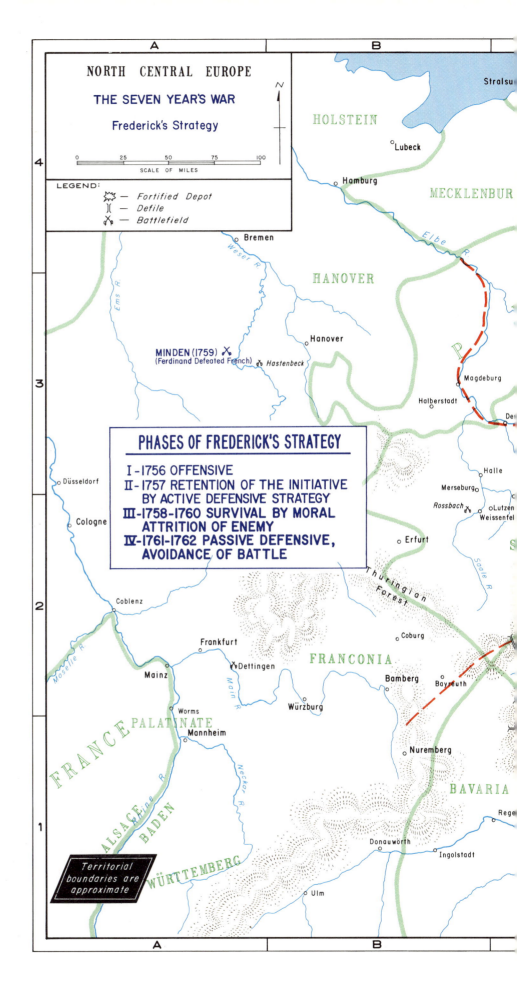

NORTH CENTRAL EUROPE

THE SEVEN YEAR'S WAR

Frederick's Strategy

N

0   25   50   75   100
SCALE OF MILES

LEGEND:
— Fortified Depot
)(— Defile
— Battlefield

HOLSTEIN

Stralsu

Lubeck

Hamburg

MECKLENBUR

Bremen

Weser R.

HANOVER

Elbe R.

Ems R.

Hanover

Magdeburg

MINDEN (1759)
(Ferdinand Defeated French)   Hastenbeck

Halberstadt

Des

Düsseldorf

Halle

Merseburg

Rossbach   Lutzen
Weissenfel

PHASES OF FREDERICK'S STRATEGY

I - 1756 OFFENSIVE
II - 1757 RETENTION OF THE INITIATIVE
BY ACTIVE DEFENSIVE STRATEGY
III - 1758-1760 SURVIVAL BY MORAL
ATTRITION OF ENEMY
IV - 1761-1762 PASSIVE DEFENSIVE,
AVOIDANCE OF BATTLE

Erfurt

Cologne

Saale R.

Thuringian Forest

Coblenz

Coburg

Frankfurt

FRANCONIA

Moselle R.

Dettingen

Bamberg   Bayreuth

Main R.

Mainz

Würzburg

Worms

PALATINATE

Nuremberg

FRANCE   Mannheim

Neckar R.

BAVARIA

Rege

Rhine R.   ALSACE   BADEN

Territorial
boundaries are
approximate   WÜRTTEMBERG

Donauwörth

Ingolstadt

Ulm

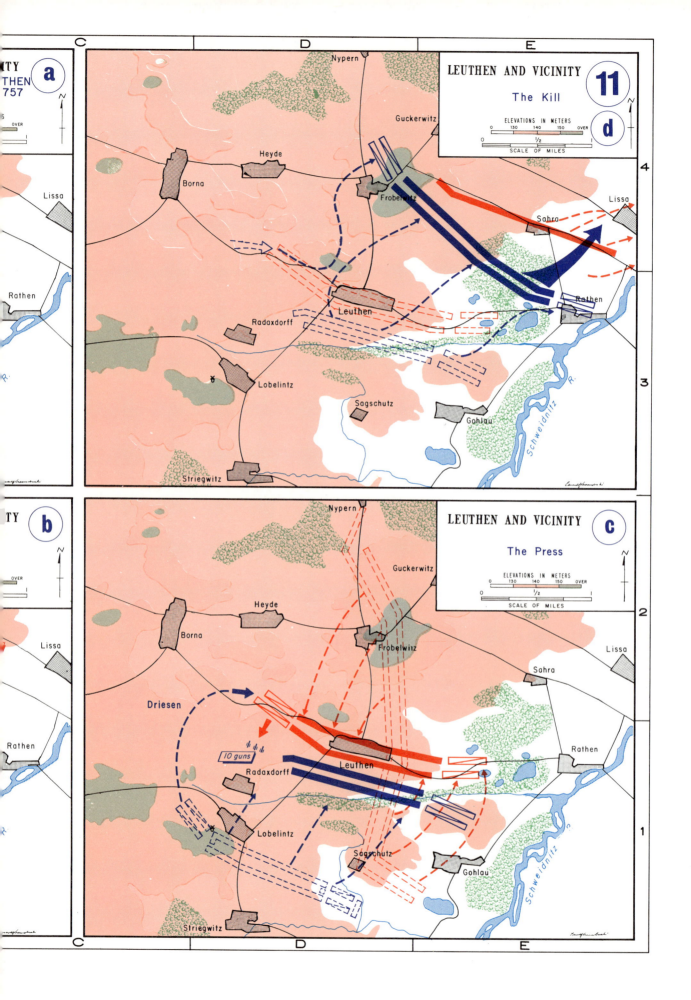

a

LEUTHEN AND VICINITY
THEN
1757

11 d

LEUTHEN AND VICINITY

The Kill

ELEVATIONS IN METERS

130 140 150 OVER

0   1/2   1

SCALE OF MILES

Labels (top map): Nypern, Guckerwitz, Heyde, Borna, Frobelwitz, Lissa, Sahra, Rathen, Leuthen, Radaxdorff, Lobelintz, Sagschutz, Gohlau, Striegwitz, Schweidnitz R.

b

c

LEUTHEN AND VICINITY

The Press

ELEVATIONS IN METERS

130 140 150 OVER

0   1/2   1

SCALE OF MILES

Labels (bottom map): Nypern, Guckerwitz, Heyde, Borna, Frobelwitz, Lissa, Sahra, Rathen, Driesen, Leuthen, Radaxdorff, 10 guns, Lobelintz, Sagschutz, Gohlau, Striegwitz, Schweidnitz R.

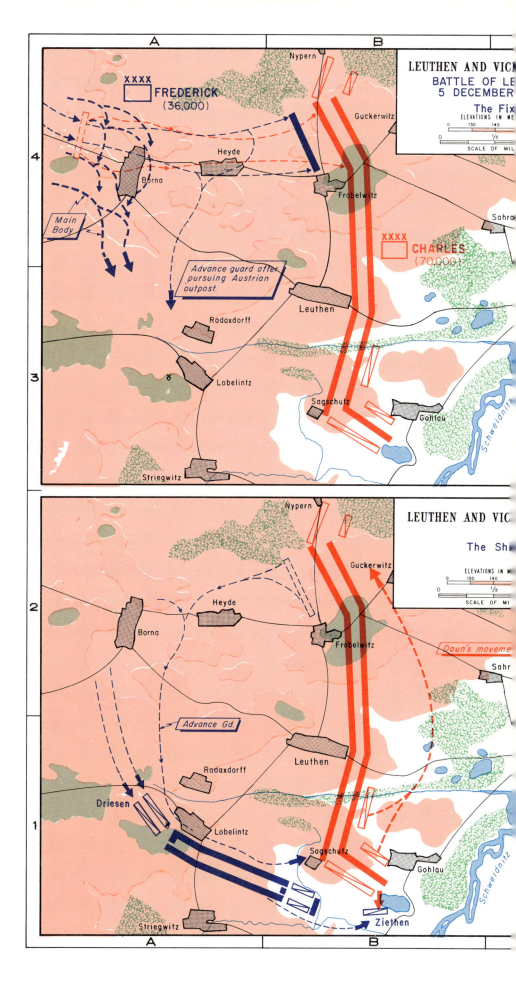

LEUTHEN AND VIC
BATTLE OF LE
5 DECEMBER
The Fix
ELEVATIONS IN ME
0   130   140
0   1/2
SCALE OF MIL

XXXX
FREDERICK
(36,000)

Nypern

Guckerwitz

Heyde

Frobelwitz

Borna

Sahra

Main
Body

XXXX
CHARLES
(70,000)

Advance guard after
pursuing Austrian
outpost.

Leuthen

Radaxdorff

Lobelintz

Sagschutz

Gohlau

Striegwitz

Schweidnitz

LEUTHEN AND VIC

The Sh

ELEVATIONS IN M
0   130   140
0   1/2
SCALE OF MI

Nypern

Guckerwitz

Heyde

Frobelwitz

Borna

Daun's moveme

Sahr

Advance Gd.

Leuthen

Radaxdorff

Driesen

Lobelintz

Sagschutz

Gohlau

Striegwitz

Ziethen

Schweidnitz

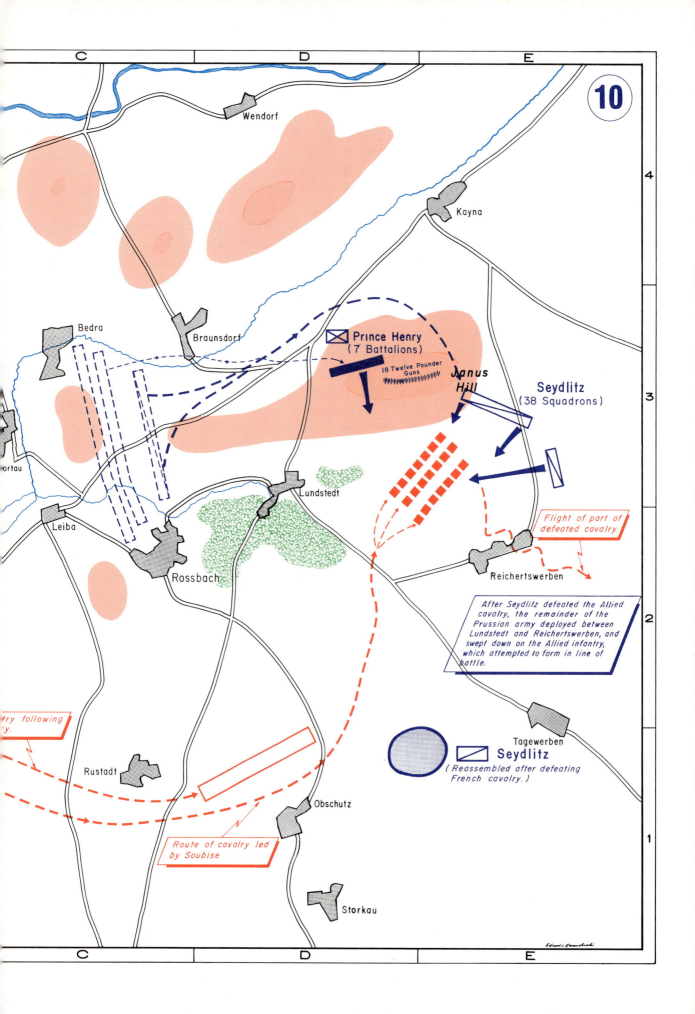

Wendorf

Kayna

Bedra

Braunsdorf

◻️✕ **Prince Henry**
(7 Battalions)

18 Twelve Pounder
Guns

Janus
Hill

Seydlitz
(38 Squadrons)

ortau

Lundstedt

*Flight of part of
defeated cavalry.*

Leiba

Rossbach

Reichertswerben

After Seydlitz defeated the Allied
cavalry, the remainder of the
Prussian army deployed between
Lundstedt and Reichertswerben, and
swept down on the Allied infantry,
which attempted to form in line of
battle.

2

ry following
y.

Tagewerben

Seydlitz
(Reassembled after defeating
French cavalry.)

Rustadt

Obschutz

*Route of cavalry led
by Soubise*

1

Storkau

10

ROSSBACH AND VICINITY

THE BATTLE OF ROSSBACH

The Trap
5 November 1757

ELEVATIONS IN METERS

0   150   160   OVER

0   ½   1

SCALE OF MILES

Eichstadt Stream

Grumpa

Mücheln

Gröst

Almsdorf

Branderoda

St. Germain

Int
cav

Zeuchfeld

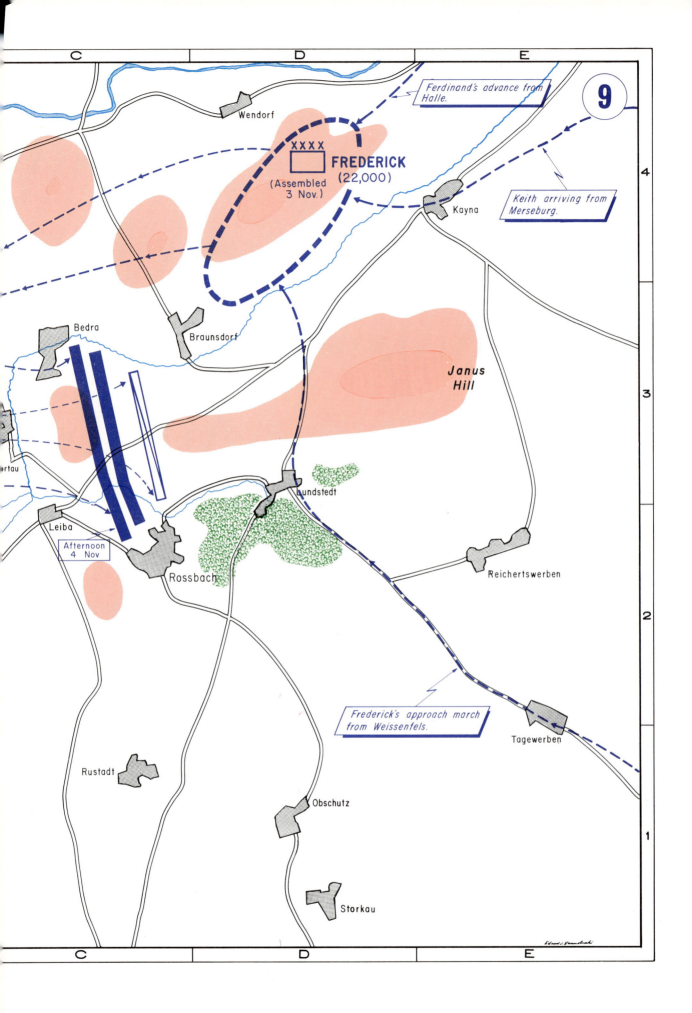

9

Wendorf

Ferdinand's advance from Halle.

XXXX
FREDERICK
(22,000)
(Assembled
3 Nov.)

Kayna

Keith arriving from Merseburg.

Bedra

Braunsdorf

Janus
Hill

Lundstedt

Leiba

Afternoon
4 Nov

Reichertswerben

Rossbach

Rustadt

Frederick's approach march
from Weissenfels.

Tagewerben

Obschutz

Storkau

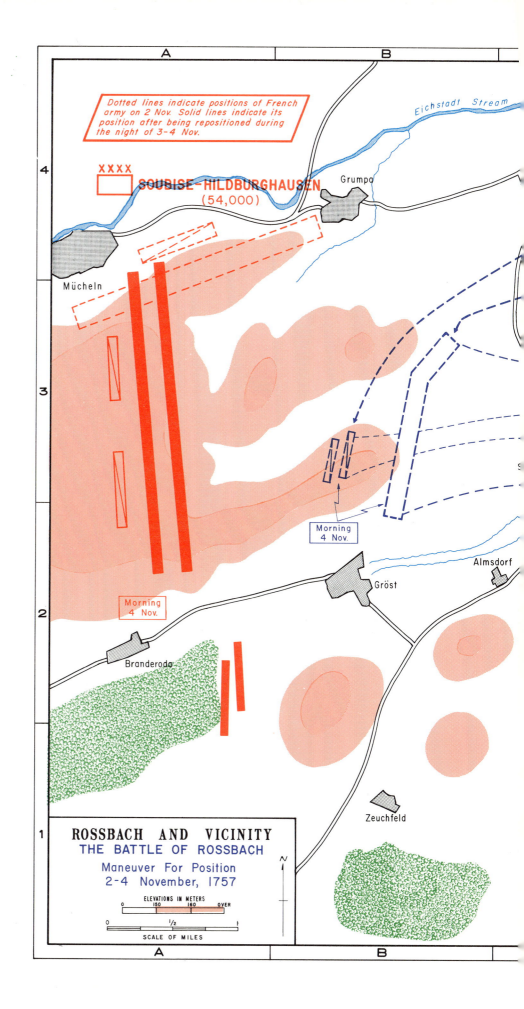

Dotted lines indicate positions of French army on 2 Nov. Solid lines indicate its position after being repositioned during the night of 3-4 Nov.

Eichstadt Stream

4

XXXX
SOUBISE-HILDBURGHAUSEN
(54,000)

Grumpa

Mücheln

3

Morning
4 Nov.

Almsdorf

Gröst

Morning
4 Nov.

2

Branderoda

Zeuchfeld

1

ROSSBACH AND VICINITY
THE BATTLE OF ROSSBACH
Maneuver For Position
2-4 November, 1757

N

ELEVATIONS IN METERS
0   150   160   OVER

0   1/2   1
SCALE OF MILES

A   B

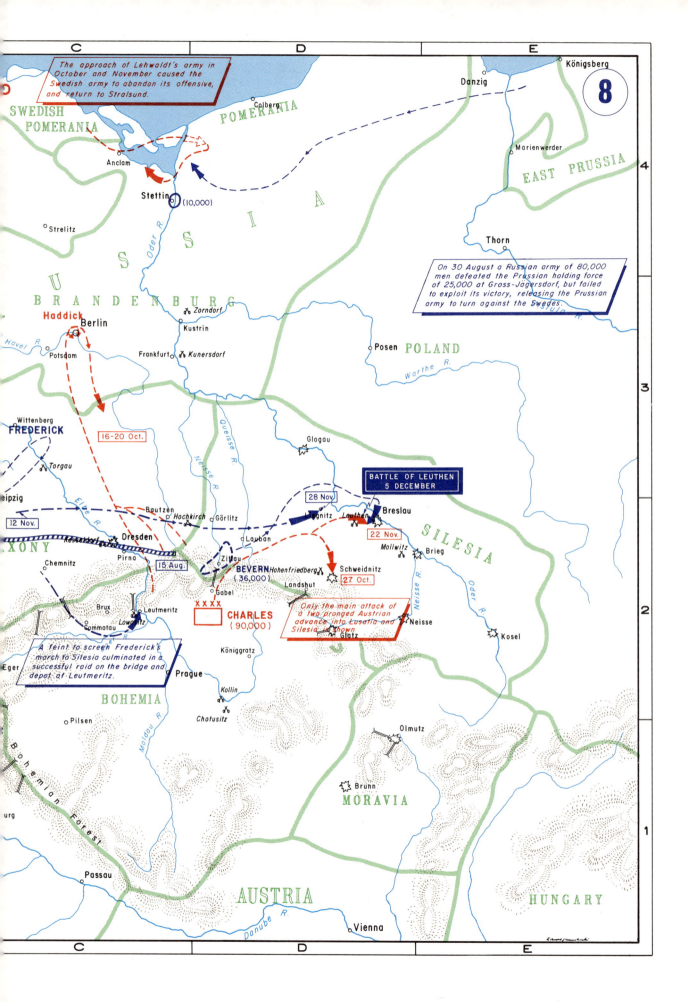

C   **D**   **E**

Königsberg

Danzig

8

The approach of Lehwaldt's army in
October and November caused the
Swedish army to abandon its offensive,
and return to Stralsund.

Colberg

POMERANIA

SWEDISH
POMERANIA

EAST PRUSSIA

Marienwerder

Anclam

4

Stettin (10,000)

Strelitz

Thorn

On 30 August a Russian army of 80,000
men defeated the Prussian holding force
of 25,000 at Gross-Jägersdorf, but failed
to exploit its victory, releasing the Prussian
army to turn against the Swedes.

B R A N D E N B U R G

Haddick
Berlin

Zorndorf

Kustrin

Posen POLAND

Havel R.

Potsdam

Frankfurt

Kunersdorf

Warthe R.

3

Wittenberg

FREDERICK

Torgau

16-20 Oct.

Glogau

BATTLE OF LEUTHEN
5 DECEMBER

eipzig

Bautzen
Hochkirch

Görlitz

28 Nov.

Liegnitz Leuthen Breslau

SILESIA

12 Nov.

Dresden

Lauban

Mollwitz

22 Nov.

Brieg

XONY

Reselsdorf

Pirna

15 Aug.

Zittau

BEVERN Hohenfriedberg
(36,000)

Schweidnitz

27 Oct.

Chemnitz

Brux

Lowositz

Leutmeritz

Landshut

Königgratz

XXXX CHARLES
(90,000)

Gabel

Neisse R.

Neisse

Glatz

Kosel

Commotau

Eger

A feint to screen Frederick's
march to Silesia culminated in a
successful raid on the bridge and
depot at Leutmeritz.

Prague

Only the main attack of a two-pronged Austrian
advance into Lusatia and
Silesia is shown.

BOHEMIA

Kollin

Pilsen

Chotusitz

Olmutz

MORAVIA

Brunn

1

AUSTRIA

Passau

Moldau R.

HUNGARY

Bohemian Forest

Danube R.

Vienna

C   **D**   **E**

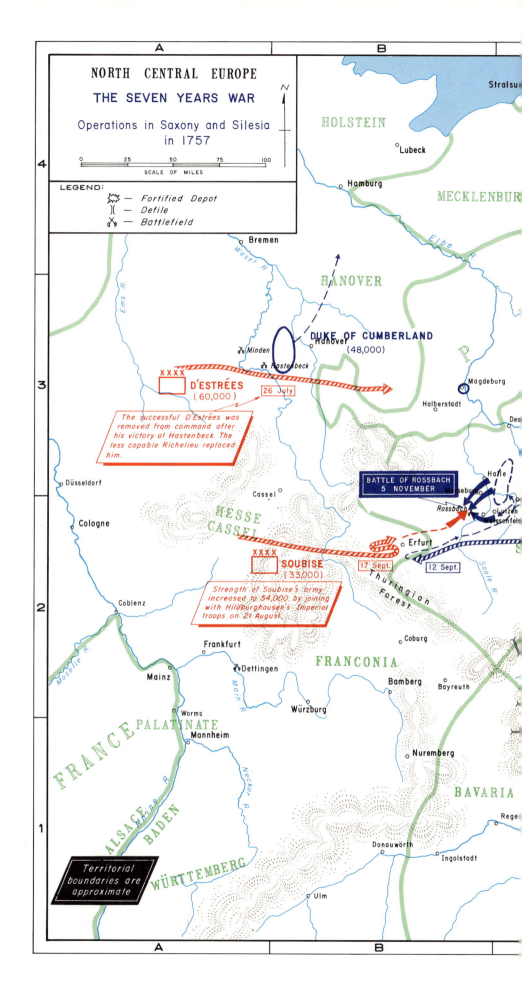

NORTH CENTRAL EUROPE

THE SEVEN YEARS WAR

Operations in Saxony and Silesia
in 1757

0   25   50   75   100
SCALE OF MILES

LEGEND:
☼ — Fortified Depot
)(— Defile
⚔ — Battlefield

HOLSTEIN

Stralsu...

MECKLENBUR...

Lübeck

Hamburg

Bremen

Weser R.

Ems R.

HANOVER

DUKE OF CUMBERLAND
(48,000)

Hanover

Minden

Hastenbeck

Magdeburg

Halberstadt

Des...

XXXX D'ESTRÉES
(60,000)

26 July

The successful D'Estrées was
removed from command after
his victory at Hastenbeck. The
less capable Richelieu replaced
him.

Düsseldorf

Cassel

BATTLE OF ROSSBACH
5 NOVEMBER

Ha[lle]

Merseburg

HESSE
CASSEL

Rossbach

Lützen

Weissenfels

Cologne

Erfurt

17 Sept.

12 Sept.

XXXX SOUBISE
(33,000)

Saale R.

Thuringian
Forest

Strength of Soubise's army
increased to 54,000 by joining
with Hildburghausen's Imperial
troops on 21 August.

Coblenz

Coburg

Frankfurt

FRANCONIA

Bamberg

Bayreuth

Dettingen

Moselle R.

Mainz

Main R.

Würzburg

Worms

Nuremberg

PALATINATE

Mannheim

FRANCE

Neckar R.

BAVARIA

Rhine R.

ALSACE

BADEN

Rege...

Donauwörth

Ingolstadt

Territorial
boundaries are
approximate

WÜRTTEMBERG

Ulm

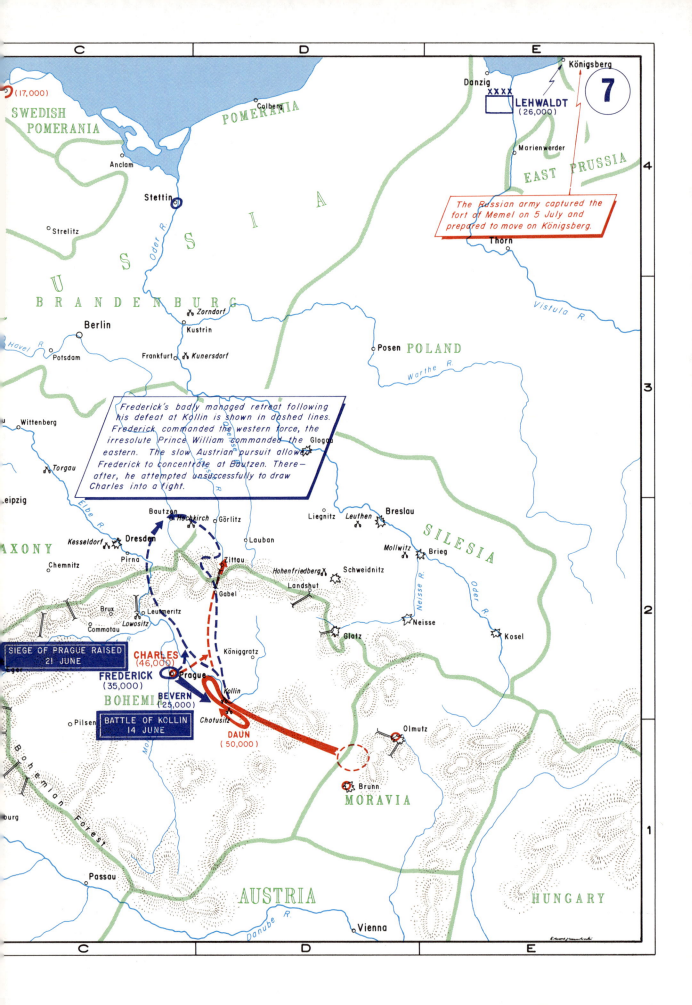

SWEDISH POMERANIA

(17,000)

POMERANIA

Anclam

Colberg

Strelitz

Stettin

Danzig

XXXX LEHWALDT
(26,000)

Königsberg

Marienwerder

EAST PRUSSIA

The Russian army captured the
fort of Memel on 5 July and
prepared to move on Königsberg.

Thorn

P R U S S I A

Oder R.

B R A N D E N B U R G

Berlin

Zorndorf

Kustrin

Havel R.

Potsdam

Frankfurt

Kunersdorf

Vistula R.

Posen

POLAND

Warthe R.

Wittenberg

Oder R.

Torgau

Frederick's badly managed retreat following
his defeat at Kollin is shown in dashed lines.
Frederick commanded the western force, the
irresolute Prince William commanded the
eastern. The slow Austrian pursuit allowed
Frederick to concentrate at Bautzen. Thereafter, he attempted unsuccessfully to draw
Charles into a fight.

Leipzig

Elbe R.

Bautzen

Hochkirch

Görlitz

Liegnitz

Leuthen

Breslau

SILESIA

SAXONY

Kesseldorf

Dresden

Pirna

Lauban

Zittau

Mollwitz

Brieg

Chemnitz

Hohenfriedberg

Schweidnitz

Neisse R.

Brux

Leutmeritz

Gabel

Landshut

Commotau

Lowositz

Königgratz

Glatz

Neisse

Oder R.

Kosel

SIEGE OF PRAGUE RAISED
21 JUNE

CHARLES
(46,000)

Eger

FREDERICK
(35,000)

Prague

BEVERN
(25,000)

BOHEMIA

Pilsen

BATTLE OF KOLLIN
14 JUNE

Kollin

Chotusitz

Olmutz

DAUN
(50,000)

Moldau R.

burg

Passau

Brunn

MORAVIA

Bohemian Forest

AUSTRIA

HUNGARY

Danube R.

Vienna

C   D   E

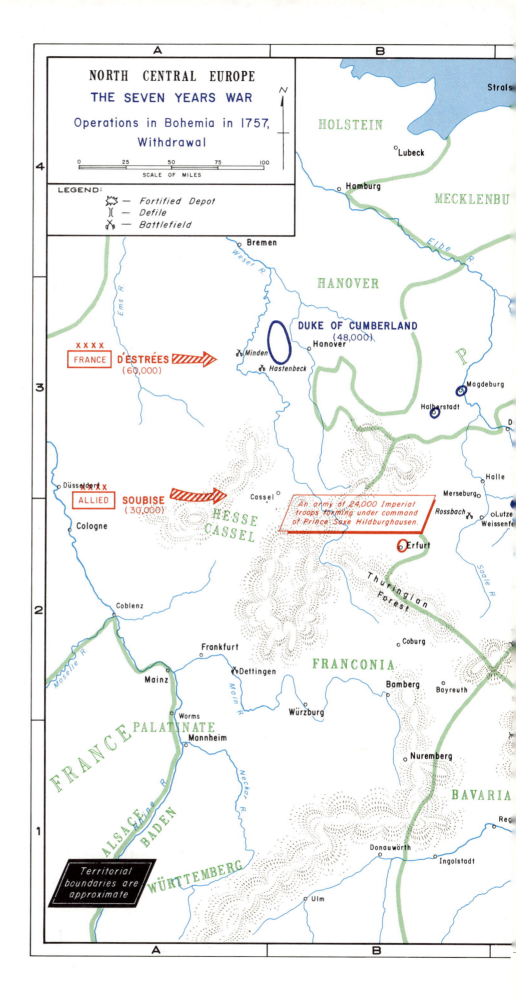

NORTH CENTRAL EUROPE
THE SEVEN YEARS WAR
Operations in Bohemia in 1757,
Withdrawal

N

| 0 | 25 | 50 | 75 | 100 |
SCALE OF MILES

LEGEND:
- ✳ — Fortified Depot
-)(— Defile
- ⚔ — Battlefield

HOLSTEIN

Strals

°Lubeck

MECKLENBU

○ Hamburg

○ Bremen

HANOVER

Wesel R.

Ems R.

DUKE OF CUMBERLAND
(48,000)
Hanover

P

XXXX
FRANCE   D'ESTRÉES ▱▱▱▷
(60,000)

⚔ Minden

⚔ Hastenbeck

Magdeburg

Halberstadt

D

Düsseldorf X
ALLIED   SOUBISE ▱▱▱▷
(30,000)

Cassel

Halle

Merseburg○

Rossbach ⚔   ○Lutze
Weissenfe

An army of 24,000 Imperial
troops forming under command
of Prince Saxe Hildburghausen.

HESSE
CASSEL

○ Cologne

○ Erfurt

Thuringian
Forest

Saale R.

○ Coblenz

Moselle R.

○ Coburg

Rhine R.

Main R.

○ Frankfurt

⚔Dettingen

FRANCONIA

○ Mainz

Bamberg   Bayreuth○

○Worms   Würzburg

FRANCE PALATINATE
○Mannheim

○ Nuremberg

Neckar R.

BAVARIA

ALSACE
BADEN

○ Donauwörth   ○ Ingolstadt   Reg

Territorial
boundaries are
approximate

WÜRTTEMBERG

○ Ulm

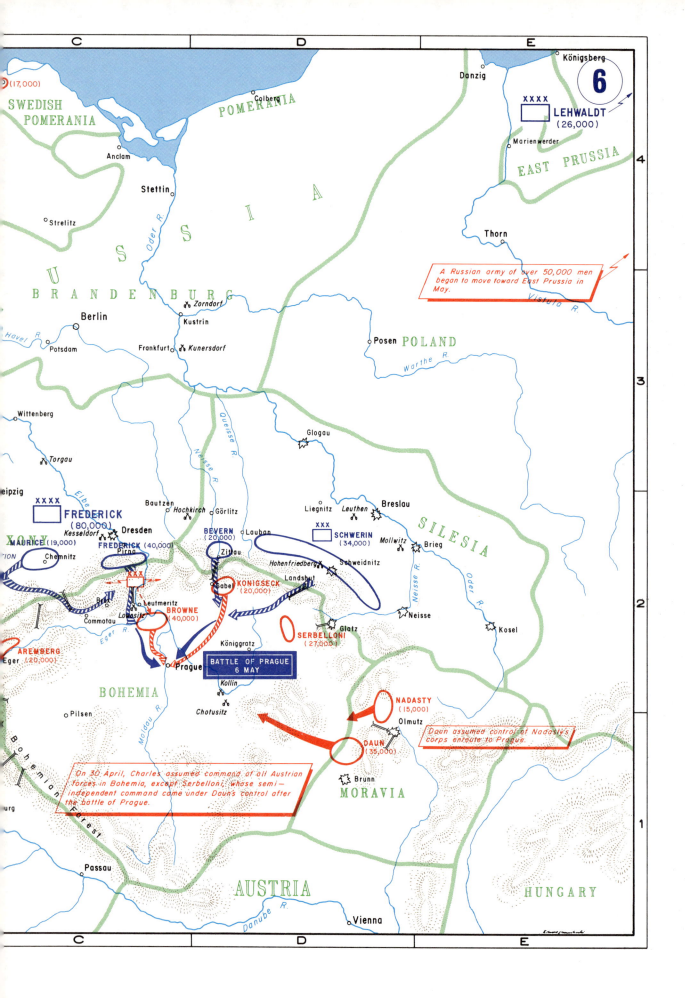

SWEDISH POMERANIA
(17,000)

POMERANIA

Königsberg

6

Danzig

Colberg

Anclam

Stettin

Strelitz

EAST PRUSSIA

Marienwerder

Thorn

XXXX
LEHWALDT
(26,000)

A Russian army of over 50,000 men began to move toward East Prussia in May.

Vistula R.

BRANDENBURG

Berlin

Potsdam

Havel R.

Zorndorf

Kustrin

Frankfurt

Kunersdorf

Posen POLAND

Warthe R.

Wittenberg

Torgau

Queisse R.

Glogau

Leipzig

Neisse R.

Liegnitz

Leuthen

Breslau

XXXX
FREDERICK
(80,000)

Kesseldorf

Dresden

Bautzen

Hochkirch

Görlitz

BEVERN
(20,000)

Lauban

XXX
SCHWERIN
(34,000)

Mollwitz

Brieg

SILESIA

XONY

MAURICE (19,000)

Chemnitz

FREDERICK (40,000)

Pirna

Zittau

Hohenfriedberg

Schweidnitz

Landshut

Neisse R.

Oder R.

Neisse

Kosel

Brux

Leutmeritz

Gabel

KÖNIGSECK
(20,000)

Commotau

Lobositz

BROWNE
(40,000)

Königgratz

SERBELLONI
(27,000)

Glatz

AREMBERG
(20,000)

Eger

Eger R.

Prague

BATTLE OF PRAGUE
6 MAY

Kollin

BOHEMIA

Pilsen

Moldau R.

Chotusitz

NADASTY
(15,000)

Olmutz

Daun assumed control of Nadasty's corps enroute to Prague.

DAUN
(35,000)

On 30 April, Charles assumed command of all Austrian forces in Bohemia, except Serbelloni, whose semi-independent command came under Daun's control after the battle of Prague.

Brunn

MORAVIA

Passau

AUSTRIA

HUNGARY

Danube R.

Vienna

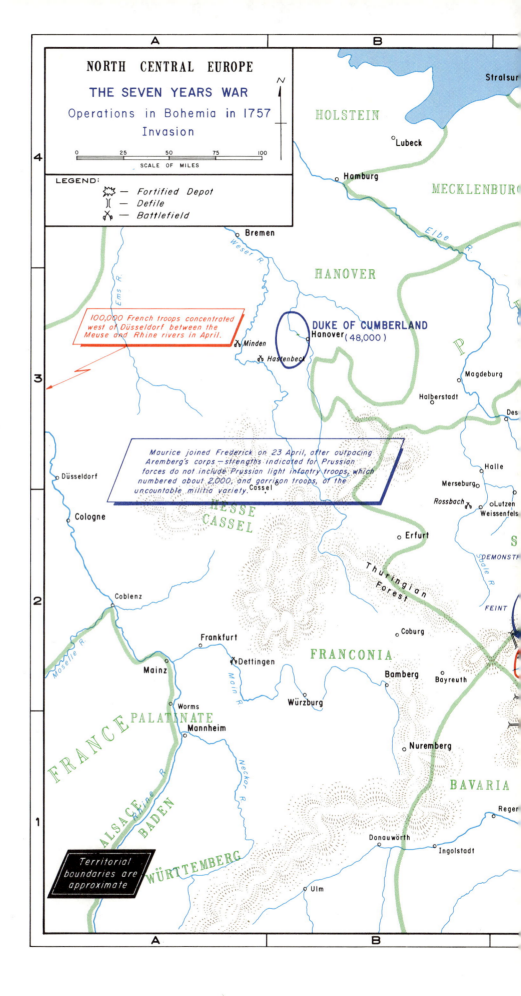

NORTH CENTRAL EUROPE

THE SEVEN YEARS WAR

Operations in Bohemia in 1757
Invasion

SCALE OF MILES
0   25   50   75   100

LEGEND:

— Fortified Depot
)(— Defile
— Battlefield

100,000 French troops concentrated
west of Düsseldorf between the
Meuse and Rhine rivers in April.

Maurice joined Frederick on 23 April, after outpacing
Aremberg's corps — strengths indicated for Prussian
forces do not include Prussian light infantry troops, which
numbered about 2,000, and garrison troops, of the
uncountable militia variety.

DUKE OF CUMBERLAND
Hanover (48,000)

Territorial
boundaries are
approximate

HOLSTEIN

Stralsur

Lubeck

Hamburg

MECKLENBURG

HANOVER

Bremen

Minden
Hastenbeck

Magdeburg

Halberstadt

Des

Düsseldorf

HESSE
CASSEL

Cassel

Halle

Merseburg
Lutzen
Weissenfels

Rossbach

S

Erfurt

DEMONSTR

Spale R.

Thuringian
Forest

FEINT

Cologne

Coblenz

Coburg

FRANCONIA

Bamberg   Bayreuth

Moselle R.

Frankfurt

Dettingen

Main R.

Mainz

Würzburg

Nuremberg

Worms

PALATINATE
Mannheim

FRANCE

ALSACE

Rhine R.

BADEN

Neckar R.

BAVARIA

Reger

Donauwörth

Ingolstadt

WÜRTTEMBERG

Ulm

Elbe R.
Weser R.
Ems R.

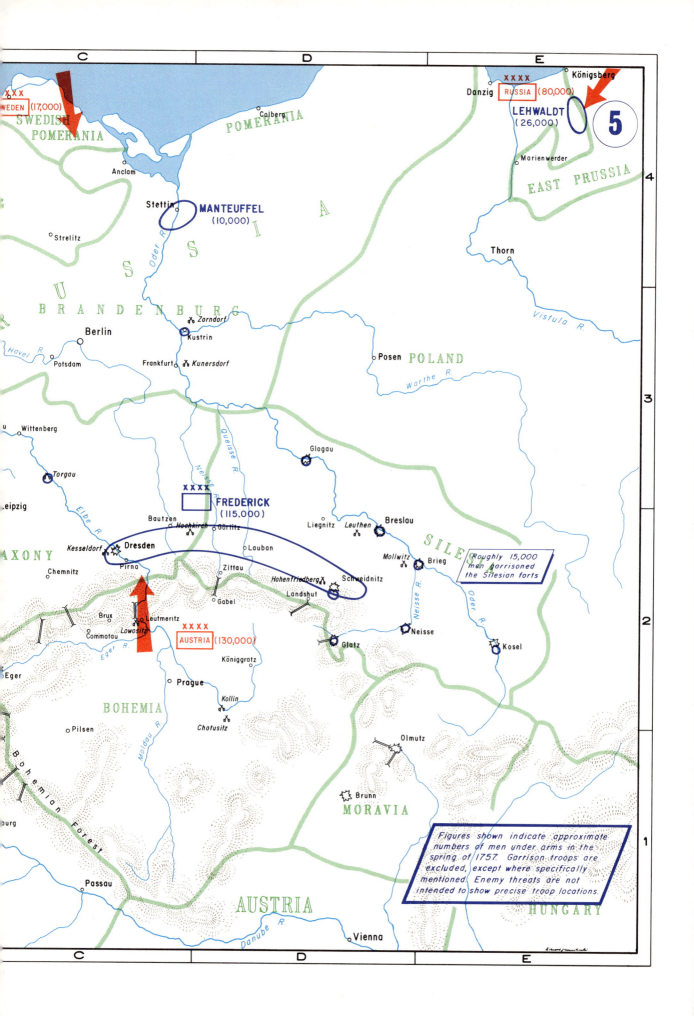

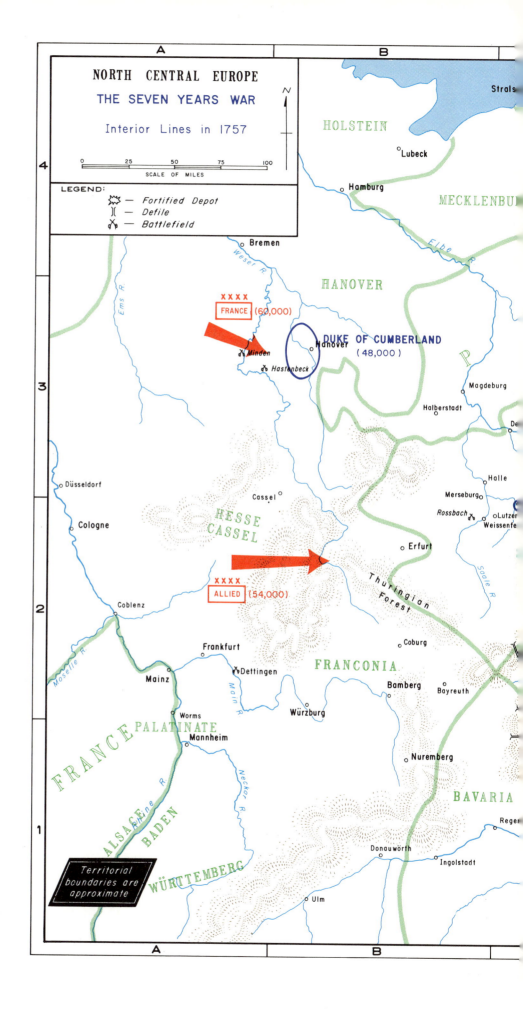

HOLSTEIN

Strals

Lubeck

MECKLENBU

Hamburg

Bremen

HANOVER

XXXX
FRANCE (60,000)

DUKE OF CUMBERLAND
(48,000)

Minden
Hanover
Hastenbeck

Magdeburg

Halberstadt

De

Halle

Düsseldorf

Cassel

Merseburg

Rossbach
oLutzer
Weissenfe

HESSE
CASSEL

Cologne

Erfurt

Thuringian Forest

Saale R.

XXXX
ALLIED (54,000)

Coblenz

Coburg

FRANCONIA

Frankfurt

Dettingen

Bamberg

Bayreuth

Mainz

Würzburg

Worms
PALATINATE

Mannheim

Nuremberg

FRANCE

BAVARIA

ALSACE
BADEN

Reger

Donauwörth

Ingolstadt

Territorial
boundaries are
approximate

WÜRTTEMBERG

Ulm

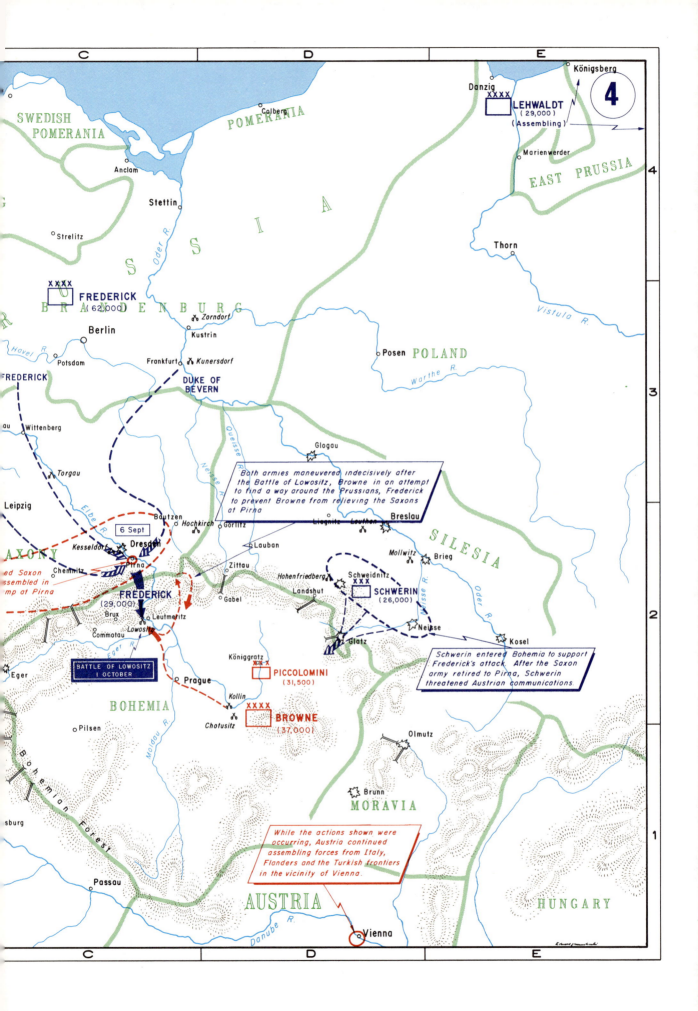

4

SWEDISH POMERANIA

POMERANIA

Königsberg

Danzig

XXXX LEHWALDT (29,000) (Assembling)

Marienwerder

EAST PRUSSIA

Anclam

Stettin

Strelitz

Thorn

Oder R.

P R U S S I A

Vistula R.

XXXX FREDERICK (62,000)

B R A N D E N B U R G

Berlin

Havel R.

Potsdam

Zorndorf

Kustrin

Posen POLAND

Warthe R.

FREDERICK

Frankfurt Kunersdorf

DUKE OF BEVERN

Wittenberg

Queisse R.

Glogau

Both armies maneuvered indecisively after the Battle of Lowositz. Browne in an attempt to find a way around the Prussians, Frederick to prevent Browne from relieving the Saxons at Pirna

Breslau

S I L E S I A

Torgau

Neisse R.

Bautzen

Hochkirch Görlitz

Liegnitz Leuthen

Leipzig

Elbe R.

6 Sept

Dresden

Lauban

Mollwitz Brieg

Kesseldorf

Zittau

Hohenfriedberg Schweidnitz

XXX SCHWERIN (26,000)

S A X O N Y

Pirna

Chemnitz

Gabel

Landshut

Neisse R.

Oder R.

ed Saxon ssembled in mp at Pirna

FREDERICK (29,000)

Leutmeritz

Neisse

Kosel

Brux

Lowositz

Glatz

Commotau

Eger R.

Schwerin entered Bohemia to support Frederick's attack. After the Saxon army retired to Pirna, Schwerin threatened Austrian communications.

Eger

BATTLE OF LOWOSITZ I OCTOBER

Königgratz

XX X PICCOLOMINI (31,500)

Prague

Moldau R.

Kollin

Pilsen

Chotusitz

XXXX BROWNE (37,000)

BOHEMIA

Olmutz

Brunn

MORAVIA

Bohemian Forest

sburg

Passau

While the actions shown were occurring, Austria continued assembling forces from Italy, Flanders and the Turkish frontiers in the vicinity of Vienna.

HUNGARY

AUSTRIA

Danube R.

Vienna

C   D   E

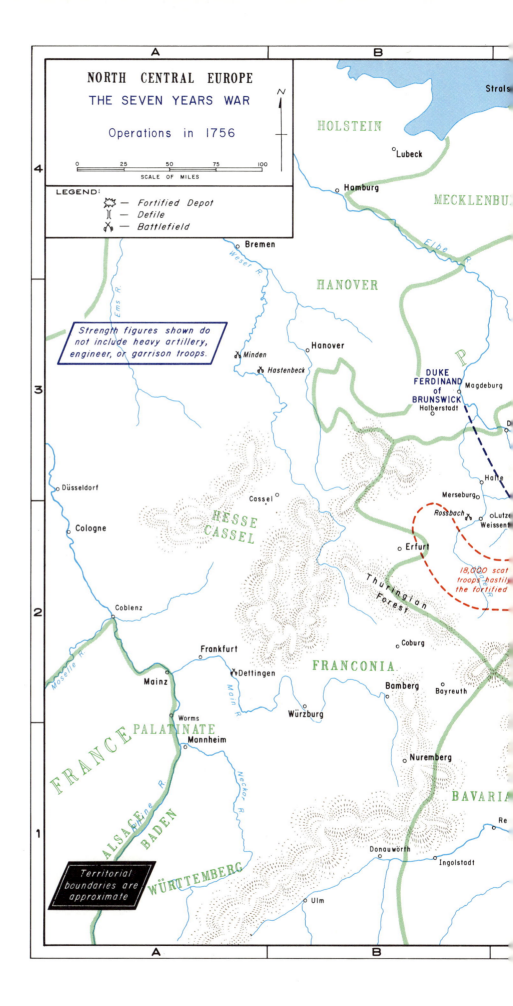

NORTH CENTRAL EUROPE

THE SEVEN YEARS WAR

Operations in 1756

N

SCALE OF MILES
0   25   50   75   100

LEGEND:
— Fortified Depot
)(— Defile
— Battlefield

Strength figures shown do
not include heavy artillery,
engineer, or garrison troops.

Territorial
boundaries are
approximate

HOLSTEIN

Lübeck

Stral

MECKLENBU

Hamburg

Bremen

HANOVER

P

Hanover

Minden

Hastenbeck

DUKE
FERDINAND
of
BRUNSWICK

Magdeburg

Halberstadt

D

Halle

Düsseldorf

Cassel

HESSE
CASSEL

Merseburg

Rossbach

Lutze

Weissen

Cologne

Erfurt

18,000 scat
troops hastil
the fortified

Thuringian
Forest

Coblenz

Coburg

Frankfurt

Dettingen

FRANCONIA

Bamberg

Bayreuth

Mainz

Würzburg

Worms

PALATINATE

Mannheim

Nuremberg

FRANCE

BAVARIA

BADEN

Donauwörth

Re

ALSACE

Ingolstadt

WÜRTTEMBERG

Ulm

Weser R.

Ems R.

Elbe

Moselle R.

Rhine R.

Main R.

Neckar R.

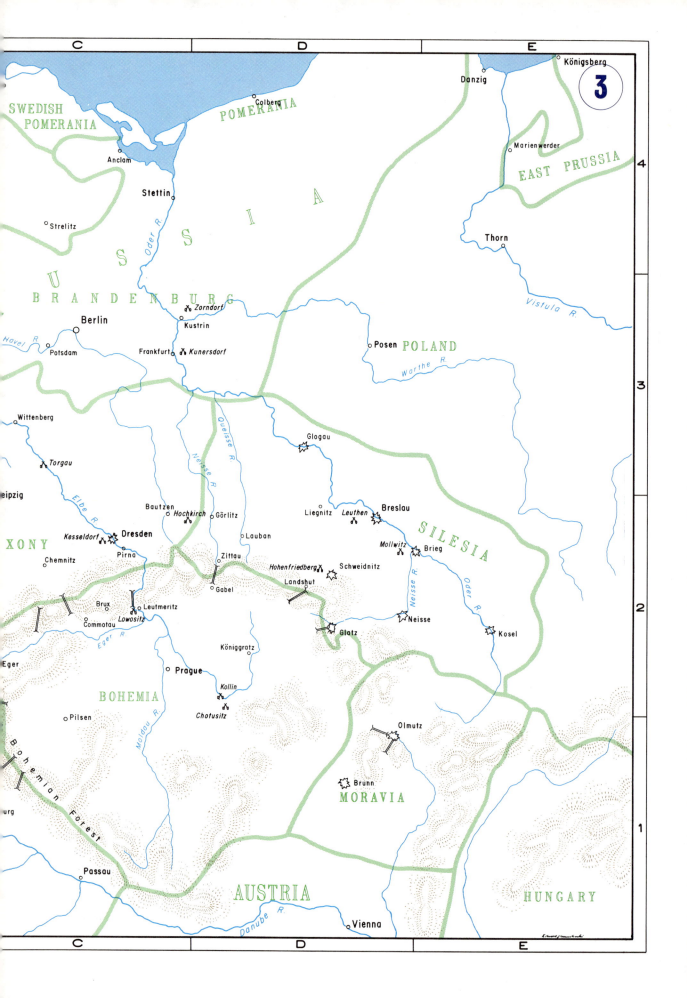

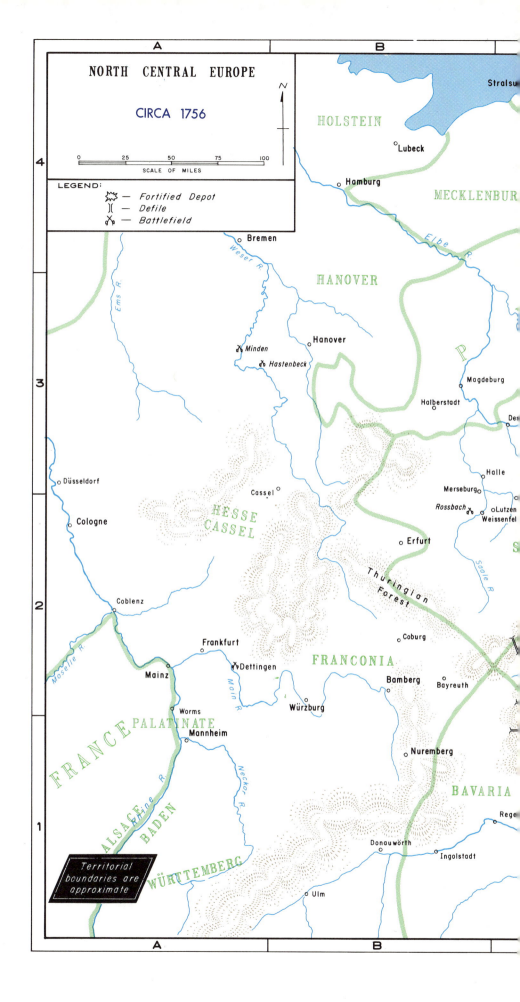

A   B

NORTH CENTRAL EUROPE

CIRCA 1756

N

0   25   50   75   100

SCALE OF MILES

LEGEND:

— *Fortified Depot*

— *Defile*

— *Battlefield*

HOLSTEIN

Stralsu

○ Lubeck

MECKLENBUR

○ Hamburg

Elbe R.

Weser R.

○ Bremen

HANOVER

P

○ Hanover

Ems R.

Minden

Hastenbeck

○ Magdeburg

○ Halberstadt

Des

○ Halle

Merseburg ○

Rossbach   ○Lutzen

Weissenfel

○ Düsseldorf

Cassel ○

HESSE
CASSEL

S

○ Cologne

○ Erfurt

Saale R.

*Thuringian
Forest*

Moselle R.

○ Coblenz

○ Coburg

○ Frankfurt

FRANCONIA

Dettingen

Bamberg ○   Bayreuth

○ Mainz

Main R.

Würzburg ○

FRANCE PALATINATE

○ Worms

Mannheim ○

○ Nuremberg

Neckar R.

Rhine R.

ALSACE BADEN

BAVARIA

Rege

○ Donauwörth

○ Ingolstadt

Territorial
boundaries are
approximate

WÜRTTEMBERG

○ Ulm

A   B

Selected Bibliography

Warfare in the Middle Ages

Cantor, Norman F. *Medieval History*. 2nd edition. London, 1969. Though a general history of the period, this reference offers excellent insights into the relationships between warfare and society.

Earle, Edward Meade (ed.). *Makers of Modern Strategy*. Princeton, N.J., 1941. Felix Gilbert's excellent chapter on Machiavelli is well worth reading.

Hollister, C. Warren. *Anglo-Saxon Military Institutions on the Evening of the Norman Conquest*. Oxford, 1962. Excellent coverage that does not get bogged down in detail of the campaigns.

———. *The Military Organization of Norman England*. Oxford, 1965. Short but highly readable and thorough.

Oman, C. W. C. *The Art of War in the Middle Ages*. Edited by J. H. Beeler. Ithaca, N.Y., 1953. This condensation of Oman's 1924 two-volume study is an excellent introduction to the subject of the title.

Spaulding, Oliver L., Hoffman Nickerson, and John W. Wright. *Warfare: A Study of Military Methods From the Earliest Times*. New York, 1925. A thorough and interesting description of warfare in the feudal period is provided within the general framework of warfare in its totality.

Naval Warfare

de la Varende, Jean. *Cherish the Sea: A History of Sail*. New York, 1956. Organized by countries, rather than chronologically. Vessel descriptions are accurate and clear.

Elliot, J. H. *Imperial Spain, 1469–1716*. New York, 1964. A good exercise in placing seapower in its perspective as a part of national power.

Lewis, Michael. *The Spanish Armada*. New York, 1960. Scholarly and with excellent background on principal personalities. Detailed orders of battle.

Marcus, G. J. *A Naval History of England: The Formative Centuries*. Boston, 1961. For the serious student.

Mattingly, Garrett. *The Armada*. Boston, 1959. Well documented from primary sources, this detailed work is a very readable narrative.

Mordal, Jacques. *Twenty-Five Centuries of Sea Warfare*. New York, 1965. Excellent description of major campaigns and battles.

Potter, E. B. and C. W. Nimitz (eds.). *Sea Power: A Naval History*. Englewood Cliffs, 1960. The current favorite as a naval history text.

Robertson, Frederick L. *The Evolution of Naval Armament*. London, 1921. Excellent descriptions and extensive tables of capabilities of early ordnance.

Robinson, S. S. and M. L. Robinson. *A History of Naval Tactics from 1530 to 1930*. Annapolis, 1942. Besides describing tactics, this volume enumerates the reasons for evolution and change.

Rodgers, William L. *Naval Warfare Under Oars*. Annapolis, 1939. Excellent on types of galleys and weapons; plans of ships. Not accurate in descriptions of battles.

Southworth, John Van Duyn. *The Ancient Fleets*. New York, 1968. Colorful and descriptive, filled with anecdotal material and insight into personalities.

———. *The Age of Sails*. New York, 1968. The best single volume for coverage of military and political situations, as well as ships and weapons. Excellent on explorers. Entertaining sidelights and anecdotes.

Stirling-Maxwell, William. *Don John of Austria*. London, 1883. Difficult to procure, but an excellent source on the Lepanto Campaign.

Gustavus Adolphus

Dodge, Theodore A. *Gustavus Adolphus*. Boston, 1895. A highly readable work which covers other great soldiers of the period as well.

Mitchell, John. *The Life of Wallenstein, Duke of Friedland*. London, 1837. Reprinted in 1971 in *The West Point Military Library* Series. A biographical treatment of the great mercenary. A view of Gustavus from the enemy camp.

Roberts, Michael. *Gustavus Adolphus: A History of Sweden, 1611–1632*. 2 Vols. New York, 1953. Rather heavy going in places, but nonetheless the most authoritative work on the subject.

The Wars of Louis XIV

Ashley, Maurice. *Louis XIV and the Greatness of France*. New York, 1965. A concise and accurate account of the reign of the "Sun King."

——. *The Greatness of Oliver Cromwell*. London, 1957. A look at the Great Protector, his New Model Army, and the English Civil War.

Churchill, Winston S. *Marlborough, His Life and Times*. 6 Vols. New York, 1935. Churchill writes glowingly and well of his famous ancestor. This is probably the best work on Marlborough. (Condensed into a single volume in 1968 by Henry Steele Commager.)

Earle, Edward M. (ed.). *Makers of Modern Strategy*. Princeton, N.J., 1941. Vauban's life and work is neatly presented in a chapter.

Klyuchevsky, Vasili. *Peter the Great*. Translated by Liliana Archibald. New York, 1958. The leading study of Peter and his reforms.

Luvaas, Jay (editor and translator). *Frederick the Great on the Art of War*. New York, 1966. Frederick evaluates the generalship of Charles XII on pages 339-360. It is unlikely that anyone has done it better.

Nicholson, G. W. L. *Marlborough and the War of the Spanish Succession*. Ottawa, 1955. A brief presentation of the military campaigns and battles of that war.

Peckham, Howard H. *The Colonial Wars, 1689–1762*. Chicago, 1964. A fast-moving presentation of the Anglo-French clash in North America.

Taylor, Frank. *The Wars of Marlborough, 1702–1707*. 2 Vols. Oxford, 1921. Excellent treatment of the Duke's battles.

The Era of Frederick the Great

Carlyle, Thomas. *The History of Friedrich II of Prussia*. 6 Vols. London, 1886. This rambling account of Frederick's life is invaluable for its insights and wealth of detail.

Delbrück, Hans. *Geschichte der Kriegskunst im Rahmen Politische Zeit*. 6 Vols. Berlin, 1920. Delbrück's monumental work remains one of the greatest treasuries of knowledge on military history. Its translation will be a major contribution to the study of war. See Vol. IV, pp. 304-332 for a concise description of eighteenth century tactics, and pp. 426-439 for an excellent interpretation of Frederick's strategy.

Dorn, Walter. *Competition for Empire*. New York, 1963. An excellent volume in the *Rise of Modern Europe* Series. Chapter 5 relates the interconnection of political, economic, and military factors influencing contemporary warfare.

Earle, Edward M. (ed.). *Makers of Modern Strategy*. Princeton, N.J., 1941. R. R. Palmer's chapter on Frederick is excellent.

Jomini, Baron. *Treatise on Grand Military Operations*. Translated by Colonel S. C. Holabird. 2 Vols. New York, 1865. Jomini wrote with a firm grasp of the eighteenth century pattern of war, but one must be careful not to mistake his system for Frederick's.

Luvaas, Jay (editor and translator). *Frederick the Great on the Art of War*. New York, 1966. This comprehensive study of Frederick's writings is easy to read and contains many pertinent observations by both Frederick and the editor.

Ritter, Gerhard. *Frederick the Great: An Historical Profile*. Translated by Peter Paret. Berkeley, 1968. A superb and concise study of Frederick's character.

Index